Frer

The Death of Otto Zehm

For Marsha,
with love and gratitude!
Billy

Frenzy and Cover Up:

The Death of Otto Zehm

Andrew Gabriel Britt

Edited by Samantha Uliano

Cover Design by Jeremy Nivison

ISBN 978 0 9859036 3 3

Frenzy
and Cover Up is
dedicated to the family
and friends of Otto Zehm, the
Center for Justice in Spokane, the
United States Department of Justice,
Spokane Mayor David Condon,
and the makers of video
surveillance
systems.

This story concerns the death of Otto Zehm, a gentle and unassuming man who lived in Spokane, Washington. Despite learning disability and mental illness, he was a devoted son, cherished friend, dedicated worker, and accomplished musician.

Rather than a peaceful passing comforted by loved ones, Otto's death was a tormented, police-initiated homicide by beating, Taser, restraint, and suffocation.

Considering that some of the individuals involved in the fatal incident or the tangled events that ensued lied to investigators or under oath in legal proceedings, I did not interview the participants. This narrative is based on reliable information in the public record; sources are indicated when not apparent.

The incident that resulted in Otto's death and how the public was misled about it were meticulously researched and are described with scrupulous objectivity. Nevertheless, some individuals involved may argue that statements or actions attributed to them are not accurate. Correcting the public record is the responsibility of those individuals who perceive it to be in error.

Persons with strong anti-law enforcement or anti-government opinions should not construe this account to be broadly supportive of their views. It concerns a single incident and the response of one city's management and police department to that incident only.

Invaluable assistance was provided by several people. Paula Rickett offered chapter-by-chapter feedback with a keen eye for unnecessary detail and wordiness. My editor, Samantha Uliano, enhanced the work immeasurably, shining what was dull, recycling material that had some usefulness, and taking out the trash. I believe that Otto, a janitor, would have enjoyed those metaphors.

My parents, Anne Schmitt and Bill Britt, provided unwavering encouragement and support during this project and my father, a neurologist, explained the medical conditions that were such important aspects of this story.

Sarah Genung willingly suffered from lack of companionship for the last two years. I am especially grateful for her sacrifice and love.

A number of individuals emerge very much larger for the roles they played in these events. When the mountain yet to climb seemed unscalable, their actions inspired me to push on. I am a storyteller here. It is they who did justice to Otto's memory.

Andrew Gabriel Britt

February, 2015

CHAPTER ONE

Spokane is the commercial, medical, and cultural center of northeast Washington. The "Lilac City" was founded in the nineteenth century at the site of a Native American settlement beside the falls of the Spokane River, which flows east to west bisecting the present city. Situated on what is now a large park adjacent to the falls, a world's fair, Expo '74, brought Spokane international attention.

The downtown business district is located just south of the river, and stately neighborhoods can be found nearby. A number of residential developments featuring contemporary northwest homes, many with an expansive view of mountains and prairies, have been built at the city's perimeter.

North of the river across from downtown are a university district and the Arena, home to beloved minor league hockey and Arena League football teams. That area, north central Spokane, isn't seedy. But it's not high end, either. Like much of the city, it's filled with blue collar neighborhoods. This is where Otto Zehm lived.

The northeast corner of the state has four distinct seasons. On late winter afternoons it gets dark early, and the temperature falls quickly after the sun goes down. People going outdoors then wear layers of clothing and warm coats.

Early in the evening of Saturday March 18, 2006, a young woman riding in a friend's car in north central Spokane placed a call from her cell phone to 911:

911 Operator: "Spokane 911. What's the location of the emergency?"

Caller: "Um, I'm on Ruby and Baldwin and there's some guy... We're at the bank and he's like, walking over, and he was trying to get into this car, and he's like messing with... We drove off so he wouldn't do anything, and now he's messing with their ATM."

911 Operator: "'Kay, Ruby and... Ruby and Baldwin? What's the name of the business?"

Caller: "Uh, it's Washington Trust Bank."

911 Operator: "Washington Trust?"

Caller: "Yeah."

911 Operator: "And what's your phone number you're calling from?"

[Omission in the recording]

Caller: "Yeah, and I didn't know if I was supposed to call 911."

911 Operator: "Yeah, that's right. So you saw a male messing with the ATM machine?"

Caller: "Well, no, we were...we, uh, saw him when we...we were going to the ATM to get money out, and we saw him across the parking lot and then we pulled up, and she already put her card in and was putting something, and he came over to the window and was getting way too close to us and talking and...and playing with the ATM, so we drove off, 'cause I thought he was going to do something to us and it was scary, and he's over by the ATM machine messing with it now."

911 Operator: "What do you mean, 'Messing with it'?"

Caller: "Uh, I...he was pressing buttons and she put her card in and stuff. I...I don't know."

911 Operator: "Do you think he was trying to get into the ATM?"

Caller: "I don't know what he...he was getting too close to us, and..."

911 Operator: "Okay."

Caller: "It scared me so we drove off, and I don't know if..."

Caller's friend: "We don't know if he got money out."

Caller: "Yeah, I...I don't know if he's gonna take money, because she already entered her pin number and stuff. We drove off because he was like, trying to get..."

911 Operator: "She took her card though, right?"

Caller: "Yeah." (to friend) "You have your card, don't you?"

Caller's friend (to Caller): "Yeah."

Caller: "Yeah. But that guy's creepy, so I thought..."

911 Operator: "Sure, one second here while I type this in."

Caller: "Okay."

[Omission in the recording]

911 Operator: "Okay, let me get the description of him. Was he a white male?"

Caller: "Yeah."

Caller's friend: "White male."

911 Operator: "How old did he look?"

Caller (to friend)**:** "Uh, how old do you think he was?"

Caller's friend: "Probably like forties."

911 Operator: "Forties? Do you remember..."

Caller: "He has, um, like long blondish, red hair, like blondish hair. Yeah. He's still at the ATM."

911 Operator: "Okay. Can you see him any longer?"

Caller: "I can see him bending over right now, like we're in the drive-through. But I can't see his face. I can't tell what he's doing. I can see his back."

911 Operator: "But he's right by the ATM?"

Caller: "Yeah."

911 Operator: "'Kay. What's he wearing?"

Caller: "Uh, like a black jacket. A cop just drove by."

911 Operator: "Black jacket and what?"

Caller: "Uh, I don't...I think he's wearing jeans."

911 Operator: "Black jacket and jeans? So right now the male is bending down at the ATM?"

Caller: "Yeah, I don't know what he's doing. He's...he has long blond hair, so...it's long."

911 Operator: "And this is the drive-through at Washington Trust Bank?"

Caller: "Yeah."

911 Operator: "The drive-through ATM, excuse me."

Caller: "Yeah, the drive-up ATM."

911 Operator: "And the vehicle that he was near, what kind of car is it?"

Caller: "Oh, it was the one we're in. It's a..."

911 Operator: "Oh, it was the one you were in?"

Caller: "Yeah! We were in the car at the ATM, and he came over to us."

911 Operator: "Oh, okay."

Caller: "That's why we drove off, 'cause it scared us and he was like getting way too close. So I told her to drive..."

911 Operator: "Okay."

Caller: "'cause he was trying to talk to us, and..."

911 Operator: "Did he seem high or intoxicated?"

Caller (to friend)**:** "Do you think he was like..." (to Operator) "I don't think he was drunk. I...he's on something. I don't..."

911 Operator: "Okay."

Caller:" I wouldn't know, but..."

911 Operator: "Can you still see him?"

Caller: "Not right now, but I didn't see him walk away. 'Cause I'm on like the other side of the ATM, so I could only see him like when he bent over."

911 Operator: "Are you in the same parking lot as him then?"

Caller: "Uh, we're at, like the end of the parking lot, like we're a little ways away."

911 Operator: "Okay."

[Omission in the recording]

Caller: "But we drove out and then backed back in, so...I, I don't know what he's doing. There's a car trying to go up to the drive-up ATM right now and..."

911 Operator: "There's...okay. And do you see the guy?"

Caller: "Oh God, he's walking aw---what does he have? He has something and he's walking away from the ATM right now, and all her stuff was in it."

911 Operator: "What do you mean he has something?"

Caller: "Like a paper and a ton of stuff in his hands. And he's walking away."

Caller's friend (in the background): "I just put money in."

Caller: "I think he has, he has, he has money."

Caller's friend (in the background): "Oh, God."

911 Operator: "He has money?"

Caller: "I think so. I think he got her money. He's walking away. He put a ton of stuff in his coat. See where he's going."

911 Operator: "Which way is he walking?"

Caller: "Um, he...I don't...he's walking down...Um, he's in the back of the parking lot. He's running! Dude, he's running!"

911 Operator: "Which way is he running?"

Caller's friend: "He's running towards New Harbour."

Caller: "He's...New Harbour on, like Division and..."

911 Operator: "New Harbour? What's that?"

Caller: "Division and...he's...It's a restaurant. Indi...Indi...Division and Indiana."

Caller's friend: "Indiana! Indiana!"

Caller: "That's where we are right now and he's...he's running."

911 Operator: "'Kay. I'm gonna transfer you over to Police Dispatch. What's your name?

11

[Omission in the recording]

Caller: "Yeah. Don't...yeah. Oh God! He's like, coming towards our car."

911 Operator: "'Kay. Hold on. I'm gonna transfer you into Dispatch. I'm gonna talk to them first, okay?"

Caller: "Okay."

[Omission in the recording]

Police Operator: "Police Emergency. Hello?"

Caller: "Hi. Um, there's some guy, and he came up to us when we were at the ATM. And uh, he like was trying to get in our car and stuff, so we drove off, but we already put the card in, and he... he was there messing with it forever, and then he..."

Caller's friend (to caller): "Where the fuck am I supposed to go now?"

Caller (to friend): "I don't...go that way."

Caller: "He's walking down Division. He...he walked off with like, stuff. Like he got money out of her ATM, and then when we started coming at him he ran. And now he's walking down Division. And I think he took a ton of money out of her ATM."

Police Operator: "So she'd already put her pin in?"

Caller: "Yeah, 'cause, and then he...he came over to us and was like, trying to get in the car, so we drove off 'cause we didn't know what to do. Yeah, and he took off running and, but he's walking now down Division.

[Omission in the recording]

Police Operator: "Okay, and you went back to your vehicle when he approached you?"

Caller: "Uh, no, we were in the car at the drive-up ATM and he came in..."

Police Operator: "Oh, okay."

Caller's friend: "We just drove off."

Caller: "Yeah. And we drove off when he wouldn't go away. And he's right here, just like walking. Like we'd started driving after he'd started walking off with like the money, and he didn't know where to go, and now he's just walking-he ran, and now he's walking, down Division."

Police Operator: "And you said south on Division?"

Caller (to friend): "Uh, is that south?"

Caller's friend (to Caller): "Yeah."

Caller: "Yeah. Division and Nora right now. Yeah. And he has like, really long blond hair and a black jacket, and okay, now he's turning. Or maybe it's red hair, I don't know. He's walking down Nora now."

Police Operator: "Which way?"

Caller: "East."

Police Operator: "East?"

Caller: "Yeah."

Police Operator: "Okay. What does he look like?"

Caller: "He has like, long blondish..."

Police Operator: "Is he white?"

Caller: "...reddish hair. He's white, um, and he is wearing a black coat and jeans and boots. His hair's like, really long, like past his shoulders long."

Police Operator: "Okay, and you said a black jacket and boots?"

Caller: "Yeah."

Caller's friend (to caller): "Are they sending someone?"

Caller (to friend): "I think so."

Police Operator: "And did you get the card back, or did he take that, too?"

Caller (to friend): "You have your card, right?" (to Operator): "Yeah, she has her card."

Caller's friend (to Caller): "I hit cancel, but I don't know if it actually..."

Caller: "Yeah. Well, she thought she hit cancel, but then he was messing with it forever, and then when we saw him walk away he had like a slip, like, it was like the slip they give back. And he had like a big wad of something, so I think it was money. And then he put it in his jacket, and when we started driving to see where he was going, uh, he ran."

Police Operator: "Okay. So then you went back around to the ATM and got the card?"

Caller: "She already had the card. She...she put it in and took it out, and entered the pin, and..."

Police Operator: "Oh, okay, so it's not one where you leave the card in."

Caller: "Huh-uh."

Police Operator: "Okay. I see. I see."

Caller: "Yeah. She has her card, but she had already put her pin in and stuff, and now he's walking up Ruby and we can't go that way. It's just a one-way. Now he's walking south down Ruby."

Police Operator: "Southbound?"

Caller: "So, against traffic."

Caller's friend: "Yeah...Is he running now? He's running now."

[Omission in the recording]

Caller (to friend): "Stop right here."

Police Operator: "Um, where is he going?"

Caller: "He's turning in to..." (to friend) "Where is he going? What is this place?" (To operator again) "He just turned, like into the grass or something, and..."

[Omission in the recording]

Police Operator: "What side of the street is he on?"

Caller: "Yeah, uh, he's walking like through a parking lot at White Elephant and, like I think he's trying to get away 'cause we're following him. And now he's like hiding, I think."

Police Operator: "At White Elephant?"

Caller: "Yeah. White Elephant and...(indistinct) gas station. There's a gas station. It's in between, uh, Division and Ruby on, and Nora, and...I don't know."

Police Operator: "Okay, so are you on Division then?"

Caller:" Uh, we're...we're on Nora. Yeah."

Police Operator: "Hold on just a second, okay?"

Caller: "Okay. He's walking over into a gas station."

Police Operator: "Okay. Hold on just a second. The officers are asking something, okay?"

Caller: "Okay. There's a cop here."

[Omission in the recording]

Caller: "The cops just ran into the gas station after him."

Police Operator: "Okay, are you still there?"

Caller: "Yeah. The cop just ran into the gas station after him."

Caller's friend: "Oh my God. They're struggle... Oh, my God!"

Caller: "Oh my! He's like...yeah, I think he's getting arrested."

Police Operator: "Are the officers out with him?"

Caller: "Uh, they're...the...one cop got out of the car and ran into the gas station. We're outside the gas station. I guess they're...struggling. Yeah, he's on the ground."

Police Operator: "Okay."

Caller: "Cop's on him."

Police Operator: "Okay. All right. Um, and what kind of car are you in?"

Caller (to friend): "Uh, what kind of car are we in?"

Caller's friend (to Caller): "Dodge Intrepid."

Caller: "Dodge Intrepid, white. Are...if they took the money, what are we supposed to do?"

Police Operator: "Well, where are you right now? I was going to have you wait there, and we'll send an officer over to talk to you.

Caller: "Um, we're right outside the gas station where they are, a 76 on Division by White Elephant."

Police Operator: "Okay, we'll have someone come out and talk to you, okay?"

Caller: "Okay, thank you."

Police Operator: "All right. Bye-bye."

*

The radio traffic between Police Dispatch and officers on patrol pertaining to the 911 call began at 6:15 pm:

Unknown police operator: "Channel 242 traffic."

Original police operator: "Can you signal 8 radio?"

Original operator: "25 (Stephen Braun) and 26 (Zachary Storment)."

Officer Braun: "25, and it's a call at Baldwin and Ruby. I'll check and advise."

Original operator: "325, copy. 26, you can."

Original operator: "325, a white male in his forties with long blond hair, wearing a black jacket and jeans."

Officer Braun: "Copy."

Original operator: "325, he's still bent down messing with the ATM machine, and the complainant thinks he appears to be high."

Officer Braun: "25, copy."

Police dispatcher: "Adam, 325."

Officer Braun: "Go ahead."

Police dispatcher: "He's got some sort of money in his hand, and now he's taken off running towards New Harbour, and now they're gonna transfer the call into us. You sure you don't want a 13?"

Officer Braun: "Yeah, you can start one."

Police dispatcher: "322 (Timothy Moses)."

Officer Moses: "22, Francis and Nevada."

Officer Braun: "25, I'm in the area."

Police dispatcher: "Copy."

Police dispatcher: "The 25 is walking southbound Ruby against traffic now."

Officer Braun: "...W. Try to get down there."

Officer Braun: "...Happen to know which side of the street he's on, east or west?"

Police dispatcher: "I'll check. Stand by."

Police dispatcher: "And he's actually at the White Elephant now, and the complainant did get her card back."

Officer Braun: "Copy, and just to confirm, he took her money?"

Police dispatcher: "Affirm."

Officer Thompson: "Edward 252 (Officer Karl Thompson)."

Police dispatcher: "Edward 252."

Officer Thompson: "Could be out at the White Elephant. I'll check on the Ruby side."

Police dispatcher: "Copy."

Officer Thompson: 252. He's just walking into the Zip Trip."

Police dispatcher: "Uh, so now the complainant's advising she's not entirely positive that he did get her money. She did not get a chance to go back and check."

Officer Braun: "...He's fighting pretty good."

Officer Thompson: "Code 6."

Police dispatcher: "Code 6 at the Zip Trip on Division."

Officer Moses: "...22, a couple of blocks off."

Officer McIntyre: "Edward 257 (Officer Sandra McIntyre), we're... slow 'em down."

Police dispatcher: "Edward 257, I copied: slow it down to the Zip Trip."

Officer Walker: "...216 (Officer Joey Walker), we have enough units at the Zip Trip now."

Police dispatcher: "Copy. Enough units at the Zip Trip. Is it okay to go back to normal?"

Officer Walker: "Ah, just hold traffic for a second, but you can tell everybody else to slow down though."

Police dispatcher: "Copy."

Officer Moses: "...2, where's our complainant?"

Police dispatcher: "Should be waiting right outside there in a white Dodge Intrepid."

Officer Moses: "Outside the Zip Trip here?"

Police dispatcher: "Affirm."

Officer Moses: "Copy."

(Unintelligible contact from Officer Ronald Voeller to dispatch.)

Police dispatcher: "Copy. Is it gonna be a de–Taser deployment?"

Officer Voeller: "Affirmative."

Police dispatcher: "And where did the Tasers go to?"

No response.

Police dispatcher: "They need to know where on his body the Tasers went."

No response.

(Call to Emergency Medical Service initiated)

Officer Braun: "325, we'll need a Corporal here as well."

Police dispatcher: "Copy. 12-314s still en route, and can you advise where the Taser probes went?"

Officer Braun: "In his upper torso. He was balled up. Couldn't tell exactly where they went."

Police dispatcher: "Copy."

*

The Computer Assisted Dispatch (CAD) classified the call, "SUSCIR," for "suspicious circumstances."

The CAD tracked the movements of Otto Zehm from the ATM into the Zip Trip. The 6:25 entry indicated, "Subj is fighting," and at 6:27, "Still need more units, inside the store." One minute later, "Enough units," was dispatched.

"Taking the male to Deac (Deaconess Medical Center)" was dispatched at 6:58, and at 7:01, "Strassenberg going to hospital in ambulance." Reports of Zehm's condition were communicated periodically by CAD. At 10:17, "Male still has a BP/pulse due to active CPR..." Later, "Male is in CT scan, appears more stable but still in very bad condition." At 12:12, "Moved to critical care, also hospital keeps asking if family has been notified." Then, "Hospital staff advised it is OK to contact subject's family if they have info."

The last CAD entry was dispatched at 12:44: "Subject moved to CCU...still critical...he is on ventilator."

*

Acting Police Chief Jim Nicks arrived at the Zip Trip about 7:30 pm. After he was briefed by officers at the scene, he triggered the Critical Incident Protocol, which is utilized when there is an officer-involved serious injury or fatality.

Evidence from the scene was gathered, marked, and labeled, and the officers involved in the incident were placed on leave. Detective Terry Ferguson, a senior Spokane Police Department major crimes investigator, was appointed lead investigator.

That evening Chief Nicks spoke with Assistant City Attorney Rocco Treppiedi, the Spokane Police Department's legal adviser and the city's Risk Manager. The media was contacted, and the first official statement pertaining to the incident was released.

Later that evening newscaster Kalae Chock announced on the KXLY television news broadcast, "A man is in critical condition after a fight with Spokane police at a local convenience store. Acting Police Chief Jim Nicks says the man lunged at an officer as he was responding to a suspicious person call. Nicks says it took between four and five officers to take down the man and that even Tasers and batons couldn't keep him down. Nicks says once the suspect was contained, emergency crews checked him for injuries."

In a recorded video shown on the broadcast, Nicks said, "Because of the nature of the fight, they were concerned about possible injuries that may have been caused to him due to the very horrific fight actually between him and the officers."

Ms. Chock added, "Nicks says it was about ten minutes after that when the man stopped breathing. EMTs performed CPR on the suspect and rushed him to the hospital, where Nicks says he's in critical condition tonight. Authorities are not releasing the name of the suspect but do say that he has a history of run-ins with police."

*

Three days later the city's daily newspaper, The Spokane Spokesman-Review, published this synopsis:

MAN WHO FOUGHT POLICE DIES IN HOSPITAL

A 35-year-old man who was hospitalized Saturday after fighting with police died about 3:30 pm. Monday at Deaconess Medical Center.

An autopsy is planned to determine the cause of death for Otto Carl Zehm.

Acting Police Chief Jim Nicks said the fight was under investigation, but, "appropriate defensive tactics were used by the officers to subdue this man who fought violently."

Nicks said Taser stun guns were ineffective after Zehm attacked one officer shortly after 6 pm. Saturday and fought several more.

The incident began when a woman reported a man behaving suspiciously at Ruby and Indiana.

A police officer approached Zehm at the Zip Trip store at Division and Augusta, and Zehm lunged at the officer, according to Cpl. Tom Lee.

It took four or five officers to subdue Zehm, who gave an address of 1934 N. North Center Street, Lee said.

Zehm began having trouble breathing, Lee said, and was taken to Deaconess.

CHAPTER TWO

In Washington state, Spokane is not considered a very progressive community. Its residents routinely complain about the high gasoline taxes they pay to support transportation projects like a ferry system and new bridges on the more populous west side. In general, its voters turn out every few years to elect conservative candidates and reject the improvement taxes proposed by the city, county, or school system. That is particularly true of less prosperous areas like north central Spokane, where damage to the asphalt streets from the winter's freeze-thaw cycle is patched piecemeal year after year and its neighborhoods, with small lots and older homes in varying states of repair, can look, well, shabby.

In 2013 the budget for Spokane County's general fund was $140 million, 74% of which was spent to pay for criminal justice programs-the sheriff's office, jail, court system, prosecutor and public defender offices, and probation services. Calls for a larger jail are frequent from those seeking election. As the county commissioners have no intention of bringing the unpassable tax increase required to the ballot, politicians can espouse strong law and order views knowing they will never be expected to get out front and sell the funding to the public.

As part of the Critical Incident Protocol, detectives from the Spokane Police Department and the Spokane County Sheriff's Office came to the Zip Trip that evening, the latter to ensure that the city's detectives followed the proper procedures and obtained information in an objective manner. However, the city's detectives began the investigation prior to the arrival of their shadows from the county. Detective Ferguson was briefed by Spokane Police Officer Timothy Moses, then she and Police Detective Mark Burbridge interviewed the store clerk, Leroy Colvin. Burbridge indicated later, "We determined we would not wait for county detectives to arrive... because we were concerned about possible contamination of his statement."

While their reports of the Colvin interview differed, both recorded very strong statements made against Zehm. According to Ferguson, Colvin became aware of the activity in the corner of the store, looked over, and heard Officer Thompson tell Zehm to put down the pop bottle. Then Zehm started yelling at Thompson, and the two "became engaged in a fight."

According to Burbridge, however, "Colvin said the first thing he remembered seeing was the large guy with the long hair holding up a two-liter Pepsi bottle. Then he saw the officer take that subject to the ground." Burbridge recorded that Colvin said he heard verbal commands by Thompson before the confrontation began but did not see aggressive action from Zehm at that point. Both detectives reported that Colvin described Zehm as angry, aggressive, and noncompliant later and saw Thompson striking Zehm with his baton, Burbridge recording "two or three times."

Detective Burbridge oversaw the processing of the scene, numbering evidence, recording placements, and supervising other detectives and forensic specialists. That night he and his shadow from the Sheriff's Office, Detective Douglas Marske, interviewed an additional witness, Andrew Schmidt. A security guard, Mr. Schmidt was washing his car at a distance from the Zip Trip and did not enter the store until the back-up officers had arrived and Zehm was hogtied. He said that the subject was "cussing and fighting" and described the fighting as, "wiggling around, trying to get the leg restraints off." Burbridge asked Schmidt what the subject was screaming, and both he and Detective Marske recorded, "The suspect continued to yell things like, 'Fuck this!' and called the officers 'a bunch of assholes.'"

Detective Ferguson and her shadow, Sheriff's Detective Charles Haley, went to Police Department headquarters to examine and tactically debrief the officers involved in the incident. They found the officers sitting together talking. Lieutenant Lundgren, a friend of Officer Thompson who had driven him there, had stayed to make sure the officers involved "didn't collaborate too much." Ernie Wuthrich, a representative of the Spokane Police Guild, and Officers McCabe and Walter were also present.

"Tactical debriefing" is the process for retrieving evidence that might have been missed by the forensic team or must be taken from officers' persons, such as weapons used or damage to uniforms. The Critical Incident Protocol specifies that any discussion during tactical debriefing pertain solely to evidence procurement. Ferguson indicated that the protocol was followed.

Officers Thompson and Braun presented injuries. Thompson had "a scrape/scratch above his right eyebrow, a scratch/gouge near his third knuckle on the outside of the right little finger, and redness on his inside left and right knees." He said his right arm near the inside of the elbow was becoming sore and that Corporal Ty Johnson, who had taken photographs of him at the scene, had mentioned a possible injury to his right cheek. Officer Braun had only a small red spot on one knee, which was beneath a scuff on his pants.

Lieutenant Scott Stephens, head of the Spokane Police Department's Major Crimes Unit, had gone to Deaconess Medical Center to relieve Officer Braun. On arrival he learned from a nurse that a CT scan of Zehm's head and heart testing had been done and that neither provided much insight into his condition. In his report he stated, "I asked (Emergency Department RN Brian) Rogge if he had noticed any obvious signs of trauma of any kind that might be a causal factor to Zehm's condition, and he stated that he did not observe any obvious signs of trauma to Zehm."

During the next few weeks, Detective Ferguson procured the audio and print dispatch records, obtained the ATM surveillance footage, collected the reports of the police officers and EMTs involved in the incident, interviewed two witnesses, and examined Zehm's personal, medical, and work history. She conducted the recorded interviews of Officers Braun and Thompson.

Several officers assisted Detective Ferguson with the investigation. Detective Lesser reviewed the Police Department's Taser policy, and Detective Miller spoke briefly with Zehm's bosses and sat in on the autopsy. Officer Bowman reviewed the surveillance video from the Zip Trip, analyzing the force used during the incident with Ferguson's direction.

Between March 18 and 22, Detectives Burbridge and Marske interviewed eight witnesses, Alison Smith, Mackenzie Murcar, Patrick Conley, Justin Balam, Carrie Coyle-Balow, Russell Balow, and two who had already spoken to the media, Michael Dahl and Kristina Turner.

Pertaining to what transpired at the ATM, the Murcar and Smith interviews confirmed that Zehm had walked up to their car, had mentioned "$500," spoke loudly and incoherently, and frightened them. They thought he was on drugs. When they followed him out of the bank's parking lot, he noticed them and started yelling.

According to Burbridge, after Zehm had entered the Zip Trip, "Murcar said she saw the officer walk up to the male and the male punched the officer... [then] she saw the officer pull the male to the ground and the officer struck the male with his baton two or three times." In a follow-up call the next day, Murcar changed her statement to say that Zehm was "swinging his arms like crazy" but denied seeing Zehm hit the officer. Detective Marske reported Murcar saying she saw two or three baton strikes while they were on the ground and that Smith said she saw the baton rise and fall over the aisles approximately ten times. Burbridge corroborated this report: "The officer took the male to the ground. Smith said that she saw the officer swing his baton 'over and over.' She said she thought he used it approximately ten times."

Detective Burbridge reported that Patrick Conley "said the officer appeared to be telling the subject something and all of a sudden the subject went to the ground... He saw the subject on the floor swinging his arms at the officer and kicking at him. Conley said he saw the officer use his club to hit the subject on the shoulders and stopped about the time a second officer arrived on scene." He described the subject as swinging at the officer with closed fists and the baton strikes used by the officers as jabs instead of full swings. Regarding two of the other witnesses, "Conley mentioned that while he was watching outside, a guy and a girl whom he thought looked a little shady (he referred to them as possible drug dealers in the neighborhood) commented that the police were picking on the guy just for stealing a Pepsi bottle and he didn't deserve what they were doing. Conley told us he commented to them that the guy didn't have to fight with the police and maybe he deserved exactly what he was getting."

Justin Balam said he never heard any conversation between the two, though he added that he could have not been paying attention. He described Zehm turning quickly toward Thompson, to which Thompson responded with a baton strike to Zehm's shoulder. Regarding the initial Taser application, "Balam said that for several seconds the Taser appeared to work and then Otto became enraged and began kicking violently." Reflecting on the incident, Balam admitted he thought Zehm was resisting arrest but perceived that Zehm was trying to get away or defend himself from the officers rather than assault them. He thought Thompson used too much force and had several opportunities to make the arrest.

The Balows saw the incident in their rear-view mirrors when pulling away from a gas pump at the store. Both said that Zehm was holding a pop bottle in front of him, and neither saw Zehm make an aggressive move. They saw Thompson do something before the initial baton strike-Carrie thought she saw Thompson say something, and Russell thought he saw Thompson stop momentarily. Burbridge reported that the couple did not agree on the details of what occurred before the first strike and did not mention how the baton strikes were delivered or, in the case of Carrie Balow's interview, where they landed. The detective's report stated that Russell said the strikes landed on Zehm's shoulder and did not include any mention of either of the Balows seeing strikes to Zehm's head.

Shortly before Zehm was declared dead, Detective Ferguson learned that two customers in the Zip Trip during the incident had given interviews to local news crews in which they claimed the official police version was grossly inaccurate. The following day Detectives Burbridge and Marske interviewed Michael Dahl and Kristina Turner in their home after having the other family members sit outside on the curb. Burbridge implied in his report that he and Detective Marske showed these unreasonably defensive and suspicious witnesses only professionalism and courtesy.

Dahl indicated he was standing on the south side of the register and had a clear view from the start of the encounter. Zehm was not resisting Thompson initially. Thompson gave a quick command before hitting Zehm in the chest with the baton, and Zehm went to the ground. While Zehm was down, he saw Thompson strike him with the baton "maybe 5 or 6 additional times while the guy was on the ground...in the knees, legs, and arms and a couple of times in the head." He did not see whether Zehm's hands were closed but heard Zehm screaming and saw him kicking his feet "all over" in attempts to "just get away." Dahl never heard Thompson tell Zehm to stop fighting and thought Zehm was a little "slow." Then Burbridge recorded that Dahl "got very angry and complained about officers driving fast with and without their lights on and pulled into the parking lot almost striking parked cars. Dahl was angry and commented that this was not safe."

Kristina Turner was even closer to the encounter than Dahl. She said she saw Thompson walk up behind Zehm and say, "Drop the soda," at which point Zehm turned around and Thompson hit him on the shoulder with his baton. Thompson stood over him and struck him several more times with the stick while Zehm shielded his face with the pop bottle. Then Thompson dropped the stick and punched Zehm with his fists about twenty times. After Braun arrived, Thompson got his stick back and struck Zehm five or ten times on the body and four or five times on the head. She never heard Thompson say, "Stop fighting," or Braun say anything. Turner added, "The officers didn't need to do this and she thought there were several times when the officers could have taken the gentleman into custody. One of those was right after the first tasing and again after he was tased several more times."

Burbridge recorded, "Detective Marske and I explained to her what the video of the incident showed and how the fight did not all occur near the south side door. In fact, the majority of it occurred in the center aisle near the west side door. Turner got a little angry and could not explain the discrepancy between her statement and the video." He also asked if she actually saw Thompson strike Zehm on the head, to which she replied that she saw him strike Zehm several times on the upper body and assumed he was struck on the head but never actually saw the blows connect. Burbridge indicated he told her that the video shows Officer Braun arriving after Thompson and Zehm had moved from the south aisle to the center and asked her if she could explain the discrepancy in what she had seen. At that point she said she "didn't want to make misstatements to have us discredit everything she saw because she knows what she saw." At another point in the interview she said that the news people had warned her that the police would try to discredit her. The two detectives assured her that that was not their intention and that they merely wanted to "make sure she was telling us what she actually saw and not confusing it with what she had heard other people say."

*

The investigation required reports from each of the officers involved. Officers Steven Braun and Karl Thompson were interviewed, and written reports were obtained from the others.

Braun's interview, the first taken by Detective Ferguson, started at 2:30 pm on March 20, 2006. In attendance was Spokane County Sheriff's Office Major Crimes Detective Doug Marske. Ferguson started by verifying that Braun had had an opportunity to discuss the interview with his Spokane Police Guild representative and that he and she had discussed the incident prior to the recording.

Braun indicated he had been a police officer for a little over six years and was a member of the crowd control team and a field training officer. He acknowledged he had been trained in the use of force and specifically, of Tasers and side handle batons.

He logged off work about 2:25 am on March 18th, slept seven to eight hours, and returned to work shortly after 3 pm. Roll call lasted twenty to twenty-five minutes. Six or seven officers were on patrol that night. He was in a one-man car assigned to the north side of Spokane. His call sign was Adam 325 and patrol vehicle, 386.

He responded to a call from a woman about a domestic altercation soon after he started patrol around 4:30 pm. He became aware of the call leading to the incident at the Zip Trip when he was driving and pulled up the calls holding in his patrol car. He did not remember if the call had been labeled "trouble unknown" or "suspicious person." He saw that a woman called indicating a man was "messing with" the ATM at the Washington Trust Bank at the corner of Ruby and Baldwin Streets. While reading about the complaint, his call signs and that of Officer Zach Stoment came from Radio. He replied that he would respond and that another unit was not needed. While in route to the bank he was advised that the callers were watching the man and that he may have gotten some of their money, "But it wasn't clear."

He radioed that he would take another unit in response to the call if one were available but did not hear anyone else being asked to respond. He continued past the bank when he arrived there because he had heard on the radio that the man was running east on Nora.

He was advised initially that the man had long blond hair and subsequently, long red hair. Then he learned that the man was near the White Elephant, a retail store on Division. While changing directions he recognized the voice of Officer Thompson on the radio indicating that a man matching that description was walking into the Zip Trip, a convenience store next to the White Elephant.

Braun parked on the south side of the Zip Trip, put his flashlight in his left side pocket, and secured his baton in the ring on the left side of his duty belt. Not having seen another patrol vehicle or Officer Thompson in the area, he walked to the south entrance of the Zip Trip. As he approached, he saw three or four customers standing across the counter from the store clerk. To avoiding putting his gun side toward the customers and to get a clear view of the entire store, he walked around to the west entrance from where he could see Thompson wrestling with the suspect near the south shelf in the center of the store. He knew that Thompson had fired the probes of his Taser as the wiring was lying on the floor and realized that Thompson had to have been fighting with the suspect for at least 30 seconds for the wiring to be discarded and for Thompson to be back on the suspect. He believed he needed to "get in this and... [keep] Officer Thompson from getting injured." He added, "I need to keep Mr. Zehm from getting injured at all if that is possible. Need to get him under control and try to calm down the situation and then figure out what's going on."

Braun pulled out his baton as he was coming through the door. Thompson was bent over or kneeling on the right side of Zehm, who was lying on his back between the shelves. As he approached, he saw Zehm's left hand in a fist. "I told Zehm to stop fighting, stop resisting." Braun delivered "three or four power jabs" with his baton to Zehm's left ribcage, to which Zehm did not react. He saw "some sort of paper that was white or off-white" in Zehm's left hand and thought it was U.S. currency. Braun did not recall Thompson saying anything to him prior to delivering the jabs.

After the jabs he stepped back "just to try and do an assessment to see if there was any, any weapons, if he was still fighting." He saw that Zehm was still fighting with his left hand in a fist and that Thompson did not have any control over Zehm. "His arms were moving, his legs were moving." He thought then, "This is going to be a, a big fight... I am a larger man and I used my side handle (baton) to deliver 3 or 4 power jabs and they had no effect. It's like he didn't even know I was there."

When Braun attempted to reengage in the struggle, Zehm rolled. Braun delivered "two or three more power jabs" to Zehm's left ribcage, which had "zero effect." Then he heard Thompson say, "Get your Taser out. Use your Taser. You might have to take a second to try and get a good shot." Braun understood Thompson to mean he needed to achieve enough spread between the two probes to have an effect sufficient for them to handcuff Zehm. He recognized he had to avoid shooting Thompson as that would take him out of the fight.

At that point Thompson was still on Zehm's right side and Zehm was "still fighting and wrestling." Braun turned off the safety on his Taser and the point of red light showing where the top probe will strike appeared. He aimed the light "maybe just a half an inch below his sternum," and fired.

Braun had seen people hit with the probes before, "And every time that I've seen it, the person makes kind of an 'uhhhhh' sound and just kind of locks up and gets really tense and then has no control. Just kind of falls over or lays there, but isn't able to move their arms or throw punches or anything like that."

However, he did not know if the probes hit as Zehm was "still moving around...still flailing. He didn't make any sound other than the groans and moans he had been making the whole time when I had been there." Braun turned the safety back on and removed that cartridge from his Taser. While attempting to insert a new cartridge, he saw Zehm's left knee bend. "My initial reaction was that he was going to kick me." Zehm looked at him, which Braun interpreted to indicate, "[Zehm] was acquiring a target." He felt Zehm's kick contact his left knee, after which Thompson said, "something to the effect of, 'Do a touch stun, do a drive stun.'"

Braun put his Taser into the left side of Zehm's neck and pressed the trigger for up to six seconds. He believed he delivered "at least one, but no more than two 5 second bursts with my Taser to the left side of Zehm's neck. He made a loud groaning noise... [but] his left hand was still in a fist. I could still see that he was pulling back and forth on Officer Thompson. He was still fighting in my opinion... The drive stun had no effect."

Then he saw Zehm put his left fist over his head. "I don't know if he was trying to punch me, [or] if he was trying to protect his face... I then delivered a drive stun into the area of his left armpit. As soon as I depressed the trigger, I took my finger immediately off of the trigger so I know, I feel very confident that there was only one 5 second burst delivered that time."

Braun indicated Zehm was wearing a gray T-shirt, a leather jacket that was unzipped and open in front, and blue jeans. He acknowledged that the drive stun in the armpit would have been through the jacket and T-shirt. "That again didn't work... and he was still fighting. I took a step back... Zehm was now in a seated position with his back to me and Officer Thompson." Thompson asked him to try to get a neck restraint. Braun dropped his Taser and "got my right hand near Zehm's right jaw trying to put a neck restraint on." However, he feared getting bitten and contracting a bloodborne pathogen or losing a finger, so he did not complete the maneuver.

After a short break in the interview, Braun stated, "I should go back a little to when I first walked in. Another one of the things I remember thinking was that this guy was wanting to fight and not, he was trying to flee or get away. He was trying to fight and with that, trying to injure somebody... That became very clear to me when he looked up at me like he was getting a target and actually kicked me. I thought he was trying to hurt me."

Braun was asked about his observations of Zehm's interaction with Officer Thompson. "He was fighting. I mean that, that, if Officer Thompson had to use a Taser and that didn't work and, you know, the way that this guy had both of his hands...he was there to fight and, and to injure somebody and not just, 'Leave me alone, I don't feel like going to jail.' He was there to fight."

Detective Ferguson reviewed Zehm's failure to comply with Braun's command, "Stop fighting, stop resisting," and the lack of effect of the Taser probes and drive stuns. Braun indicated, "[Zehm] didn't say, 'Ow,' didn't say, 'Stop,' didn't say, 'Leave me alone,' didn't say anything, just kind of grunting."

Braun stated that after he aborted the attempted neck restraint, he pushed Zehm to the right, and Zehm ended up lying on his right side with his head toward the floor. Braun put his right shin across the left side of Zehm's jaw and both hands on Zehm's left arm. He was able to use his right hand to radio for more units. Then he heard Thompson "get on the air and say, 'Code 6,' which means, 'We need a heightened response, we need a couple of units. We need them to come here using their emergency equipment, overhead lights, audible signal to get here because we need help immediately.'"

"Then somehow, Zehm was on his back and I was no longer on him... I no longer had control over him at all, but I don't know or cannot remember exactly how it is that I was no longer in that position... I then put my left knee either on his left forearm or left rib cage above his arm, but some place where I felt I had at least some control over his left hand so that he didn't have the ability to punch me or Officer Thompson. His right hand in a fist then came up over his face. I don't know if he was trying to punch me. I don't know if he was trying to pull away from Officer Thompson... I immediately grabbed, used my right hand to grab his right wrist from the pinkie side and put my left hand either on his forearm or near his elbow and just to control that hand so that I didn't get punched, Officer Thompson didn't get punched, and to try to get some control so the fight would end. I then started to twist his pinkie so his pinkie would have been twisting up toward his face in a counterclockwise motion. My hope was that I was going to be able to twist his arm in that way. Straighten his arm out, pull him to get him to a prone position so we could handcuff him and get control and end the fight...or lower the possibilities of somebody getting injured, whether it was law enforcement or Zehm... I wasn't able to straighten out his arm. I wasn't able to pull him over, and I remember saying something to the effect of, 'This isn't working and if I twist too much more, I'm going to break his arm,' and I didn't want to break his arm. And then shortly after I said that, I saw another officer come in and start helping to get control, and then a split second later there were 4 or 5 other officers trying to control Zehm, and I was no longer directly involved in the altercation nor did I have any physical contact with Zehm."

He recognized the others as Sergeant Torok and Officers Uberuaga, Raleigh, and Dahl. He said they could not immediately get Zehm on his stomach for a prone handcuffing position. During their interaction with Zehm, he did not see any baton strikes or Taser use.

Braun picked up his baton and Taser. He thought he would have to "get back in to try and control Zehm," but then saw Zehm on his back getting handcuffed. He heard someone ask, "Do we need to leg restrain him?" He indicated that he and someone else responded that Zehm needed to be leg restrained. Braun described seeing Zehm on his stomach in handcuffs "kind of flailing about...still kicking." He heard a couple of different voices say, "Stop fighting, stop kicking..." Then he saw somebody put leg restraints on Zehm.

Braun noticed Officer Thompson's straight baton near the southwest corner of the store. He walked outside, saw Corporal Johnson, and asked him to take a photograph of the boot print on his pants. After the photograph was taken, he walked back into the store and heard Officer Uberuaga say, "The guy is not breathing. He is turning blue."

He knew EMTs had been there to remove the Taser darts. He ran out the west entrance of the store, saw one and yelled, "The guy's not breathing. We need help."

After emergency personnel reentered the store, Braun talked with other officers about what had happened. He saw Officer Sandra McIntyre pick up what looked like a couple of pieces of mail that they believed Zehm had dropped. He asked Officer Moses, who arrived after the first group of backup officers, to contact the original complainant and get a statement from her.

Before Zehm stopped breathing, he had heard Officer Strassenberg say that American Medical Response was needed for ambulance transport. Braun thought that necessary because, "I thought he was high on methamphetamine just 'cause of the way he was acting and no pain compliance, nothing."

He stated that medics were called "almost immediately after Zehm was placed in handcuffs, possibly before the leg restraints went on. It was very early on."

Braun followed the ambulance to Deaconess Medical Center "with my overhead emergency lights on so that I could stay directly behind the ambulance in case Zehm came to and started fighting again and (the ambulance) had to pull over."

He was asked if he had seen any blood on Officer Thompson or himself. "After everything was over, I saw there was some dried blood or that Officer Thompson had been bleeding in his lip, in his lower lip." He acknowledged

31

that the leg restraint did not immobilize Zehm. "He was still flailing around, and I remember hearing somebody...saying that he was stretching the leg restraints."

Ferguson concluded Braun's interview with the question, "Was there any point during the struggle with Mr. Zehm that you thought you were going to get hurt?"

"As soon as I walked in and saw the Taser on the ground, I knew... 'Oh, shit, this guy's fighting to fight and to injure, not to flee,' and then when I struck him with my side handle baton and had zero effect... I'm a large guy and I'm fairly strong and if I'm hitting somebody with or power jabbing with a side handle baton and they act like they didn't know I was there...the chance of me getting injured or Officer Thompson getting injured, I felt, were pretty high."

Braun's interview was concluded at 3:56 pm. During the interview Otto Zehm was declared dead at Deaconess Medical Center. His pancreas, spleen, kidneys, and adrenal glands were harvested for transplantation before his body was transported to the county morgue for a forensic autopsy.

CHAPTER THREE

Detective Ferguson interviewed Karl Thompson on the afternoon of Wednesday, March 22, 2006, in the presence of Spokane Police Guild representative Jeff Harvey, Guild attorney Hillary McClure, and Spokane County Sheriff's Detective Bill Francis. She began, "We are discussing the situation that occurred at the Zip Trip on Saturday on the 18th and we have already had an opportunity to discuss it... On occasion Detective Francis and myself will be referring to the notes that we took to make sure we address the same things we did in the pre-interview."

Officer Thompson was asked to describe his experience in law enforcement. He indicated that he began his career with the Los Angeles Police Department in 1969. During the 10 years with that department, he was a hostage negotiator and spent the last five and one-half years in a special assignment of SWAT. He moved to Idaho in 1979 and worked with the Kootenai County Sheriff's Department as a deputy, a State Police detective, and an administrator. He spent seven years working privately as an arson and fraud investigator for insurance companies before joining the Spokane Police Department in 1997. His assignments in Spokane had included Patrol, Field Resource Officer, TAC Team for crowd control, Crisis Intervention Team for dealing with the mentally ill, Critical Incident Management Team, Field Training Officer, and hostage negotiator. His current position was patrol officer on the 11 am-9:40 pm shift and his primary area, the north side of Spokane.

He described having had ongoing training with TAC, "which includes defensive tactics," and recent training within Patrol that consisted of "refresher training in defensive tactics...close contact and ground fighting." He acknowledged having had extensive baton training and stated that he carried his baton "on most of the calls and contacts that I have."

He had been trained in the use of force and indicated that he preferred a straight baton. His certification to use a

Taser had included training in which he was "shocked by the 50,000 volts from a Taser...something that was very forceful and very effective on me." He had used his baton and Taser "many times" in situations Detective Ferguson referred to as "lawful law enforcement activities."

Thompson carried his Taser in a thigh holster on patrol and had both discharged the probes and administered drive stuns in the course of his work. Discharged probes "had always produced successful incapacitation." He described the drive stun impact as "creating an amount of pain in which you're seeking compliance" and acknowledged that his results with that technique had been inconsistent.

On March 18th, roll call started at 11:00 am. Thompson's call sign was Edward 252, and he was in a one-man patrol car. On his duty belt he was carrying "my Glock sidearm, ammunition, 2 handcuffs...a small flashlight...my portable radio, my baton. I also have a multi-tool pliers-knife that's on my belt, OC or pepper spray, and then I normally carry an additional sidearm concealed as a backup."

He responded to several calls that day, one a hit-and-run collision and another in which he recovered a gun. He picked up a couple of hamburgers and went to the North Central COP Shop to eat dinner. It was there that he heard the first radio traffic concerning the Zehm call. "I heard Adam 325, which I recognized was Steve Braun's call sign. It was dispatched to a north side call... Shortly after I heard his call sign going on a call, I heard radio broadcast that the suspect was running or walking towards the New Harbour Restaurant... Because that's fairly close to where I was at, I walked outside to...pull up the call on my computer, my car computer, to read the circumstances and be prepared."

He acknowledged that more information was available on the CAD screen. He read, "'The complainant was at an ATM...when she saw a male approaching in a, in a aggressive manner that frightened her to the extent, she had already punched in her pin number, but she was frightened enough that she left the ATM machine to get away from this individual who was coming, walking towards her.' It also gave the description of the complainant's car... [and] of the subject, uh, white male, I believe it said 40's, long reddish hair, black jacket... and the possibility that he may have withdrawn cash under her PIN that was already punched in."

Ferguson asked, "So what did you understand was the fundamental nature of this call?"

Thompson replied, "Even though it...began as it was titled a suspicious person, this information led me to believe that a crime may have been committed, either that or premature robbery attempt based on the complainant's description of the mannerism of this individual... I believed that it was...likely that...a crime may have been committed."

He was driving in the direction of Division and Indiana Streets when he learned that the suspect was approaching the White Elephant, a retail store. He turned south and, as he entered the driveway between the White Elephant and the Zip Trip, saw the complainant's car at the east end of the lot. Then he saw "a white male, 35-40, long reddish hair, black leather jacket, dark trousers, coming from the east...and entered the store. This person, this male matched the description that had been broadcast.

"It was evident that I was the first officer who was in a position to actually see the suspect... I advised radio that the suspect was entering the Zip Trip." He parked his car beside the gas pumps, got out, and grabbed his baton. "I was assuming that the suspect may have seen me drive approaching him in my police car as he was walking through the door... I got out and ran to the north door." Thompson claims he was concerned the suspect would leave the store by one of the other exits "and we were going to have a foot pursuit." Through the windows he saw the suspect "walking to the west end of the store, turning and walking south towards the corner." Thompson entered and immediately ran to the west and turned south. "The suspect initially had his back towards me and appeared to be reaching for something off a shelf. As soon as he turned around, I could see that he was holding a large two-liter bottle filled with a dark liquid."

Ferguson asked him to "back up to the clothing description and specifically, the jacket."

Thompson described it as "a heavy black leather jacket...waist length...like a motorcycle jacket...a kind of soft body armor. If the situation developed and an officer had to use force, leather is going to protect the person wearing it... If there is a Taser application, during the training, one of the things we were advised of, that leather can be somewhat defeating of the electric current...of a Tasing situation. So those are things that were in my mind as well as the fact that a coat also conceals what is underneath."

When asked how Zehm was holding the bottle, Thompson said, "With both hands... parallel to the floor...at chest level, his arms...back toward his body. His elbows were down in what I would describe as a loaded position or where your muscles are tensed back. It's the first thing I recognized and, number one, it was a very unusual way in which to hold a bottle. The second thing I recognized is that this person now has the capability of being in a position...where he can attack me... The distance I closed to was within four feet... I had my baton in my right hand."

Ferguson questioned, "Why did you have it in your hand instead of in the holder?"

"When I entered the store, there were other considerations that I was making that I normally do from training and experience. One is that I was going into a store that created some confinement... I knew that there were canned items, there were glass items as well as all the other soft packaging. There were potential weapons within arms reach... I also realized that I had seen a clerk at the...register as well as what I thought was several patrons on the south side of the counter... I realized that the suspect was wearing a leather coat. I needed to be prepared...to defend myself if necessary and also to control and subdue. My intent was to control this person and physically detain them in handcuffs so we could continue our investigation as to whether there was...clear evidence of a crime and if he was armed. And I knew I was alone and, that being said, I wanted to be prepared especially being alone that I had a less lethal weapon available in case I, either I was attacked or I felt that an attack was imminent."

Ferguson then asked if he'd ever been alone when confronting someone in a suspicious circumstance call, and he indicated that he had. Referring to confronting Zehm, he said, "When I stopped and...was about 4 feet from him, the baton would have been in a...loaded position or cocked position that I if I do have to strike with the baton, it is ready to go and this is also aside from training, this is a ready position. Part of the purpose here is also that when verbal commands are given in a heightened risk situation...the subject receiving the commands, also understands your intent is to project force. You want them to know the urgency of your commands."

When asked what made this situation a heightened risk at this point, he answered, "Circumstances of the call. The fact that the complainant was so alarmed that not only had they sought safety by leaving the ATM, and continuing to maintain surveillance of this person... The fact that I was alone. There were no other officers present and the fact that I, from experience and training, have to be prepared if the person does have a weapon to safely respond, and there were bystanders in the store.

"The individual holding the bottle was holding it in a very tense manner... We made immediate eye contact when he turned around. We were both staring at each other. When I came to a stop, I immediately told him, I ordered him...in a forceful voice, 'Drop it.' He immediately replied, and during this short discourse, we both did not break eye contact. His eyes were wide. He was looking straight at me.

"He said, 'Why?' It was a forceful response... He didn't break eye contact, and my first impression was, here I am in full uniform. I'm displaying the baton in a manner that shows that I'm prepared to strike, I'm ordering him to drop the bottle, and he tells me, 'Why?' And I immediately said, 'Drop it now.' I said it twice as loud and he said, 'No.' It was, again, looking straight at me, clearly without any provocation, that was his response.

"In my mind at that point, in our proximity, my belief was that he was preparing to assault me. When he turned around and saw me entering, he, he did not immediately flee. He picked up an object and it was held in a manner that...he could use it as a significant weapon against me."

Thompson was asked to describe the look on Zehm's face. "The look...did not display any fear...any confusion. Because the eye contact, there was no breaking of eye contact...his voice didn't waiver...he wasn't licking his lips...his facial appearance was deliberate...resolute and, and noncompliant, defiant. I think defiant would be an accurate term, that clearly, he was not going to comply...with my orders.

"I believed that he was preparing to strike me and the recognition there is that normally there is about ¾ of a second reaction time. The person who decides to act first had the advantage...in whatever offensive action they take... Within that distance, I knew he had the advantage and that he had a potential weapon that he could reach me either by swinging or throwing and if it were to hit me in the face, that he would achieve a huge tactical advantage. Realizing that, I decided to strike his leg with my baton to preempt what I believed was about to happen... My hope was to be able to buckle his leg and put him down on the ground there.

37

"The strike was meant to try and incapacitate him, to subdue him and drop him down to the floor, where I could continue verbal instructions with him to lie on the floor, put his hands behind his back, where I would have maintained distance, a guarding position, and advising radio that I had one that I was guarding and maybe for a unit to step it up.

"He immediately pivoted to the right. He didn't drop the bottle because I could see that he hadn't dropped the bottle, and he was turning away from me. I grabbed the back, probably the collar of his jacket...and pulled myself closer. I delivered another strike to his right leg.

"I don't believe I had yet described, in addition to the position he was holding the bottle in, was the stance that he held that was again, I believe I did say it was not a passive stance. It was a very resolute stance... His whole body suggested that it was tensed and prepared to respond either by pushing, throwing, or charging me. That, that's the interpretation that I recognized. The snapshot that I had from, from a lot of experience and training... It's clearly my intention to physically detain him when I made contact with him in the store to continue the investigation.

"Once I had engaged and I struck him, I started yelling orders that, you know, 'Drop it,' 'Stop fighting,' 'Get down,' continually ordering him to cease and to obey what I directed him to do.

"On the second strike and I'm again yelling at him, 'Drop it." He says, 'No,' one more time. That's the last time I remember hearing him tell me anything. Beyond that there were a lot of growls and, and roars, and, and screams...of somebody who is typifying a high level of commitment to resisting or attacking."

When asked what happened next, Thompson stated, "We started thrashing off both shelves...spinning, thrashing, slamming my back into shelves... I'm yelling commands. It's not until the end of the aisle that he drops the bottle. So I am still striking him with the baton using one hand, holding with another, holding the back of his jacket as we're now spinning. At that point....in this first aisle, while he is on his feet, his fists are clenched and he starts boxing me. And he starts swinging both of his fists, and I do feel blows on my upper chest area... My strikes are coming up and hitting on the shoulder, on the torso...wherever I can except the head."

Thompson acknowledged that he was not in a deadly force situation. Then he continued, "When we get to the end of that aisle...I am able to get him, to knock him down. He goes down on his back, and I go down on top of him. He clearly at that point is swinging both his fists at me. I remember pulling back away to get some distance to get away from his punches and I was on my feet, and I also realized that I had just moments if I was going to be able to tase him. And his jacket was not zipped, so in that position, the leather jacket was not covering his torso. I drew my Taser and probably from about three feet I fired...with my left hand with my Taser. I heard the Taser activate and, looking at him, he's still swinging his fists. I hear growling. I'm not seeing the normal reaction I get when I've had to use the Taser. In other words, I'm not seeing that freezing of the body where the muscles are locked up by the electric charge. He's still moving. He rolls and gets to his feet, and I don't remember again at that point if I just dropped the Taser realizing that he may have broken a wire, dislodged a probe, but it's clearly not effective at this point. And the Taser, I don't remember if I reholstered or just dropped it, but I still had the baton in my right hand."

Ferguson asked, "What was your expectation when you discharged the Taser?"

"I thought that the fight was over as soon as I fired the Taser into him. I thought this is what, the point to get to, to tase him. It, it'd be over now. I can control him physically with the Taser."

"And what happened?"

"It didn't work. He kept moving and he started getting up."

"Do you still have your baton in your hand?"

"Yes."

Ferguson continued, "What happened as he started to get up?"

"I started striking him again, and I also know that I didn't have the Taser in my hand when he started to get up...and he's moving away from me. As I'm closing distance he turns around, and this would have been where he...started swinging at me. As I approached to get close enough again to try and push him or knock him down to the floor, he's standing there boxing with both fists, throwing punches."

"And this would have been the second time that he was throwing punches?"

"Yes. That would have been the second time. And it was in this, I clearly remember it was in this first aisle way."

"Did he actually hit you?" Ferguson asked.

"Yep, he hit me. He hit me because, again I was trying to get a grasp on him to be able to spin him or force him down as I'm striking him with the baton. And at this point, you know, I would have been striking his torso and, and any legs or torso or arms as an available target. Realizing that again the strikes while he's got that leather jacket on are not going to be all that effective. Because I'm swinging, I'm not using jabs which would have...required 2 hands. I was using one hand swings."

Then she asked, "How did you end up back down and/or around to the center aisle?"

"We wound up on the next aisle to the north. What I don't clearly remember is the direction we took to get around to that next aisle. I just don't, I don't remember. I do know that I grabbed a hair hold, which is how I was able to stay with him as he's writhing, you know, spinning, and swinging and again, we're banging into the shelves and I'm still yelling at him and striking him, trying to get his legs to buckle. We wind up in the next aisle. He goes down. I knock him down, push him down. He loses his balance and...goes back down on his back, and his head now is oriented somewhat toward that Division St. door, entrance/exit. At this point I realize that I've weakened, the suspect and I have both been going at it full bore and to me it seemed like about a minute, and I realize that I've expended a lot of energy and I'm starting to get tired. I get on top of him and essentially I'm straddling him and I sit on him... I'm using my body weight to try and hold him down. I grabbed his right wrist and tried to move it. He's got both fists clenched up, his fists are still clenched. They're in front of his chest, and I cannot move his, his hand off his chest.

"At this point he's not, he's no longer flailing at me or striking or punching at me. There's a couple of seconds where I was able to get on my shoulder mike. I put out a code 6. That was the first time I was able to get on the radio during, from the time the fight started. When I realized that I couldn't pull his hand off of his chest and that he was not going to respond to verbal commands, then I knew that I, alone, was not going to be able to handcuff him."

Ferguson asked, "Did you see Officer Braun come in?"

"Yes. He came in through the, would be the west door... Again, when I have the suspect down...I had that momentary quiet time to get on the radio, he was kicking and trying to roll out from underneath me. And when Braun came in, first thing he tried to do was grab his, the suspect's left hand, pull it back for handcuffing. Well, he couldn't get his hand off of his chest either...and I know he has considerable strength. So I told him, 'Use your baton, start hitting him.' He started making power jabs in the suspects, would have been his shoulder area, back area, side area, on the left hand side. He tried. He did a number of those. I don't know how many, but then he tried the hand again. There's still no compliance. I told him, 'Use your Taser.'

"Steve stood up, drew his Taser and I could see the muzzle, he was trying to track the suspect because again the suspect is kicking, he is writhing on the floor... He fires, he hits. I hear the Taser activated, but...there's absolutely no effect on the suspect... I saw him strip the cartridge and as soon as he did that, I know he's preparing to do a drive stun, and he comes down and I said, 'Hit him in the neck with it.' And I do see him put it in, in the suspect's, would have been on the left side of his neck and I hear the suspect roar.... Excuse me, I think before we went to the tasing, after the baton strikes by Steve, I told Steve, 'See if you can get a choke on him..' ...And he tried, but he couldn't... Then I believe he went to the Taser and after that was unsuccessful, I was again still astride of the suspect. And I told Steve...'Get your knees on him. Just get him pinned.' I got back on the radio. I said we need another unit inside, and I said the best thing we can do is to just keep our body weight, keep him pinned on the floor until we get some assistance here."

Thompson said that Braun may have applied a second a drive stun to the suspect's torso or underneath an arm. "Once, once Steve, we just went to the pinning mode, Steve again grabbed the suspect's, it would have been his left hand because I had his right hand, and we both just held his wrists until units came in there and joined in.

"Three to four officers came through the west door at the same time... I saw arms grabbing the suspect's arms and start forcefully pulling them back, pulling the suspect's arms off his chest, and they started rolling him, which meant I had to get off of him. Someone handed handcuffs, and I put the first cuff on his right wrist and then handed the other cuff to another officer because I couldn't even see his left arm... Once I knew that the second cuff was on, then I kind of pushed myself away from the suspect and from them and got up and realized that the fight was over at this point and went outside to catch my breath.

"As soon as he was handcuffed, I and at least one officer said, 'Get medics, get on the air, get medics. We've done a Taser application, impact weapons have been involved.' And they did arrive and I went in and out of the store several times. But when medics did arrive, I know that they withdrew the probes because I saw that there were probes on the floor. The medics gathered their equipment and left the store, and I remember hearing an officer say, 'He's not breathing.' I walked over by his head and bent over and someone, one of the other officers moved the subject on his side, and I could see that the discoloration in the face was a dark purple... Someone else said as well, 'Get the leg restraints off of him,' and an officer actually cut the leg restraints. Another officer went out into the parking lot, retrieved the medics before they left, got them back inside and then started the resuscitation attempt."

Then Ferguson asked, "With the experiences and the training you had, especially with the advanced training dealing with mentally incapacitated people, I think you had mentioned that in the beginning... was there anything throughout this incident that suggested an incapacitation on the part of the suspect?"

Thompson replied, "No, nothing, I saw nothing that I've ever picked up on leading up to and during the confrontation gave me any indication that there was any incapacitation there. As I said before, at the point we locked eyes, there was no appearance of confusion. There was, he was, gave me the impression of being resolute, forceful, both in his reply and in his actions... I have the training to adjust accordingly, and I still would have to control the person, still have to subdue the person. It wouldn't have changed the tactics, the physical tactics, because you still have to do what you have to do, and that means physical control in some form."

Thompson was asked that if the suspect had not had something in his hand and still did not comply with his initial verbal commands, would he have used his baton? He answered, "No. The appearance...and how he held the bottle...and then gauging his responses from the two commands, that's how I came to that conclusion... The single reason I hit him with the stick is...I thought I was about to be attacked, and I was going to preempt that and try to gain some tactical advantage."

When asked if he had been injured, Thompson replied, "My right elbow was hurting at the end of this...aside from a scuff on my knuckle and I had some scuffs on my knees, I didn't have any serious or treatable injuries... One over my right eye or cheek that's also photographed."

Ferguson sought then to clarify several points. "When the suspect was down the first time...and he had punched you, at which point you were able to move yourself back and stood up, why did you continue to engage?"

"I still had other bystanders in the store. I hadn't searched him to know if he had other, had weapons concealed, and we still had to detain this person because there, the very basis of the contact was the belief that a crime may have occurred."

"Had a crime occurred independent of the original complaint to this point?"

"My only knowledge, it was connected to the complaint...the caller's information."

"Had there been anything else that had occurred since you made contact with this gentleman?"

"Oh, yeah, yeah, once I engaged and he refused lawful commands...during my attempt to subdue to him, he assaulted me. We had at the very least felony assault on an officer."

"When the other officers arrived after you and Officer Braun had him pinned...for detainment purposes, did you tell them anything?"

"I said, 'Make sure you check him for weapons. We have not searched him for weapons.'"

Two days later Detective Ferguson checked the recorded interview against the practice run and noted an omission from the recording, that Thompson continued to beat Zehm with his baton after tasing him "as it was distracting Zehm and the officer wanted to keep surrender as Zehm's only option." Further clarification added three days later was that Thompson's first strikes were horizontal, and he only delivered diagonal strikes to Zehm's chest after Zehm started punching him. Thompson indicated that he changed targets from Zehm's legs to his shoulders, arms, and wrists only to deflect incoming strikes, and that he never aimed at the soda bottle. Instead, he was trying to strike one specific nerve in Zehm's leg. Thompson also indicated that he carried a unique, extra-long ironwood baton because it allows him "to have distance from a threat."

The transcript of the interview was reviewed and signed by Officer Thompson on March 27, 2006.

Heavier and more durable than the standard materials used in police batons, ironwood has to be crafted with metalworking tools due to its hardness.

*

Officers Zachary Dahl, Sandra McIntyre, Erin Raleigh, Daniel Strassenberg, Jason Uberaga, Ronald Voeller, and Joey Walker and Sergeant Dan Torok had responded to the call from the Zip Trip for backup. The scene they came upon was alarming. Shelves had been knocked out of place and, looking exhausted, Officers Thompson and Braun were sitting on the still struggling Zehm. Several officers noticed that Thompson's uniform was scuffed and dirty, and two noticed blood on his lip. Some described Zehm as trying to hit or kick Thompson and Braun and others as just screaming at them. His shouts were described as "a crazed yell" and "a piercing, rhythmic scream."

Of the four officers who restrained Zehm, two officers pinned Zehm's arms to the ground while another rammed his thumb into a pressure point behind an ear, but Zehm continued "bucking and kicking with superhuman strength." The officers managed to flip Zehm onto his stomach, reposition him in the aisle, and handcuff his hands behind his back. Zehm was calm for a moment, but as soon as the officers got off of him he started kicking, rocking, and trying to get up. Two officers held down his trunk. Two others each put a shin against the back of one of Zehm's knees and hoisted on his feet, trying to get his legs to bend. Zehm held his legs straight, and their efforts lifted his trunk off the ground. Finally the officers were able to bend his knees, and Officer Dahl restrained his legs by wrapping a thick nylon strap around his feet, coiling the slack in the strap around the handcuffs, and securing the hog-tie with a claw clamp.

American Medical Response emergency personnel were called to remove the Taser darts. Zehm started kicking his legs back and pulled so hard against the nylon strap that it stretched a couple of inches. When his hands turned white, the officers feared he would break bones in his hands and get free. They put a second set of handcuffs above the first and took up the slack in the leg restraint. Then they rolled Zehm onto his side. Two officers remained on top of him while waiting for EMS to arrive and remove the Taser darts. At that point Zehm was heard to say, "All I wanted was a Snickers."

Spokane Fire Department paramedics McMullen and Cappellano and EMTs Giampetri and Griffith responded to the American Medical Response call. They understood they were to remove a Taser dart from a male in police custody. They found Zehm "very belligerent, fighting wildly, spitting, kicking, and screaming," and noticed that his face was bloody. Griffith removed one Taser dart and noticed a puncture from another that had fallen out. Abrasions on Zehm's chest were noted and assumed to be from the fight with police officers, who told them batons had been used. Zehm's vital signs were not checked because he was continuing to struggle against the restraints.

Described as "hostile and yelling unintelligibly," Zehm was moved onto his stomach, his legs still tied to the handcuffs. The EMS personnel and police officers discussed the safest means of transporting the suspect. Due to concerns about substance use because of Zehm's extreme strength and seeming immunity to pain and the fear of possible medical complications from the effort he had put forth, it was decided that Zehm would be transported to the hospital in an ambulance with a police escort.

Officer Raleigh requested a mask "to prevent Zehm from continuing his resistive, assaultive, and unruly behavior and possibly utilize the saliva and fresh blood in his mouth to spit on me or other officers." Griffith had a hard time hearing Raleigh's request over Zehm's yells, so Raleigh placed a cupped hand over his nose and mouth, gesturing for a mask. Griffith went to his truck and grabbed a plastic re-breather mask intended for use with supplemental oxygen. He stripped the oxygen tubing from it, leaving a nickel-size hole for breathing. When the mask was slipped over Zehm's mouth and nose, he immediately started screaming and bucking.

The EMS personnel left Zehm hog-tied in police custody. Officer Raleigh put a knee into the small of Zehm's back, and Officer Uberaga placed a shin across the back of his neck. After a couple of minutes the officers noticed that Zehm was silent and still. They rolled him onto his side and saw that his face and neck were purple and that he was not breathing. Braun ran out of the store to get the EMS personnel. One officer cut off the leg restraint while another removed the handcuffs. The officers rolled Zehm onto his back and moved out of the way. EMS personnel found Zehm without pulse or respiration. Cardiopulmonary resuscitation was initiated, and within minutes Zehm was in an ambulance speeding to Deaconess Medical Center.

Officer Sandra McIntyre did not participate in the struggle with Zehm. She interviewed the store clerk, Lee Colvin, who told her he heard Thompson tell the suspect to stop and put the pop bottle down but could not see the fight. It was she who picked up the paycheck and hourly pay statement Zehm had dropped during the incident.

The store supervisor, Angela Wiggins, came to the scene and made a copy of the surveillance video at the direction of Officers Walker and McIntyre. That videotape was given to Officer Timothy Moses, who also helped secure the scene and took the complainant's statement. He asked the complainant and her friend to return to the ATM and determine if the suspect had taken money out of the friend's account. They ascertained that no money had been taken and found a book and compact disk at the ATM, which they gave to Officer Moses.

The reports of what the backup officers saw and did were written several days after the incident. Three officers wrote their reports together with a Spokane Police Guild attorney who was present to advise them.

One officer ripped a seam in his pants during the incident. None of the backup officers or EMS personnel were injured.

CHAPTER FOUR

The life of Irish author James Joyce is celebrated annually on June 16, "Bloomsday," named for Leopold Bloom, the protagonist in Ulysses. *Don Kardong, who founded Spokane's Lilac Bloomsday Run in 1977, later explained that* Ulysses *was the inspiration for the name.*

Held every year since on the first Sunday in May, the 12 kilometer race is an international competition for men and women. But the majority of the participants are area residents who begin training in March after the snow has melted off the roadways and sidewalks. The event has become a collective expression of civic pride and the commemorative T-shirt given to every finisher, a symbol of personal achievement. The 2006 Bloomsday Run had 44,756 participants.

The Spokane Police Department's investigation continued into early May. Detective Burbridge titled his investigative notes, "Assault," referring to Zehm's alleged assault of Officer Thompson. Detective Ferguson initially titled hers, "Officer Involved Fatality," but changed her investigative intent to Zehm's assault of Thompson three days later. She changed the heading back to "Officer Involved Fatality" in mid-April.

Detectives Miller and Marske attended the autopsy, and Ferguson was informed of the preliminary findings. According to her notes, "Detective Miller advised there was no indication that blunt force trauma caused the death of Zehm, but rather he likely died of a cardiac arrest. However, the manner and cause of death remain undetermined pending toxicology results." She did not reference Miller's notes of extensive bruising over Zehm's body and the Medical Examiner's indication that further examinations in addition to the toxicology reports would be needed before she ruled on the cause of death.

Detective Burbridge interviewed three witnesses to the incident, Britni Brashiers, Greg Lakarish, and Tracy LeBlanc. Britni Brashiers was a teenager at the time, had been inside the Zip Trip, and had paid careful attention to the encounter. Her mother contacted the media shortly after the first television broadcast reporting the incident. Britni had told her mother that the "horrific fight" described by Chief Nicks had not involved a "lunge," "boxing stance," or any verbal exchange before Thompson's first blow landed. Detective Ferguson contacted Britni's mother, who indicated she had been advised to talk to an attorney before allowing investigators to talk with her daughter as the police had lied about what had taken place, and she was concerned the police would discredit or try to change her daughter's statement. The Brashiers' attorney contacted Ferguson, who had Burbridge pursue the matter. His interview of Britni Brashiers took place in the presence of her mother and an attorney. Although she may have had the best view of any of the witnesses, the record of her interview has not been made available to the public.

Greg Lakarish, an engineer for Burlington Northern Railroad, acknowledged that he had not wanted to be at the Zip Trip and had not paid much attention to the incident. He was not perceived as having a discernible bias against law enforcement. However, he described two contradictions to the official version of the incident. Lakarish said the first thing he heard was the command from Officer Thompson, "I told you to get down." Then he heard a similar command just before Thompson delivered two baton strikes to the right side of Zehm's head. He described Zehm "cradling the Pepsi bottle as if he were carrying a football," stated that Zehm never said a word, and did not see any aggressive behavior from Zehm. He was asked, "Did any of the other customers say anything while this was going on?" Lakarish responded that he spoke with a black man at the scene, and they both questioned why the officer did not just get Zehm down and handcuff him.

The black man was Tracy LeBlanc, a local bouncer. According to Burbridge's notes, LeBlanc saw Thompson strike Zehm seven or eight times with his baton but had no idea where the strikes landed. He described Zehm's resistance to handcuffing, including that his "hands were closed in fists, and his feet were kicking." LeBlanc believed Zehm was trying to hurt the officer and get away.

The investigators searched Zehm's background for a motive for the assault of Officer Thompson. They interviewed high school friends, coworkers, bosses, his landlord, and his mother and reviewed his medical and work records, focusing particularly on Zehm's attitude and demeanor and on his mental health issues. They learned the history of a well-liked, partially-disabled but functional individual.

48

For the previous five years Zehm had worked for Skils'Kin, an employment service for mentally-disabled adults, as a member of the janitorial crew at Fairchild Air Force Base just west of Spokane. Three managers of Skils'Kin were interviewed initially, Controller Cindi Dillon, Human Resources Manager Julie Orchard, and Human Resources Specialist Shirley Bader. All described him as a cheerful and kind employee who had an exceptionally good work record until about two weeks before the Zip Trip incident. According to Orchard, Zehm's work-related problems involved his inability to stay on task and to do his work properly. Dillon and Orchard reported, "Although Zehm had not been himself recently and had trouble with his work, he had not been argumentative...and had not had any disputes with co-workers or staff." Orchard said Zehm had not been to work since March 7, 2006, which was the first time he had missed work in the one and one-half years she'd held her position.

Zehm's work records indicated that he had had two minor confrontations in the years he been employed by Skils'Kin. One occurred when he was behaving strangely at a bus stop and was almost attacked, and the other when he yelled at a coworker he believed to have stolen items from his backpack. Craig Lewis, Zehm's direct supervisor, and other managers at Skils'Kin were interviewed subsequently. They stated that Zehm's behavior had changed in late February or early March. He stopped singing in the van on the way to work, lacked focus, daydreamed on the job, and was unusually slow to respond to verbal commands. They advised him to schedule an appointment with his doctor, but Otto did not realize anything was different and told them only that his medication was making him sleepy.

Ferguson recorded, "The (Skils'Kin) staff explained to me that (psychiatric evaluation at) Sacred Heart Medical Center is a tremendous threat to many of their workers because it could result in being sent to Eastern State Hospital. They were not surprised that Zehm did not voluntarily agree to go. They could not establish that Zehm was a danger to himself or others, or that he was gravely disabled, therefore these supervisors could not involuntarily place him at Sacred Heart."

On his last day at work, Zehm arrived at the wrong gate and "got chewed out." His bosses told him to see a doctor and sent him home, deciding he could not return to work until he could follow basic rules. A few days later Zehm returned to the base, presenting again at the wrong gate. His supervisor reiterated that he could not return to work until he'd seen a doctor. The day before the fatal incident, Zehm's bosses contacted his mother and, when they realized she had not heard from him, either, asked her to file a missing person report. She told them it was too late in the day to file a report and that there was nothing else she could do.

One of Detective Ferguson's final entries concerning the work-related interviews was, "All of the staff...repeatedly stated that Zehm had never exhibited any aggressive behavior and that they could not believe he would ever be aggressive. There was a general acknowledgment that his odd behaviors and physical presence could be viewed as threatening to people unfamiliar with Zehm. It was apparent...that the staff was very fond of Otto Zehm and deeply disturbed by his death."

Otto's mother, Ann Zehm, insisted on being interviewed in the presence of her lawyer, Terri Sloyer. She related that Otto had a learning disability but had attended regular classes and graduated from North Central High School. He had never had disciplinary issues or been in any kind of trouble. At age 19 he was diagnosed with the schizoaffective-type of schizophrenia. She indicated that Otto called her every evening and gave her money to help with her living expenses. In the weeks prior to his death, she had noticed Otto's schedule slipping. He called her less frequently and did not return her calls. She indicated that she was certain that what happened at the bank must have been a misunderstanding. Detective Burbridge reported her to say, "If Otto were confronted by an authority figure like a policeman, she didn't know what he would do, but...if the officer were too close to him, he might fight."

During the investigation the Police Department's use of force policy was reviewed. Detective Ferguson confirmed, "Baton strikes are authorized when dealing with an assaultive subject. 'Assaultive' is defined as 'noncompliance perceived as, or resulting in, an actual assault on an officer.'" She also noted that the Department's training regarding leg restraint is to use as many officers as necessary to control the subject while applying the restraint and to constantly monitor the subject once restrained.

The investigation of Taser use during the incident touched on assaultive cues that would allow its legitimate use. According to Detective Lesser, who reviewed the Department's policy and training concerning Taser use, "We discuss that there are certain assaultive behavior keys that allow the officer to apply the probes prior to actually allowing the subject to assault the officer." Taser International, maker of the weapon, suggests the neck and pelvic areas for application while warning that those areas are sensitive to mechanical injury. The carotid artery could be crushed, for example. "Those areas should only be targeted when officers are defending themselves from violent attacks."

Three of the EMS personnel were interviewed. All three claimed they saw Zehm spitting. Two of them said they saw no sign of mental illness yet admitted hearing Zehm ask, "Hello, is anybody there?" when they were removing a Taser dart from his body. Paramedic McMullen summarized the consensus view that they saw "an out of control guy mad at the cops for busting him for stealing from those girls." In regard to possible head injury, one reported seeing Zehm "bouncing his head around and easily could sustain a head injury from hitting his head on the floor or shelf." Interestingly, EMT Cappellano stated that he "would not have a subject remain on his stomach once leg-restrained."

The record of the medical appointment shortly before the incident indicated that Zehm wanted to reduce his dose of olanzapine, an antipsychotic medication. Ferguson noted that the Deaconess emergency physicians said that a cardiac condition caused his death and that there were several fresh bruises, although she did not specify their location.

The last investigative note in Detective Ferguson's file indicated that the Medical Examiner, Dr. Sally Aiken, was awaiting additional materials before making her final decision. However, because she could not rule out the use of restraints as a cause of Zehm's cardiac arrest and death, Dr. Aiken's final ruling was expected to be that he died at the hands of another person. His death was a homicide.

*

Dr. Aiken, a forensic pathologist and the Medical Examiner for Spokane County in 2006, was known for efficiency in her work and directness in her reports and testimony. She reviewed the video surveillance tape from the Zip Trip, the interviews of Officers Thompson and Braun, the written statement of one backup officer, Otto Zehm's outpatient records from the Community Health Association of Spokane, the pre-hospital care report from American Medical Response, the records of the hospitalization at Deaconess Medical Center, and the records of the organ procurement agency. She performed the autopsy herself, and the report included hundreds of photographs and numerous references to scientific literature.

She began the report with a brief clinical summary: "A 37-year-old male involved in an altercation with Spokane Police

Department officers on March 18, 2006. During the altercation, a Taser was used on the decedent and he was struck with a baton. He eventually was placed in four-point restraint with his hands handcuffed behind his body and his legs secured with a flexible cuff, which was attached to the handcuffs. [He was] placed in the prone position...The Fire Department intubated the decedent. He was then transported to a local Spokane hospital. He was found to be brain dead and eventually expired. The decedent was an organ donor."

The lack of blood flow to the brain for as little as five minutes can trigger a cascade of biochemical events in the tissue leading to death of the entire organ. When the brain is dead, no blood flows into it, and it does not produce any electrical activity. But the heart continues to beat, pumping blood to the rest of the body. The person is comatose and does not breathe spontaneously, so oxygenation of the blood has to be maintained by mechanical ventilation. The hopeless prognosis lead to the establishment of brain death as a legal definition of death in every state, and it is from such individuals that organs are removed for transplantation.

Brain death from cardiopulmonary arrest has characteristic autopsy findings. Microscopically, dead nerve cells throughout the brain are swollen, which causes swelling of the entire organ. The resulting increases of pressure inside the skull pushed the cerebellar tonsils at the base of the brain down into the upper spinal canal.

The hypothalamus normally produces antidiuretic hormone, which circulates to the kidneys and concentrates the urine. The production of antidiuretic hormone stops when the brain dies, so the production of a large volume of dilute urine ensues, a condition termed diabetes insipidus.

Dr. Aiken began the summary of Zehm's autopsy findings by stating that the cause of brain death was "hypoxic encephalopathy due to cardiopulmonary arrest while restrained (total appendage restrained) in prone excited delirium." She supported that statement by referring to the clinical documentation of a comatose state and diabetes insipidus prior to death, marked swelling of the brain with herniation of the cerebellar tonsils into the upper spinal canal on gross inspection, and the typical findings on microscopic examination of brain tissue.

She reported two pathological findings pertaining to the heart. The first was moderate atherosclerosis in the left anterior descending coronary artery. There was no evidence of blocked arteries or heart muscle damage typical of a heart attack. She also found hemorrhagic myocardial necrosis of papillary muscle. Papillary muscles are attached to valves in the heart and prevent the backflow of blood. Dr. Aiken stated that that particular finding is often present after lengthy cardiopulmonary resuscitation as had occurred in this case.

She noted that there were "multiple blunt force injuries to the lower extremities and left flank" but indicated that full body x-rays did not identify any fractures.

Testing on a blood sample obtained when Zehm arrived at Deaconess Medical Center was performed by the Washington State Toxicology Laboratory. Caffeine and nicotine were found in the specimen, but no alcohol, drug of abuse, or other drug was detected.

In her discussion of the autopsy findings, Dr. Aiken reviewed the concept of excited delirium. She concluded, "The decedent's behavior and actions in the convenience store are consistent with a state of excited delirium, which has been defined as 'a state of extreme mental and physiological excitement characterized by extreme agitation, hyperthermia... hostility, exceptional strength and endurance without apparent fatigue.' Although excited delirium is often a result of illicit drug intoxication, review of the medical literature indicates that excited delirium 'frequently occurs in psychiatric patients without any positive toxicologic findings.'"

She considered the possibility that Otto Zehm experienced the neuroleptic malignant syndrome, which can produce symptoms similar to excited delirium in patients treated with antipsychotic medication. However, this syndrome includes "hyperthermia and muscular rigidity, signs not exhibited by the decedent upon hospital presentation." She mentioned that while olanzapine has been associated with disturbance of the heart rhythm, she judged that drug to be an unlikely cause of Zehm's cardiopulmonary arrest as it was not found in his blood.

Referring to the baton injuries and Taser applications, she stated, "Multiple, patterned contusions were noticed on the decedent's extremities and over the left flank. However, there were no associated significant internal injuries, no evidence of trauma to the chest, abdomen, neck, or brain. No injuries were seen during organ donation. The autopsy demonstrated three sets of pattern injuries attributable to the application of the Taser. Two were found on an upper extremity consistent with Taser dart marks, and pattern injuries were located on the right lower chest and the left upper chest typical of drive/stun application.

Because multiple minutes transpired between the application of the device and the decedent's cardiopulmonary arrest, and in the intervening time between application and cardiopulmonary arrest the deceased continued to struggle vigorously, it is unlikely that the device resulted in disturbance of the heart rhythm."

She reiterated the investigative history that a neck hold had not been applied. Then she discussed four-point restraint in the prone position. "For more than two decades, cases have been described in the medical literature in which sudden death and cardiopulmonary arrest have occurred in individuals while in states of excited delirium who are restrained. Research into these deaths include the effect of restrained position on oxygenation, blood pressure, and pulse, has been conflicting and somewhat controversial. Evidence of an association of mechanical asphyxia from being restrained in the circumstance of excited delirium is largely based on observational autopsy reports. However, it is likely in this case...that restraint itself placed the decedent at a risk for cardiopulmonary arrest. **In light of the circumstances, the death is attributed to hypoxic encephalopathy while restrained (total appendage restraint) in a prone position for excited delirium.**"

She concluded, "Forensic pathologists in multiple jurisdictions have considerable debate about the appropriate certification of the manner of death in similar instances. In some jurisdictions the manner of death in such cases will be **undetermined** because of lack of significant scientific knowledge about the cause of such events. Many other jurisdictions choose to determine the manner of death in these cases an **accident** because the apparent lack of intent and because of the unpredictability of these cases of sudden death in those with episodes of excited delirium.

"In this jurisdiction, by convention, similar deaths are characterized as **homicide**. This is partly to ensure heightened sense of scrutiny that deaths occurring under the auspices of police agencies require. As unpredictable as this death may have been, it is not likely to have occurred without the prone restraint and total appendage restraint position. For statistical purposes, certifying manner of death on a death certificate, 'homicide' means death at the hands of another. It does not imply culpability or intent.

"In keeping with these considerations, the manner of death is homicide."

*

54

Detective Ferguson's report of the investigation was released on May 31, 2006, and forwarded to the County Prosecutor's Office. The report began with a review of Otto Zehm's medical history and work records. She stated that he suffered from a mental disorder that had been diagnosed when he was in his teens. He has been treated with a medication regimen and had required two psychiatric hospital commitments. She acknowledged that he had been "functioning acceptably" on medication and "maintained employment and independent living."

He had been "employed by the Skils'Kin Center as a janitor for approximately five years until his death. He was dependable, friendly, well-liked and performed his job well." He was taking medication during his employment, "reportedly with good results. When his behavior did vary to unacceptable levels (hallucinations, lack of focus), he responded positively to verbal directions. Otto Zehm...was habitual in terms of task performance and personal activities. Zip Trip clerks from the Illinois/Perry store reported that Zehm stopped by every evening for a Pepsi and dinner.

"In mid February, 2006, Skils'Kin supervisors observed unusually disturbing behavior from Otto Zehm. Their records mention increased confusion, distraction, disorientation, poor work performance, need for increased work supervision, nonsensical responses and verbal aggression. On 3/2/06, staff investigated an involuntary placement for him, however, he reportedly did not meet mental health criteria." She indicated that the Skils'Kin staff knew of his reduction of medication and persuaded him to contact his doctor for an appointment.

Ferguson stated that Zehm had reduced his medication use in hopes of curbing his appetite and quitting smoking. She referred to his appointment at a Community Health Association of Spokane clinic on February 13, 2006, with Julie Leffler, A.R.N.P., who recorded that he felt 'too medicated.' "Leffler also questioned cognitive impairment in addition to schizophrenia symptoms based on her impressions during that consultation." Ms. Leffler procured an agreement from him to consistently take his medication and monitor his symptoms. On March 13, 2006, Community Health Association of Spokane records indicate that a call was placed to Otto Zehm as he had missed an appointment. He did not answer, and a message was left for him.

"On March 7, 2006, the decision was made by the Skils'Kin director for Zehm not to report to work until after the medical appointment. Zehm was informed of the decision but arrived to work the next day anyway, with no apparent recollection of the temporary discharge. The staff was very concerned for his welfare due to his high level of confusion and therefore tried to maintain contact with him. This included contacts with his mother, who also reported that Otto was behaving very differently and was concerned. Mrs. Zehm later advised detectives that Otto called her every night, but did not do so the last two weeks prior to his death. Despite efforts, the Skils'Kin staff did not have contact with Otto Zehm after March 7, 2006. His last paycheck was mailed to him on or about March 10, 2006."

Pertaining to the incident at the ATM machine, Detective Ferguson wrote, "This male's actions intimidated the complainant, who thought he might be intending to rob her. The complainant drove away from the ATM without completing her transaction. As the 911 call continued, the complainant stated the male may have taken the money she was trying to secure from the ATM machine as he was 'messing' with the machine as she drove away."

Ferguson noted that Officer Steve Braun was dispatched initially to the complaint and subsequently stated, "As more information was received from the complainant, including a description of the subject possibly being 'high' per his behavior, Officer Karl Thompson also responded. Officer Thompson confirmed with Spokane Police Department radio that the subject did take the complainant's money."

She stated that Officer Thompson saw the subject entering the Zip Trip and quickly followed to detain him. "Officer Thompson withdrew his baton and held it in the presentation position as a sign of force when he confronted a possible robbery and/or theft suspect." The report reiterated the details of the encounter that Officer Thompson provided in his interview, including the statement, "Otto Zehm held the 2-liter bottle of Pepsi with both hands in a horizontal position at chest level. He was wearing a heavy leather jacket capable of concealing a weapon. He looked directly at Officer Thompson, who was dressed in a full uniform, and displayed a defiant, deliberate look that was not marred by confusion or submission."

She stated that Officer Thompson's information regarding the initial complaint "required that he detain the subject for further investigation. The nature of this call and the subject's clothing made this a heightened risk contact for Officer Thompson...[who] was aware that there was a clerk and customers in the store who could be in danger if Zehm escalated to assaultive behavior. Officer Thompson ordered Zehm to drop the bottle. Zehm responded with, 'Why?' The order was given again and Zehm said, 'No'... Officer Thompson quickly considered his force options and decided to apply a baton strike to preempt an anticipated assault by Zehm. The strike was delivered to Zehm's left thigh with the expectation that it would disrupt an assaultive plan and Zehm would buckle to the ground and then be controlled with handcuffs."

The report continued with a description of the sequence of events during which Officer Thompson grabbed Zehm's jacket collar and "applied a second strike to the legs." Ferguson stated, "Zehm punched the officer in the chest a number of times with both fists. Officer Thompson applied his Taser once as Zehm punched at him...but Zehm did not react as expected and his assaultive behavior continued. Zehm again punched Officer Thompson when he regained his footing. Officer Thompson applied more strikes to the torso, shoulders, and arms as the muscle mass strikes were ineffective... Zehm did eventually go the floor as Officer Thompson struck him in the legs."

Then she described Officer Braun's use of his baton as, "several power jabs, no strikes...to Zehm's torso area, with no apparent effect... Braun then fired his Taser once at Zehm's torso, however, the subject was very active and the probe hit was unknown. Officer Braun subsequently applied a number of drive stuns with the Taser to Zehm's torso to try subdue him. These did not alter Zehm's actions. Officer Braun considered a vascular lateral neck restraint but could not safely apply it. Neither officer...could get Zehm to unclench his fists or arms to get him cuffed. There was a point where they used only their weight to control him until additional officers arrived."

The backup officers "successfully cuffed Zehm. His aggressive behavior continued, therefore leg restraints were applied. Zehm was rolled over onto his side, however, his constant movement resulted in his laying on his torso as well. Zehm pulled against and stretched the leg restraints, which allowed him to kick and present even more of a threat to officers. The leg restraints were reapplied. Officers monitored him as he lay prone; sometimes on his side, sometimes on his stomach. They noticed he was no longer breathing and immediately summoned the medics, who were still in close proximity. The leg restraints and cuffs were removed so that emergency care could be given."

Her only reference to the video surveillance tape was that it "shows a nearly 20 minute difference between the last power drive stun and recognition that Zehm was not breathing."

She stated, "Zehm was transported to Deaconess Medical Center. ER staff there successfully resuscitated him, however, he expired on March 20, 2006, when life-support was discontinued. Zehm's potassium level was very low upon admission, which was consistent with cardiac issues during an excited delirium episode."

Ferguson then reviewed the autopsy findings and toxicology report. Her conclusion restated Dr. Aiken's but changed the emphasis: "Due to a standard jurisdictional practice as regards the manner of death and the definition of homicide as 'death at the hands of another,' the manner of death was ruled a homicide. In other jurisdictions, such deaths are ruled 'undetermined' or 'accidental'."

Ferguson stated that the investigation "included contacts with direct witnesses, employers, mental health professionals, family, acquaintances, and medical personnel. Additionally, verbal or written statements were obtained from officers. Video surveillance tapes as well as 911 and Spokane Police Department radio transmissions were reviewed. Mental health, employment, medical and autopsy records were secured and incorporated into the investigation. Also, Spokane Police Department defense tactics and Taser deployment policies were reviewed. Primary instructors for these tools were also consulted."

She attributed the fatality solely to Otto Zehm. His "control and behavior deteriorated when he decreased his (medication) approximately two months before his death. He continued to deteriorate when he stopped taking (it) approximately three weeks before his death.

"Otto Zehm responded to Officer Thompson's commands with refusal and noncompliance. The totality of the circumstances then perceived by this officer with 20+ years of law enforcement experience led him to believe an assault by Otto Zehm was imminent. Per training, policy, and experience, Officer Thompson tried to prevent the assault with non-lethal baton strikes to muscle mass. The altercation escalated and other uses of force were applied as the danger to the officers increased. All uses of force were ineffective. Only sheer numbers of officers gained control of Zehm, who exhibited exceptional strength.

"There is no evidence to support that excessive force was used. Although... this was an exhausting, very physical altercation, deadly force was not applied. Zehm was monitored after leg restraints were applied and a medical response was requested. When it was discovered that Zehm was not breathing, medics were summoned immediately and the restraints were removed. There is no evidence of criminal negligence reference responding to Zehm's medical needs.

"In conclusion, there is no investigative finding of criminal activity on the part of the involved officers."

*

Detective Ferguson's report was defective in these respects:

- She did not mention the reports of a number of witnesses whose descriptions of the encounter were very different from Officer Thompson's,

- She did not include the statements of every one of Otto Zehm's supervisors that he had never been aggressive or confrontational,

- She did not acknowledge that Otto Zehm had not committed a criminal act,

- While she reviewed the video surveillance tape from the Zip Trip, she made no mention of whether Officer Thompson's account of the encounter or the witnesses' statements were corroborated by the video evidence,

- She stated, "Officer Thompson confirmed with Spokane Police Department radio that the subject did take the complainant's money." But it was Officer Braun who had asked the radio dispatcher, 'Just to confirm, he took her money?" That had never been verified to the dispatcher, who initially responded, "Affirm." Soon after that exchange, however, the dispatcher broadcast, "Now the complainant's advising she's not entirely positive that he did get her money. She did not get a chance to go back and check."

- She also stated, "Deadly force was not applied as it was not warranted," omitting the statements of at least three eyewitnesses, Dahl, Turner, and Lakarish, that Officer Thompson struck Otto Zehm in the head with his baton.

- She added, "Zehm was monitored after leg restraints were applied." "To monitor" means "To observe, record, or detect an operation or condition; to oversee, supervise, or regulate; to watch closely for purposes of control, surveillance...keep track of, check continually." She was not critical of the behavior of the backup officers who placed Zehm in the prone position while in four-point restraint, affixed a hard plastic mask with a dime-sized hole for breathing over his face, and allowed two officers to press their weight down on his spine, establishing that such treatment is consistent the Spokane Police Department's policy of "constant monitoring of a restrained suspect."

Yet this report was the basis of the city's assertion for nearly six years that Otto Zehm was responsible for his death.

CHAPTER FIVE

Who was Otto Zehm?

His parents were Ann and Otto Zehm, Sr, and he had a step-sister, Carrie. Despite learning disability, Otto had attended regular classes in Spokane School District 81. After graduation from North Central High School he worked for many years as a seamster mending blue jeans and jackets.

Otto lost his father in 1999. The following year he started working as a janitor for Skils'Kin, a non-profit organization that supervises work for individuals with mental disabilities. He cleaned buildings at Fairchild Air Force Base and the Skils'Kin main office.

Otto was 5'10" tall and weighed 180 pounds at the time of his death. Most striking about his appearance was the long, light red hair parted loosely on the left and falling over his right ear to below the shoulder. He had a round face with wide features and light pink skin.

His mother told Spokane Police Department investigators that Otto had been diagnosed with "schizoaffective disorder" in late adolescence. One of the schizophrenia-spectrum disorders, the symptoms typically appear in the late teen or young adult years and have significant psychosocial impacts and health risks. Psychological disturbances commonly include false perceptions, delusions, paranoia, and disorganized speech and thinking. Social and occupational dysfunction often occur and can result in long term unemployment, poverty, and homelessness. Cognitive dysfunction develops, particularly impairment of immediate recall on tests of memory and of executive functions like planning, organizing, sequencing, and multitasking. A slow speed of mental processing is usually evident. Recurring manic or mixed manic-depressive disruption of behavior and mood distinguish the "schizoaffective" type of schizophrenia. Affected individuals have a shortened life expectancy due to medical problems and a higher rate of suicide.

Medications can diminish or alleviate the mental, cognitive, and mood disturbances of the disorder. Antipsychotic, antidepressant, and mood-stabilizing medications all have a role. However, adverse effects of these medications are frequent, and non-compliance with prescribed treatments is common. Antipsychotic medications in use currently often cause drowsiness, enhanced appetite and thirst, and weight gain. Complications of long term use of these medications include obesity, metabolic syndrome, and diabetes which result in damage to the heart, brain, kidneys, and blood vessels from atherosclerotic vascular disease. Therefore, the long term treatment of an individual with a schizophrenia-spectrum disorder requires the expertise of a psychiatrist to manage the mental, cognitive, and emotional disturbances, a general physician to monitor and treat medical complications, and a social worker/case manager to organize the support services necessitated by social and occupational dysfunction.

When Otto took his medication reliably, his behavior was well regulated. He lived alone in an apartment in north central Spokane. He went to the same convenience store every evening to get food for supper. He was an extremely dependable employee and a steady worker. He visited his mother frequently, called her nightly, and often played guitar songs to her over the phone. He regularly deposited part of his paycheck at the same branch of Washington Trust Bank, keeping enough in cash to pay his monthly rent of $380. He bought soft drinks or snacks for the members of his work crew, explaining that he had "budgeted for" that expense when asked about it. He assisted his mother with her living expenses and had $6,421.87 in his bank account when he died. The book he left at the ATM was Master Your Money by Ron Blue.

His psychiatric disorder was managed by Spokane Mental Health until 2003 when 900 people with major psychiatric illness lost eligibility for services there due to tougher federal standards. The Community Health Association of Spokane (CHAS), with two psychiatrists each working one day per week, assumed the psychiatric treatment of 600 of them, including Otto. Mid-level providers, nurse practitioners and physician assistants became responsible for the treatment of the majority.

Otto's February 13, 2006, CHAS clinic appointment was with a nurse practitioner who made him sign an agreement to continue to take his medication despite the adverse effects. However, his behavior continued to deteriorate after that appointment, and his performance at work declined. According to his supervisor, the problems "involved his ability to stay focused on his task or to do his work properly." Detective Ferguson recorded in her investigative notes, "All of them (supervisors) said it was Zehm's lack of focus, lengthy response time during conversation, and his daydreaming that alarmed them." Repeated presentation at the wrong gate at the Air Force base precipitated his suspension from work. Two weeks before his death he stopped calling his mother regularly and didn't return her calls. She described him as incoherent during the sporadic conversations she had with him in that interval.

Otto usually did his banking at a teller window in the north central branch of Washington Trust Bank. On the evening of the Zip Trip incident, however, he arrived after the bank had closed, so he tried unsuccessfully to use the ATM...

*

Otto had had a prior run-in with police or rather, once in the distant past when he had been off his medication, the police ran into him. In the early morning hours of a day in 1990, he was seen walking along a large thoroughfare by Spokane County Sheriff's Deputy Gallion. The deputy noticed that his jeans were ripped and thought he looked confused. After confronting him, he thought Otto might have a mental problem and decided to detain him in order to take him to Sacred Heart Medical Center for a mental evaluation. When Otto resisted, a physical struggle ensued. Two deputies, Zollars and Badicke, responded to Gallion's call for assistance, and eventually Otto was handcuffed, hobbled, and taken to jail.

Deputies Gallion and Zollars filed reports of the incident. Zollars reported, "Throughout the entire incident Zehm screamed that he was crazy, 'They're not the real police,' and once hobbled, he looked up to us and said, 'I love you.'"

*

Otto was an accomplished guitarist. A fellow high school student, John Duplain, used to come to the Zehm home to practice with him. At that age Otto could play the long, complicated guitar solo in "Eruption" by Van Halen. According to Duplain, "He was already, as far as I'm concerned, a master."

Otto had continued to play guitar and drums with a band of friends who gathered weekly after work, usually at his apartment and after he had verified with his neighbors that the noise would not be disruptive. He preferred rock and heavy metal music from the '80s and recorded some of the sessions, peddling the tapes for $2 each. According to Tim Byrne, a guitarist with the band, "We planned on getting on stage some day. Otto could play the six string like he was ringing a bell." The CD Otto left at the ATM the night of the Zip Trip incident was "Rage for Order" by Queensryche, an '80's heavy metal band.

In the weeks before his death, Otto began missing band practices and frequently broke down crying. Byrne thought he may have been upset about a girl named Amber. Byrne reported, "I went to a bus stop and waited for him. He got off the bus and walked right by me. He said, 'I can't do it anymore.' He took off really scared and upset. That's the last time I saw him."

Otto was esteemed by his friends and coworkers. Bob Dexter, who knew Otto for 20 years and referred to him as his best friend, said, "He had the biggest heart I have ever seen on anybody." Co-workers described him as "a gentle lion...with a golden heart" and "a wonderful man. He was proud of his work, and he had a nice smile." Another said, "He was the teacher and the protector of the guys who were maybe more disabled than he was."

Skils'Kin assistant program director Ray Lancaster summarized the feelings of Otto's supervisors and coworkers: "It's just a complete tragedy. We're all horribly dismayed by it. I think we're all diminished by him not being around."

*

Otto Zehm didn't escape poverty, but he lived independently and maintained employment almost all of his adult life. He had a close and supportive relationship with his mother, long-term relationships with many friends, and was genuinely liked and admired by those with whom he worked. He developed his talent for music and became an accomplished guitarist.

Just as Otto didn't let learning disability and mental illness define his life, others refused to let the report of the Spokane Police Department's flawed investigation of the Zip Trip incident characterize his last moments.

CHAPTER SIX

Founded in 1999 by public defender Jim Sheehan, the nonprofit Center for Justice in Spokane defines itself as "a legal advocacy organization that works to empower individuals and provides vigorous oversight and advocacy when community's rights need to be defended and community voices need to be heard." It is dedicated to "the experience of justice for those of limited resources. We work with compassion for people, a commitment to community empowerment, and with an awareness of the sacredness of the Earth."

In its early years the Center for Justice concentrated on poverty law, representing indigent mothers, parents with mental disabilities, and other underserved groups. In 2005 its litigation resources were redirected to the regional ecosystem, human civil rights, and government accountability. Its involvement with poverty law continued through the Community Advocacy Program.

Two days after Otto died, a nephew of Ann Zehm contacted the Center for Justice on her behalf. Soon afterward he delivered a letter from her to the Center, which was received by attorney Terri Sloyer.

> *The man Otto Zehm, the one that is in the news on TV and in the newspaper, is my son.*
>
> *All I know about what happened is the news, except I was not notified of his being in the hospital. The evening until the next day was about 14 hours. The hospital called about 9:00 am the next day that he was there. I told them I was coming right away.*
>
> *I have a hard time walking-I use a walker. One of the men here at the apartment house took me to the hospital. When I saw him, he was in a deep coma. They told me that there was barely life signs when*

they brought him in. He never moved any. His eyes were closed. I stayed with him as long as I could and never saw him move on his own.

When I went home that night to my apartment I broke down and cried. I knew I had to get hold of myself. I could not stand the pain-I had to turn it off. I also have a broken heart. I can't break down now.

They told me that they had to make tests to see for sure that he was brain dead or not.

I stayed the next day with him in the hospital. He was the same-no sign of moving. The heart monitor was going-his heart was beating strong, being kept alive by the life support. Tests, about five different ones, all came to the same conclusion: he was brain dead. I decided at that time, his heart was so good, for him to be an organ donor. Filled out a questionnaire. I decided to stay numb to keep up with all the paper work and decisions that have to be made if I can help my son.

He was born Oct 31, 1969. He was a quiet child, not wanting to fight. Pretty much did what he was told, went to school, graduated from high school. Got a job sewing at a factory, had an illness that put him in the state hospital at Medical Lake. Was released to a halfway house, then for a while was on SSI then got a job with Skils'Kin where he was working up until a week before all this happened to him. Something was wrong because he did not answer his phone. Sometimes he did-he sounded like a stranger trying to tell me he was ok.

Anything else you need to know, you can call me.

My grandchildren are calling me for comfort; friends are, too. I have no desire to sue-money means nothing to me, just to pay all the bills and keep his good name.

Sincerely.

Ann Zehm, Otto's mother

P.S. What I really want to know is what took his life. How did he die?

67

Ms. Sloyer discussed the letter with other members of the staff. At the suggestion of attorney Breean Beggs, the Center's director, probate was opened in the estate of Otto Zehm.

*

All records, including the surveillance video, witness interviews, and background checks, were withheld from the media and the Zehm family during the Police Department's investigation. The only information the family could access were the autopsy findings and the hospital records, their release governed by laws outside the jurisdiction of the Police Department.

On May 30, 2006, one day before Detective Ferguson's final investigative report was sent to the Spokane County Prosecutor, lawyers for the Zehm family and the City of Spokane signed a Protective Order crafted by Assistant City Attorney Rocco Treppiedi. The order released all investigative findings to the family on the condition that the information be used only for legal matters. It was further agreed that neither party would share this material without the consent of the other. The confidential material included "all photographs, and audio tape, 911 emergency call, police dispatch tape, and other evidence gathered; (and) the names and statements of all witnesses."

That same day Spokane Police Detective John Miller asked Dr. Aiken to verify certain autopsy findings so they could be accurately released at a scheduled press conference. Dr. Aiken informed him that the disclosure of any autopsy information to the public without the family's consent violated the Autopsy Privacy Act. She also advised him that she could not authorize or provide any information that might be used in connection with the Spokane Police Department's media release. The detective explained to her that it was too late for him to prevent the release of the autopsy findings.

A few hours after the Protective Order was signed by both parties, Chief Nicks held a press conference in which he attempted to defend his officers by talking about portions of the investigation into the death of Otto Zehm. With Rocco Treppiedi at his side, he discussed the autopsy report and presented excerpts from statements made by witnesses to the encounter and by the officers involved. He repeated that Zehm had "lunged" at the officer and claimed that when Zehm was "hobbled," he was on his stomach but was quickly moved onto one side, remaining in that position for either "all of the time" or "a majority of the time." Lastly, he emphasized that all of the officers involved in the encounter with Zehm had acted appropriately and according to their training.

The next day the city placed additional information regarding the case, including additional details of the autopsy, on its official website. Much of that information remained available to the public for more than three years.

One week later the Center for Justice delivered a letter to the City Attorney's office in which Breean Beggs, representing the Zehm family, claimed that Chief Nicks' press conference and the website posting violated the Protective Order and Washington State law concerning the privacy of medical records. He further claimed that Officer Thompson did not have probable cause for a warrantless search. Having reviewed the available surveillance videos, he stated:

- There had been no "lunge" by Zehm as he only noticed Officer Thompson two seconds before the first baton strike, immediately retreated, and held his hands up to ward off Thompson's blows,

- Officer Thompson did not have time to tell Zehm that he was under arrest before striking him,

- Zehm had not assaulted Officer Thompson with a dangerous weapon (soda bottle), and

- Zehm had been left on his stomach for approximately 13 minutes after being restrained.

In the letter Beggs made three requests:

- The City acknowledge that it violated the Protective Order and apologize to the family,

- Chief Nicks retract his statements that Mr. Zehm was restrained on his side during his hobbling for the majority of the time, that Mr. Zehm's lunging at and/or attacking the officer justified the assault with the baton and that any type of officer demand occurred prior to the officer's baton strikes, and

- The City remove the web posting of quotations from the Medical Examiner's Report and apologize to the family for releasing information from the autopsy report.

Two weeks later the Center for Justice received Rocco Treppiedi's reply. It began, "Your letter seeks an apology to the family. At the outset, let me emphasize once again as various City representatives such as Chief Nicks and Deputy Chief Odenthal, myself, and the investigating officers have personally stated to you and/or Mrs. Zehm – that the City and all those involved express their sympathy to the family for the loss of Otto Zehm's life. Mr. Zehm was apparently well-liked by his family, friends, co-workers and neighbors. His death was tragic. I trust you know that the expressions of sympathy have been sincere."

However, Treppiedi unequivocally disagreed with the Center's portrayal of the encounter. "Based on my initial review of the events of March 18, 2006, I believe that each of the responding officers utilized lawful tactics throughout the event and utilized good judgment based on the totality of circumstances which confronted them. When reviewing the actions of a police officer under the law, the law requires the scrutiny to be taken from **the perspective of the involved officer**. Neither judges, nor juries, nor litigants, nor anyone else can substitute their own judgment for that of the involved officer under the law."

He continued, "Your analysis does not '...embody allowance for split-second judgments – in circumstances that are tense, uncertain, and rapidly evolving – about the amount of force that is necessary in a particular situation.' While I appreciate your advocacy on behalf of the Zehm family, it appears that the analysis is nevertheless precisely the kind of hyper-critical attempt to second-guess and over analyze a tense, uncertain, and rapidly evolving situation.

"It appears your analysis takes a subjective view and fails to take into account: (a) the totality of the circumstances known by Officer Thompson at the time he entered the store... (b) Officer Thompson's training and experience; (c) Officer Thompson's direct observations of Mr. Zehm; and (d) the statements of others, such as the store clerk, who heard Officer Thompson yell commands to Mr. Zehm, and heard and observed Mr. Zehm's refusal to comply. Your analysis also leaves Mr. Zehm's actions out of the calculus. While we have all heard about Mr. Zehm's normally pleasant personality, at the time Officer Thompson dealt with him he was non-compliant and physically combative."

After referring to statements made by a number of the responding police and emergency services personnel

70

indicating that Zehm had acted violently, Treppiedi attempted to justify Officer Thompson's actions: "The analysis in your letter fails to acknowledge the rapidity in which confrontations between citizens and officers – including this one – occur. You acknowledge that '2 seconds' before he was struck by Officer Thompson that Mr. Zehm had turned and noticed the officer. Much can occur during those two seconds, as well as the few seconds preceding it. Based on the statements of witnesses, including Officer Thompson, much **did** occur. Officer Thompson is an experienced, well trained officer... The split second within which the decision to use force – how much and how applied – is not captured by the Zip Trip video... [which] does not contain audio, so any analysis based solely on the sketchy, bouncy video during which there are times when Mr. Zehm and Officer Thompson are not in view, is not definitive.

"In short, Chief Nicks will not, as you request, publicly retract what you characterize as 'misrepresentations' because they are not misrepresentations. What you have characterized as misrepresentations appear to be your own subjective view of the video and the facts."

After claiming Zehm's death was entirely unpreventable as evidenced by the immediate medical attention he received at the scene, Treppiedi wrote, "The hyper-critical focus on the officers' actions leaves out another significant part of the story. Mr. Zehm had suffered from a mental illness that has required treatment and medication. All information gathered to date...establishes the fact that Mr. Zehm had stopped taking his medications and had been acting strangely during the weeks before March 18th... The friendly Otto Zehm people had become accustomed to was not the man who interrupted the women at the ATM, was non-compliant with Officer Thompson, and was combative throughout the events in the Zip Trip. The Spokane Police Department has a well-developed protocol for working with mentally disturbed people, but here they were responding to a report of criminal activity, not merely a confused or ill individual."

Treppiedi stated that as the video was obtained by the Center for Justice from a source other than the City legal team, it was the City's position that it had not violated the Protective Order. He claimed that the City had not violated Washington State law concerning the privacy of autopsy reports because the law is that a person's privacy is violated "when disclosure of information about the person would be highly offensive to a reasonable person, and is not of legitimate concern to the public."

*

During the weeks that Treppiedi was drafting his response to the Center for Justice, legal teams were investigating the incident for the local media. According to "Accounts of Police Beating Differ," a July 13, 2006, Spokesman-Review article, "The newspaper has sought unsuccessfully since the incident occurred to obtain a copy of the surveillance video. (County Prosecuting Attorney) Tucker claims it would jeopardize his own investigation into the incident even though everyone pictured in the video has already been interviewed by detectives. The newspaper served notice Wednesday that it will file a lawsuit against Tucker if he fails to release the video by noon Friday."

That Friday the video was released to the newspaper. The next day the Spokesman-Review published two articles on its front page relating to the Zehm encounter, "Video Shows Zehm Backed Away" and "Police Admit Inaccurate Account of Fatal Beating."

The first story described the action recorded on the video, which was shown immediately on local news programs and posted on the internet. The video captured Zehm walking into the convenience store and strolling down an aisle followed soon by Officer Thompson. Zehm turned, saw the officer, and backed out of view. Four seconds later, Zehm was on the floor. Thirteen seconds later, the camera caught the blue flash of a discharging Taser. Officer Braun's arrival was recorded followed by the appearance of the backup officers. Then EMS personnel arrived and were seen exiting but soon returned and began the resuscitation effort. A few minutes later, Zehm was taken out of the store on a gurney.

The other article, "Police Admit Inaccurate Account of Fatal Beating," accompanied a press release from Chief Nicks in which he admitted he had given "inaccurate information while trying to defend his officers' actions." He was unable to "account for why he and others in the department continued to claim for months that Zehm 'lunged' with a plastic soda bottle at the first officer on the scene, when the video shows the man retreating with his hands in the air." He also acknowledged that the video directly

72

contradicted his previous assertion that Zehm was rolled onto his side after he was restrained. The article stated: "Nicks said he discovered his mistake about a month after the May 30 news conference. When asked what he did to correct the public's false impression of how the events unfolded, he replied, 'I'm telling you right now.'"

Zehm's behavior and the alleged soda bottle weapon were discussed in the second article. "From the beginning of the case, police have described Zehm as a hostile, violent crime suspect who attacked officers and refused to obey orders... At no time before being struck did Zehm 'lunge' or 'attack' the officer as police repeatedly claimed. Nor does it show him holding a plastic soda bottle, which authorities have argued was a threat to the officers' safety. No bottle of soda is visible in Zehm's hands at any point during the 35-minute video."

The dispatched message to which Officer Thompson had responded was released along with the store surveillance video, the transcript of the 911 call, and the ATM surveillance video. "The dispatcher can clearly be heard saying that Zehm was 'acting high.' But Beggs, the family's attorney, pointed out that the woman [who called 911] never described Zehm in that way on the tapes. 'There is some screw up in dispatch,' Beggs said in regard to the erroneous information going to the officers. 'That is a police screw up, not a witness screw up.'"

The article further quoted Beggs who, after reviewing the video frame-by-frame, stated that a police officer placed a mask over Zehm's face and Zehm stopped breathing three minutes later. "This is a non-medical opinion. Based on the structure of the mask and the short amount of time between placing the mask on him and his breathing difficulties, there appears to be a connection."

The next day Chief Nicks gave another press conference and claimed that, regardless of any errors in the account of the encounter the public was given initially, the officers who responded to the call did their jobs correctly. "They had the information necessary before going into the store to stop and detain Otto Zehm...and the officers did the right thing given the situation." He continued, "As time goes on, and we talk to more and more people, it supports Karl's account of the incident. The only thing that matters is what was in Karl Thompson's mind at the moment." The conclusion attributed to him was that although Zehm had not

73

lunged at the officer, his behavior at the ATM gave the responding officers reason to believe that he was a threat to himself or others.

Soon after that press conference, Spokane Mayor Dennis Hession asked the media and public to not question the validity of the internal investigation and give the County Prosecutor time to review the matter. According to the Spokesman-Review, "Hession said he has no information yet that would justify calling for an independent external investigation and that the participation of the Spokane County Sheriff's Office, as well as the independent review by the prosecuting attorney, should be sufficient to ensure an objective review. 'They each have their own credibility at stake,' the mayor said. He cautioned members of the public not to jump to conclusions that officers used excessive force. 'It's unfair to Otto Zehm. It's unfair to the police officers involved to reach conclusions based on observations from people who don't have the experience and expertise to draw those conclusions...' He also said members of the public might be shocked at the use of force, but physical confrontation is a regular part of a police officer's job. 'I am not a police officer, and I don't have their training.'"

But the media and the public continued to scrutinize the matter. Ten days after rejecting the option of an independent investigation, Mayor Hession agreed to hire an expert to examine the investigations done by the Spokane Police Department pertaining to the Zehm encounter and another, unrelated incident. However, the investigator declared in mid-October, 2006, that he was unable to investigate the Zehm case because of ongoing criminal investigations and legal action.

On August 4, 2006, in apparent violation of public disclosure law, the city released a third surveillance video of the Zehm encounter that had been taken from a different angle from the first two. According to the front page newspaper article about the additional view, "The video... was not included in a packet of information released by department officials July 13. At that time, police officials acknowledged that the surveillance tapes were inconclusive in determining whether the mentally ill janitor had the bottle in his hands, which Officer Karl Thompson used as the primary justification for his pre-emptive use of a police baton. On Thursday, in response to a second round of public records requests, city officials ...announced that the disputed pop bottle was visible in the footage."

At the news conference called to release the video, the article indicated that "(Spokane Police Department spokesman Cpl. Tom) Lee said the video shows Zehm 'clearly holding a pop bottle and clearly swinging at Officer Thompson.' A review of the video shows Zehm falling to the floor as Thompson engages him near the end of an aisle. While lying on the ground, Zehm is seen holding the base of the soda bottle with his left hand and the neck of the bottle with his right hand, which is how Thompson described it in his report. But Zehm appears to be holding the bottle in front of his face. He moves it side to side three times before the bottle falls out of view and he stops moving. It's then that Thompson applies the first Taser jolt and the two men are seen wrestling out of view. Asked later where in the video it shows Zehm 'swinging' at Thompson, Lee backed off his earlier description. Lee said 'swinging' was probably too strong a word. He said the video shows Zehm holding the bottle above his head, moving it back and forth. While the video appears to put the bottle issue to rest, it does not show other aggressive actions by Zehm as described by Thompson in his report."

This series of media releases raised questions about the Police Department's evidence-gathering process. What became of the soda bottle, and why doesn't the Medical Examiner's report mention the face mask put on Zehm three minutes before he suffered cardiopulmonary arrest? As discussed in the Spokesman-Review, "Police consider the (soda) bottle key to the case, saying in numerous public statements and reports that Zehm's aggressive use of the bottle helped justify Officer Karl Thompson's decision to pre-emptively strike Zehm with a baton." However, the department did not examine the bottle allegedly held by Zehm for fingerprints until prompted by the Center for Justice. When it was examined, none were found in spite of the fact that the smooth 2 liter bottle presented an ideal surface from which to recover prints.

The Spokesman-Review published an article on July 26, 2006, concerning the absence of Zehm's prints on the bottle. This discrepancy prompted County Prosecutor Steven Tucker to hire Grant Fredericks, a retired Canadian police officer and forensic video expert with a history of investigating law enforcement encounters. According to the

75

article, he was selected because one of the attorneys for the city had attended a seminar Fredericks had taught that addressed ways in which digital videos can be misleading.

The potential impact of the modified non-rebreather mask placed over Zehm's face had not been considered in Detective Ferguson's investigation. Discussed in the same Spokesman-Review article as the absence of fingerprints on the soda bottle, "Beggs said he wasn't surprised that Ferguson did not mention the mask, which she had a forensic specialist retrieve after it had been discarded in a trash bin for bio-hazardous material. 'The tenor of her report was that the Police Department didn't bear any responsibility for Otto's death. Failing to mention the mask was consistent with that.'"

Subsequently Dr. Aiken sent the mask to Michigan State University to be tested. She directed that the actual conditions during which Zehm wore the mask not be reproduced. Instead, two healthy college students wore it while running on a treadmill and, under those conditions, the mask did not significantly impede airflow. In late September, 2006, she ruled it out as the cause of death.

Dr. Aiken's word was final in all matters concerning autopsies conducted by the Medical Examiner's Office, and the attorneys involved in the Zehm matter did not question her conclusions about Zehm's autopsy. However, Breean Beggs protested the restrictions she specified for testing the effects of the face mask. According to a Spokesman-Review article of September 22, 2006, "Beggs...received the same report... 'They didn't put someone on their diaphragm with their legs held back and check to see what effect the mask would have on their ability to breathe,' Beggs said."

*

Emergency Medical Services is staffed by paramedics and emergency medical technicians of the Spokane Fire Department. Soon after the Zehm tragedy, Spokane Fire Chief Brian Schaeffer ordered a Medical Practice Investigation intended to "minimize any future occurrence of a similar incident." The investigation assessed system influences, educational and training issues, circumstantial influences, and human factors. The findings of the investigation were disseminated throughout the department on August 17, 2006. The report included a brief synopsis of

76

the Zehm encounter followed by a thorough analysis and set of recommendations, some of which were implemented immediately.

The analysis of system influences identified three shortcomings, the first concerning how the responding Emergency Medical Services personnel followed Taser removal procedures. The departmental protocol stated that all victims of Taser use "must be thoroughly assessed to determine if other medical problems or injuries are present." It was noted that in this particular instance, the police officers did not allow Zehm's restraints to be removed for a proper examination.

A second concern related to how responding EMS personnel should alter treatment for a restrained aggressive or violent patient. EMS personnel are not allowed to hog-tie patients. The responding personnel were not faulted as Zehm was under Police Department custody. However, when an individual is restrained, "...EMS personnel must insure that the patient position does not compromise the patient's respiratory/circulatory systems, or does not preclude any necessary medical intervention to protect the patient's airway should vomiting occur." Furthermore, "restrained extremities should be evaluated... every fifteen minutes (based on patient cooperation)." These aspects of the protocol were ignored during the Zehm encounter.

The third matter was the provision of a modified non-rebreather mask for use as a spit mask. Identified as a common practice before this report was released, no authorization existed for a non-rebreather mask to be modified and used without oxygen in any situation.

The remainder of the investigation found little in need of improvement. The educational and training issues highlighted involved the appropriate use of non-rebreather masks and the implementation of department-wide education concerning proper restraint. There were no human factor concerns, and the only significant circumstantial factor was found to be the poor communication between Spokane Police Department officers, who thought the EMS personnel would handle all of Zehm's medical needs once they were on scene, and the EMS personnel, who thought they were simply to remove Taser barbs.

After a short summary stating that there was little modern medicine could have done for Zehm by the time EMS personnel realized there was an emergency, Chief

Schaeffer listed eight recommendations for improvement. The entire department was notified that gauze rather than non-rebreather masks are to be used as "spit masks." Other recommendations pertained to improving continuing education and communication within the Fire Department and with the Spokane Police Department.

This review of policies, procedures, education, training, and communication avoided potential liability concerns while being timely, transparent, honest, and efficient.

*

From the outset, the city maintained that Zehm's behavior forced Officer Thompson to strike him and that his death, while a tragedy, did not result from deviation from the Spokane Police Department's established policies and procedures. But Zehm's death was far from the first questionable officer-involved fatality in Spokane. After a strong public push for civilian oversight in the 1980s, the Citizen's Review Committee was established in 1992 over the Police Department's objection. However, in practice the committee could only review cases forwarded by the Chief of Police. In its years of operation, the committee found only one officer to have acted unacceptably, and that officer was not disciplined by the Police Department. The victim had to file a federal civil suit and ultimately received compensation from the city. At the time of the Zehm encounter, the committee had no staff or budget and had not met in almost 10 years.

Constrained by the Protective Order, the Center for Justice was limited to requesting the city to acknowledge publicly that Otto Zehm's death was not his fault and that some form of public oversight be created to oversee the investigation of officer-involved fatalities. "We give law enforcement guns, the power to arrest and even kill," Breean Beggs said. "With that power comes accountability. The police work for the citizens of Spokane."

The city's uncompromising reply came from Chief Nicks. On June 26, 2006, the Spokesman-Review reported, "Acting Police Chief Jim Nicks wouldn't respond to interview questions but issued a prepared statement saying he believes the city's current system is 'responsive and accountable to the public...' He didn't address the public's lack of access to internal investigations, which are secret."

CHAPTER SEVEN

Spokane County Prosecutor Steven Tucker received the Police Department's final investigative report at the end of May, 2006. There was no word from his office about the matter until September, 2006, when he told Spokesman-Review reporters he would delay a decision about prosecuting any of the officers involved "because Acting Police Chief Nicks was uncomfortable with handling it with the newly appointed Chief of Police, Anne Kirkpatrick, due to take over on September 17th."

Anne Kirkpatrick was sworn in on September 11, 2006, having been selected from 43 applicants after a nationwide search. She had degrees in counseling, business, and law and had led two police departments previously. Soon after her swearing in, Deputy Police Chief Al Odenthal resigned, having been involved in a number of controversial police matters including some misleading statements after he reviewed the surveillance tapes in the Zehm case.

On January 31, 2007, the Spokesman-Review quoted Chief Kirkpatrick, "I am in perfect agreement and supportive of citizen oversight in some form." The article continued, "But re-emphasizing what she said last summer when she was a candidate for the job, Kirkpatrick repeated that the police chief still must retain the exclusive power to fire or discipline an officer for misconduct, and the department must be able to investigate complaints."

During his review of the Zehm matter, Tucker requested that the Medical Examiner perform coroner inquests in cases of officer-involved fatalities. Such inquests are legal proceedings in which the Medical Examiner presents autopsy findings to a grand jury. If the grand jury finds probable cause, the Medical Examiner issues a warrant for the perpetrator. Coroner inquests had not been held in Spokane for decades, and Dr. Aiken refused, stating she didn't believe it's her job "to decide whether law enforcement officers acted appropriately during in-custody deaths." Finally, in October, 2006, Tucker told newspaper reporters,

"I don't have enough to charge criminally and try to prove it beyond reasonable doubt." He added, "It's tough to investigate your own people."

Local elections were held in the fall of 2007. Despite considerable public criticism of his inaction in the Zehm matter and that his opponent ran almost exclusively on that issue, Tucker was re-elected County Prosecutor. Mayor Hession did not fare as well. In the aftermath of Otto Zehm's death, he initially supported the police officers' actions. But he soon decided he needed more information and commissioned two external reviews of the Police Department. When he received the results, he told the public he would respond quickly to the concerns raised. However, according to the Spokesman-Review, "The extent of the recommendations appeared to come as a bit of a surprise to the mayor," and there was little he could do. Both reviews suggested the Citizen's Review Committee be overhauled, but neither the mayor nor the Chief of Police had the power to do that because police oversight falls under "working conditions" and is subject to bargaining during contract negotiations with the Police Guild. The recommendation to modify and update investigative practices within the Police Department likewise was outside the purview of the Mayor's Office.

Mayor Hession attempted to improve the city's communication with citizens. Several panels and community discussions were held that focused on the city leaders' efforts to prevent an occurrence similar to the Zehm encounter, the centerpiece being the training of all police officers and firefighters in dealing with individuals exhibiting excited delirium.

Nevertheless, a major issue during the mayoral campaign was the inept way City Hall had handled a number of police scandals, and Mr. Hession was voted out. The new mayor, former city council member Mary Verner, had run on a "positive leadership" platform. As mayor, she ended the city's practice of filing countersuits against citizens who sued for civil rights violations. But she remained a vocal supporter of Officer Thompson and the Police Department, repeatedly stating that the officers did nothing wrong and no criminal act had occurred.

The Center for Justice entered a claim for damages against the City of Spokane in June, 2007. Commenting to the public in the only legally permissible way it could, the

Center stated that while it was asking for $2,900,000 in damages, the claim could be satisfied for much less money if the city took steps to prevent a similar tragedy from happening again.

On September 3, 2008, Karl Thompson's wife filed a petition for divorce in Kootenai County, Idaho, where the couple lived in a log home on two acres near Hayden Lake. They had been married for 38 years. Three weeks later, an uncontested decree of divorce was entered which transferred all interest in their home to her and directed that it be sold for a reasonable price. She was also awarded half of his retirement account from the City of Spokane, all of his interest in another deferred compensation plan, a motor vehicle, and other personal property. Karl Thompson was directed to pay all of their existing debts and $1500 per month in spousal support until her death. The decree provided that he could reside in the home rent-free until it was sold.

In October, 2008, in what one city councilman called "a preparedness issue," the City of Spokane authorized a retainer in the amount of $45,000 for outside legal help in anticipation of a civil suit from the Zehm family. The attorney chosen was Carl Oreskovich, a partner in a highly respected law firm in Spokane. According to the firm's website, "Etter, McMahon, Lamberson, Clary, and Oreskovich have received the highest national rating for legal ability and ethical standards. Lawyers in the firm are listed in the Best Lawyers in America and have been named among Washington state and Spokane's Best Lawyers in civil litigation, employment and criminal law."

In late February, 2009, the mayor and police chief made public statements about the Zehm family's claim. Reported on March 1, 2009, by the Spokesman-Review, "'I've looked into the details surrounding this incident,' (Mayor) Verner said, 'and I just don't think the behavior of the officer rose to a criminal behavior.'

"Kirkpatrick said Thompson 'has my unequivocal support...Based on all the information and evidence I have reviewed, I have determined that Officer Karl Thompson acted consistent with the law.'"

Shielded by the Protective Order, the attorneys for the Zehm family and the City conducted negotiations. However, the matter could not be resolved, forcing the Center for Justice to file a civil suit on March 13, 2009, five days before the statute of limitations expired. The Center gave a statement to the Spokesman-Review, "...no one on duty that day, from the dispatcher to the acting police chief, has ever offered to take responsibility for the department's role in Otto's death. The family is left with no other option of preventing future deaths among the disabled community than to fulfill the duty they owe the estate by filing a civil suit in federal court." The City of Spokane, Detective Ferguson, and all seven officers who came into contact with Zehm were named as defendants.

The presentation of the factual basis for the suit began with a discussion of Spokane Police Department training and policy that the plaintiffs claimed were violated. Included were police officers' training as to how to detain suspects, when force can be used, how to do their job without infringing on the constitutional rights of civilians, the consequences of violating those rights, and the policies to reduce the risk of in-custody death.

The discussion then turned to the 911 call and the dispatcher's confirmation that Zehm was intoxicated. The dispatcher's retraction of her previous confirmation that Zehm had taken the caller's money at the approximate time Officer Thompson came into contact with him was noted. It was emphasized that Officer Thompson did not observe Zehm breaking any law, showing any sign of delirium or intoxication, or acting in any way that would cause the officer to believe that Zehm was either armed or a danger to the public.

Then the sequence of events during the encounter, based on the review of the surveillance tapes, was presented. It was charged that Officer Thompson believed he had the authority to detain Zehm, had rushed him with his baton raised over his head, and the alleged verbal exchange between the officer and Zehm was not overheard by witnesses. The use of force policy of the Police Department that verbally refusing orders is not an excuse for police officers to use deadly force or a weapon in the detention process was quoted.

After establishing that all of the defendants knew what should have happened, the aspects of the encounter for which the suit sought redress were outlined. It was claimed, "Officer Thompson's purpose, namely to strike Zehm to the ground, was not justified under the circumstances and facts known to the officer but was substantially motivated by a purpose to punish or inflict payback upon Zehm for saying 'Why?' and 'No.' In the alternative, Officer Thompson acted with deliberate indifference to Zehm's rights in deciding to strike Zehm to the ground." To support this claim, the surveillance evidence that Officer Thompson saw Zehm turn and back away was cited. In this violation of Zehm's constitutional rights, "Officer Thompson...created the risk that Zehm would lawfully defend himself. But for Officer Thompson's preemptive and unlawful attack, Zehm would not have needed to defend himself."

It was emphasized that Zehm did not attack the officer but shielded his face as he was beaten, tased, and hit in the head with a baton. Zehm "reasonably defended himself," which "merely resulted in Thompson's further escalation of force in retaliation." It was claimed that the Medical Examiner corroborated the possibility of a head strike, which constituted the use of deadly force.

Next the video evidence of the actions of the backup officers and their reports concerning Zehm's restraint were presented. Zehm was placed in four-point restraint and left on his stomach for 13 minutes, a violation of the Spokane Police Department policy designed to reduce the risk of in-custody death. Instead of placing him on his side and not touching but carefully monitoring him, "Videos...show that Zehm's feet, though strapped loosely to his wrists, were periodically physically pinned back by an officer who was positioned at Zehm's knees, thus increasing the pressure on Zehm's diaphragm."

Then the arrival of EMS personnel, placement of the non-rebreather mask, and Zehm's eventual death were discussed. Notably, at the hospital Zehm was not found to be running a fever or to have any evidence of preexisting heart disease. The Medical Examiner was quoted, "It is likely in this case, and in similar cases, that restraint itself placed the decedent at risk for cardio-pulmonary arrest."

The Center for Justice sought compensation for the Zehm family for numerous grievances. "Upon completion of the Autopsy Report by the Medical Examiner, the City of Spokane arranged a press conference and Chief Nicks disclosed privileged portions of the Autopsy Report and other privileged and private information to the public.

"Prior to the above disclosure, the City had requested that Plaintiff agree to the entry of a mutual non-disclosure order that would have covered confidential investigatory information in the possession of the police.

"The City and Chief Nicks knew that when this non-disclosure order was signed, prior to the news conference, it created its own set of rights in favor of the Plaintiff in addition to rights established by statute.

"In addition to releasing the privileged and/or confidential information, Chief Nicks or subordinates in the Department's media relations position stated that:
- Zehm had lunged at Officer Thompson, and
- Zehm had been kept on his side for the majority of the time he was restrained.

Both statements are false. Chief Nicks' false statements placed Zehm in a negative light.

Chief Nicks made the false statements after having reviewed the security camera videotape of Officer Thompson's confrontation with Zehm. Chief Nicks made false statements knowing them to be false."

After asserting that the purpose of the Police Department's investigation was to determine whether or not the involved officers had used force appropriately, it was stated that according to Washington State law, a dead person cannot be charged with a crime. However, while conducting the investigation, Detective Ferguson obtained warrants for Zehm's medical records under the pretense of investigating Zehm's assault on Officer Thompson. According to state and federal law, obtaining a warrant for private medical records under a false pretense is an illegal invasion of privacy. "Upon belief, the above invasion of privacy was substantially and/or causally motivated in order to preemptively prepare against Zehm's estate for his in-custody death and in retaliation for exercise of federal rights."

It was stated that during the two years and 11 months since the encounter occurred, the City of Spokane publicly defended all of its involved employees. It was argued that since the official position of the City was that all of the officers had followed appropriate policies, and since the officers had acted in a way that deprived Otto Zehm of his constitutional rights, the City held policies that encouraged its agents to break federal law and is civilly liable.

Statements made in support of an alleged conspiracy included: "Tacitly or otherwise, one or more of the Defendants entered into an agreement to violate Plaintiff's

84

civil rights and committed an overt act in furtherance of that agreement. Initial police statements, including releases by both subordinates on behalf of the Department and by Acting Chief of Police Nicks, falsely portrayed Otto Zehm as the aggressor. On multiple occasions officials for the Police stated that Otto Zehm 'lunged' at Officer Thompson. Zehm's movement was plainly a retreat from the onrushing baton-brandishing officer.

"Evidence from the scene included the non-rebreather mask placed over Zehm's mouth and nose. No officer at the scene, nor senior officer reviewing Zehm's death, advised the Medical Examiner that the non-rebreather mask was used. The non-rebreather mask was not provided to the Medical Examiner for her first review. Until the issue of the non-rebreather mask was raised by third parties, the City, its Chief of Police, investigators, and the officers on the scene took no steps to preserve the mask.

"At least one interview of Officer Thompson was conducted off the record. Following the initial interview Officer Thompson was interviewed by Officer Ferguson on tape and led through a series of questions oriented toward exonerating his conduct.

"Officer Ferguson prepared and submitted a factually invalid affidavit seeking personal and privileged information for the purpose of investigating a dead person for an unprosecutable crime."

The request for damages included the premise that Otto Zehm suffered pain and death and that his injury and death caused further financial loss in the form of hospital and funeral expenses. Ann Zehm suffered damages "related to the interference in the parent child relationship, invasion of privacy in her son's records, release of confidential information to the public and false allegations regarding her son and his death." Factors specified that influenced the claim included that Otto was young, in good health, and gainfully employed and that he had provided financially for his mother while he was alive.

The Center concluded with a list of the laws the Zehm estate claimed were violated and demanded a jury trial and reward for legal fees and economic, noneconomic, and punitive damages.

One month after the civil suit was filed, the City Attorney's Office submitted its response, prepared with the assistance of Carl Oreskovich, in a point-for-point admission, denial, or clarification of each issue.

Pertaining to the training in the use of force, the defendants presented the Spokane Police Department's use of force policy and argued that, as Otto Zehm was not passively resistant, referring to refusing to comply with orders but not fighting back, the guidelines for passive resistance do not apply.

Concerning the 911 call, the defendants noted, "...the characterization of 'suspicious person' was the initial characterization, and...the nature of the call changed to a theft/robbery before the first officer was able to contact the 'suspicious person,' later identified as Mr. Otto Zehm." They acknowledged that while the caller never confirmed that Zehm had taken money from the ATM, she thought he had gotten the money. She also described Zehm's suspicious actions to the emergency dispatch operator. Accordingly, the information available to Officer Thompson changed the nature of the call "from a mere 'suspicious person' to a possible robbery."

In response to the allegation that Zehm showed no objective signs of "excited delirium" when observed by Officer Thompson, "these defendants assert the paragraph is vague as to whom and at what time Mr. Zehm showed no objective signs of 'excited delirium' and therefore deny the same... Mr. Zehm was acting in a bizarre manner – enough to scare the two complainants at the ATM, and enough for them to consider him to appear 'high' – and assert Mr. Zehm had avoided taking his prescribed medication for his long-standing medical condition, paranoid schizophrenia, which upon information and belief, was a significant predicate factor for the onset of an excited delirium episode."

The defendants' description of the encounter began with the claim that while Officer Thompson did not see Otto Zehm exhibit any bizarre behavior as he drove up to the Zip Trip, Zehm had watched the officer driving up seconds before he went into the convenience store. They stated that Officer Thompson had reason to believe that Zehm was armed and dangerous because Zehm was a possible robbery/theft suspect, might be high, was wearing a leather jacket that could easily conceal a weapon, and had evaded both the victims of the potential crime and the responding officer. Based on these assumptions and the presence of multiple exits from the store, Officer Thompson appropriately accelerated to head off a foot pursuit. They stated that Officer Thompson readied his baton for purely defensive reasons due to the possibility of a hidden weapon. Furthermore, turning the corner of the aisle, Officer Thompson found Zehm holding a pop bottle that "could be used as a significant weapon." Then they recounted Thompson's verbal exchange with Zehm exactly as recalled in his recorded interview.

Concerning the plaintiff's allegation that the witnesses to the initial encounter did not hear the alleged verbal exchange between Thompson and Zehm, the defendants retorted that some of the witnesses did hear it. The defendants agreed with the plaintiff's statement that the Spokane Police Department's policy prohibits the use of a weapon when a suspect says, "No," to an officer's command. But the plaintiff's assertions that Zehm was passively resisting and that Officer Thompson had no reason to believe that he had a weapon or was attempting to flee were denied.

Concerning the plaintiff's criticism of Thompson's use of force, "Officer Thompson decided to respond to Zehm's alleged query, 'Why,' and, 'No,' with a preemptive physical attack and use a weapon to strike Zehm to the ground." The response was, "These defendants deny the same. By way of further answer, defendants assert Mr. Zehm was, under the totality of the circumstances known to and perceived by Officer Thompson, defiant to lawful commands given clearly and repeatedly to Mr. Zehm, under circumstances that were tense, uncertain, and rapidly evolving, and that Officer Thompson would not have struck Mr. Zehm if Mr. Zehm had dropped the bottle."

The plaintiff had also alleged that Officer Thompson rushed Zehm and struck him to the ground either to punish Zehm for telling him, "No," or with deliberate indifference to Zehm's rights. The defendants answered, "What Officer Thompson observed under the totality of the circumstances was a felony criminal suspect who posed a potential danger to his and others' physical safety and who clearly repeatedly defied the commands of a uniformed officer to clear his hands of an item (several pound bottle) the suspect could use instantly to hurt or distract the officer." The defendants also denied that Zehm had backed away from Officer Thompson, was not actively resisting or preparing to fight, and only raised his arms to protect his face. Denying that Officer Thompson is responsible for the "natural consequences" of his actions, it was claimed instead that his actions "were reasonable and lawful based upon the totality of the circumstances known by and perceived by him at the time, as authorized by *Graham v. Connor*, 490 U.S. 386 (1989)." The ruling in that case established that all officers act based on the snap decisions required in rapid, tense, and evolving situations and therefore, cannot be judged in hindsight.

The response acknowledged the plaintiff's claim that Thompson used his Taser against Zehm and struck him with a baton repeatedly in rapid succession. "These defendants admit a struggle followed during which Officer Thompson gave Mr. Zehm many verbal commands such as, 'Drop it,' 'Stop resisting,' and, 'Stop fighting,' which Mr. Zehm again defiantly and angrily rejected at first by stating, 'No,' and thereafter by making loud growls, roars, and loud guttural sounds as Mr. Zehm physically resisted the officer's efforts to get him under control, and assaulted the officer by punching him and repeatedly kicking him. Defendants further admit that Officer Thompson deployed his Taser against Mr. Zehm, but that it was ineffective, and struck Mr. Zehm, pursuant to appropriate police procedure and training, while attempting to defend himself from Mr. Zehm's kicks and attempted, unsuccessfully, to get Mr. Zehm under physical control."

While admitting that one witness observed head strikes, the defendants argued that Officer Thompson never intended to or never actually did hit Zehm in the head with his baton, that the video surveillance record does not show any head strikes, and that neither the paramedics at the scene, the physicians who examined him at the hospital, or the Medical Examiner identified injuries to his head that were consistent with baton strikes. They concluded, "Mr. Zehm refused to comply, at least twice, with lawful commands from a uniformed police officer before any force was used, that the officer's commands and use of force were lawful under the totality of the circumstances known to and perceived by the officer, and that Mr. Zehm was not authorized by law to reject the officer's commands or resist the officer's efforts to obtain and maintain control of him."

The manner of Zehm's restraint and the plaintiff's specific allegations that Zehm was kept on his stomach and his legs flexed even further at times by the backup officers were addressed next. "Mr. Zehm continued to struggle until he was observed to have stopped breathing. Despite the restraints, Mr. Zehm actively moved, turned and kicked toward the officers. Mr. Zehm's struggle against the restraints was so violent at times that he was pulling his hands through the handcuffs by kicking hard with his feet, and officers had to place a second pair of handcuffs on him. Mr. Zehm was kicking so hard that he stretched the nylon strap between his wrists and feet, an act no officer on scene had ever witnessed before. The officers had to re-adjust the strap after he stretched it."

The defendants refuted the claim that Zehm had a breathing problem while the officers were holding him down by stating that Zehm had continued to "scream incomprehensibly." They added, "He was reported to have moderate atherosclerosis in his left anterior descending coronary artery of the heart. Further, according to the Medical Examiner's report, microscopic examination of the heart did demonstrate myofiber necrosis, which was non-acute, probably reflecting a period of autonomic instability or catecholamine excess prior to Mr. Zehm's entry into the convenience store."

Then the defendant's response turned to Chief Nicks' press conference, Detective Ferguson's investigation of Zehm's medical and employment records, and the city's response to the incident. The defendants claimed, "Incorrect and/or confusing information about the Medical Examiner's report had been reported by the press." Therefore, Chief Nicks was legally able to disclose information that was important to the public, and nothing that was said violated Zehm's privacy. Additionally, although Chief Nicks repeated that Zehm had lunged at Thompson and was kept on his side the majority of the time while restrained, those statements were revised later as the investigation progressed. Finally, while a deceased person cannot be prosecuted for a crime, crimes may still be investigated after a suspect has died. It was claimed that such information is sought in death investigations nationally and that Zehm's behavior prior to his death was enough of a concern for his family and friends that some of the information had been given to the media before Detective Ferguson requested records. Finally, the City disagreed with the plaintiffs, believing that the officers involved did not violate any federal or state law.

The response denied the alleged conspiracy. It was noted that the mask was eventually provided to the Medical Examiner, who found that it was not a factor in Zehm's death, and the claim that Thompson got an off the record interview before the recorded one was excused with the statement that both detectives present during the initial interview had taken notes. The defendants denied the existence of actionable damages, repeating that Zehm suffered from medical conditions and was having difficulty immediately prior to his death.

The defendants presented a summary of events, addressing specifically how 911 calls are processed, that the possible victims followed Zehm, and that individuals from the Spokane Police Department, the Spokane County Sheriff's Office, and the County Prosecutor's office have reviewed the matter. Otto Zehm's medical and work history were discussed, including his mental illness and recent difficulty at work that resulted in a forced leave of absence.

Then a detailed review of Zehm's criminal record was provided: "Mr. Zehm has a history of being physically resistive and aggressive with law enforcement officers, to the point of having to be hobbled prior to being transported to jail:

On August 3, 1990, Mr. Zehm was observed by a Spokane County Sheriff's Deputy to be wandering along an arterial in a confused manner wearing ripped clothing. The deputy drove back to investigate and determined that Mr. Zehm was lost and very confused, and appeared to have mental health problems.

Mr. Zehm answered some of the deputy's questions, refused to answer others, and did not appear capable of caring for himself safely in and along the roadway, a major arterial. The deputy determined he would have to take Mr. Zehm to Sacred Hearth Medical Center for an involuntary mental health evaluation and possible involuntary commitment for treatment.

Mr. Zehm verbally and physically resisted the deputy's efforts to either go with the deputy or remain at the scene.

When the deputy attempted to prevent him from running away, Mr. Zehm assaulted the deputy, and the deputy had to wrestle him to the ground, where the two struggled. During the struggle, Mr. Zehm twice tried to get to the deputy's gun in his holster.

The deputy twice had to use his radio to call for immediate, emergent backup assistance during the struggle. Mr. Zehm continued to fight against the efforts of the backup officers as well, and attempted to kick the first deputy in the groin area. The deputies had to hobble Mr. Zehm in hand and leg restraints, carry him to a patrol car, and transport him to jail where he was booked on the charges of third degree assault against the first deputy, and obstructing a public servant.

Mr. Zehm was not tried on the criminal charges. Instead, he was referred for involuntary mental health evaluation and treatment."

The response added that at the time of the March, 2006, law enforcement encounter with Zehm, there was no standard practice set by the Washington State Criminal Justice Training Commission requiring a hobbled suspect to be placed on his side. The defendants claimed that, according to police training, a hobbled suspect could be left in the prone position.

The response continued with affirmative defenses, beginning with the claims that the plaintiff failed to state a cause of action against a specific defendant and that the court does not have jurisdiction over the contempt of court allegations derived from Chief Nicks' press conference. Furthermore, "All force used by defendants against Mr. Zehm was lawful under the standards for reviewing the use of force by police officers established by the U.S. Supreme Court in *Graham v. Connor...*"

The defendants stated, "Each individual police officer defendant is entitled to qualified immunity from the plaintiffs' suit because each acted reasonably under the circumstances, none of the officers violated any of plaintiffs' constitutional rights, and the rights allegedly violated were not so clearly established that it would be clear to a reasonable officer that his/her conduct was unlawful in the situation he/she confronted. The qualified immunity extends to all alleged actions in plaintiffs' amended complaint, including but not limited to the detention and subsequent arrest of Mr. Zehm, any and all alleged uses of force (use of baton, Taser, handcuffs, leg restraints, hobbling device, and all other techniques and devices used), investigation, application for and execution of search warrants, and public statements."

The response concluded with the following statements:

"Otto Zehm was lawfully detained and arrested.

Probable cause existed for his arrest, and he should have known to behave properly while being arrested.

The force used during his detention was necessitated by his own actions and was 'necessary and reasonable under the totality of the circumstances known by and perceived by the officers, under tense, uncertain, and rapidly evolving circumstances.'

Any injury Mr. Zehm suffered was caused by his unlawful assault and battery on the officers attempting to arrest him and by his own negligence in caring for himself.

The allegation of inadequate police investigation is not actionable under Federal law, nor is the allegation of negligent police investigation actionable under Washington State law.

Allegations that officers or employees violated policies, procedures or training are not actionable.

The plaintiffs waived any privacy rights to Zehm's medical and mental health records.

Plaintiffs' injuries and damages, if any, were proximately caused by Mr. Zehm's own fault, including negligence, and assumption of the risk of known and appreciated dangers. (They) arise out of a condition of which Mr. Zehm had knowledge and to which Mr. Zehm voluntarily subjected himself."

The response ended with the defendants' demand for a jury trial, dismissal of the plaintiffs' case, and award of the costs incurred in defending the lawsuit.

On May 26, 2009, the Spokane City Council authorized the city staff to amend the contract for the services of Carl Oreskovich to a maximum of $200,000, deemed necessary "to assist in the representation of the City of Spokane and its employee(s) in the claim and lawsuit filed by the estate of Otto Zehm and to work with the City Attorney's Office...with additional compensation requiring further City Council action."

*

In July, 2009, the Thompson family home was listed for sale at $675,000. In April, 2010, a review of Kootenai County records indicated that the home was no longer listed for sale. Officer Thompson continued to reside there with his ex-wife.

CHAPTER EIGHT

In June, 2006, the United States Department of Justice opened an investigation into the use of force during the encounter with Otto Zehm and his in-custody death. Detective Ferguson's investigative files were requested, and agents of the Federal Bureau of Investigation and attorneys from the United States Attorney's Office began re-interviewing witnesses. The Department of Justice claimed later that despite repeated requests, a complete copy of the relevant files of Detective Ferguson and the Major Crimes Unit was not received until three years later.

Discrepancies between the Spokane Police Department's report and the newly obtained witness statements were quickly identified. Since Detective Burbridge had interviewed most of the witnesses, the federal investigators focused on his account of the witness statements. The most striking discrepancy concerned the interview of the witness who had spoken to news reporters prior to giving her statement to Detectives Burbridge and Marske. The Department of Justice stated that the detectives "felt this witness had an anti-law enforcement bias" and began the interview intending to discredit her because she had told reporters she "saw Thompson immediately strike Zehm in the head with [his] baton."

The Department of Justice wrote in a court filing, "Most of the interviewed percipient (fact) witnesses make significant changes to Burbridge reports summarizing their interviews... The revisions are more incriminating of defendant Officer Thompson's use of force than is contained in Burbridge's summaries (i.e., witnesses variously describe: immediate use of force; lack of any significant warning; lack of response time for Zehm; Zehm described as trying only to get away, not attack/assault the officer; and they describe location of baton strikes that are inconsistent with defendant's versions.) The Department of Justice later requested Burbridge's notes from interviews but was informed that he had destroyed them. Detective Marske did retain notes for several but not all witness interviews. These notes, while generally supportive, do not address all described discrepancies and/or omissions."

Ultimately, the Department of Justice found it impossible to obtain accurate witness statements. According to a court filing by Assistant U. S. Attorneys James McDevitt and Victor Boutros, "In Spring 2007, the Department of Justice also performs interviews of Spokane Fire Department personnel. During the course of the interviews, an attending assistant city attorney provides, on several occasions, his interpretive 'substantive clarifications,' which rephrase the witness' statements. These 'clarifications' likewise suggest testimony and/or statements that are adopted by the interviewed percipient witnesses. The Department of Justice decides following completion of these interviews that, if it is going to be successful in searching for accurate witness recall, untainted by representative statements and/or suggested 'clarifications,' that the Department of Justice will have to use the lengthier, more time consuming, grand jury process to perform and complete it's examination of City fire department personnel, Spokane Police Department officers, investigators, and administrators."

A grand jury was convened and the federal investigation continued in secrecy until March, 2009, when the Spokesman-Review reported that a criminal indictment against Officer Thompson could be filed in the near future. The grand jury indictment came on June 19, 2009:

COUNT ONE

*On or about March 18, 2006, in the Eastern District of Washington, the Defendant, **KARL F. THOMPSON, JR.,** then a police officer with the Spokane Police Department, while acting under color of law, struck and repeatedly struck Otto Zehm with a baton and Tasered him, resulting in bodily injury to Otto Zehm, and thereby willfully deprived Otto Zehm of a right preserved and protected by the Constitution of the United States, namely, the right to be free from the unreasonable use of force by one acting under color of law, all in violation of Title 18, United States Code, Section 242.*

COUNT TWO

*Between on or about March 22, 2006 and on or about March 27, 2006, in the Eastern District of Washington, the Defendant, **KARL F. THOMPSON, JR.,** then a police officer with the Spokane Police Department, knowingly made a false entry in a record and document, to wit: by making a false statement in an interview recorded on March 22, 2008, a transcription of which was reviewed and signed by **KARL F. THOMPSON, JR.,** on March 27, 2006, with the intent to impede, obstruct and influence, the investigation of a matter within the jurisdiction of a department and agency of the United States, that is, the Federal Bureau of Investigation, and in relation to and contemplation of such investigation, involving the violation of constitutional rights described in Count One of this Indictment, all in violation of Title 18, United States Code, Section 1519."*

The Spokesman-Review article reporting the indictment quoted Assistant U. S. Attorney James McDevitt concerning role of the Department of Justice in the case. "These are not matters that we do with any sort of glee... But where there is no local action, or where the results of the state or local proceedings are insufficient to vindicate the federal interest, a federal prosecution may be sought."

Officer Thompson was arraigned on July 9, 2009, and set a signature bond, meaning he didn't have to pay anything out of pocket but would forfeit $50,000 if he fled. In a curious turn of events, the Police Department assigned him to a desk job for which he was paid $73,000 per year to check and cross-reference daily training bulletins regarding best police practices for high-risk liability incidents, a job created by Chief Kirkpatrick specifically in response to the Zehm incident.

Soon after the release of the indictment, the City of Spokane held a press conference to express continued support of its Police Department and Officer Thompson. According to the Spokesman-Review, "'Based on the information we have, we've been supportive of not only police officers but the firefighters and the other city employees involved in that incident,' City Administrator Ted Danek said.

'I don't believe Karl acted to willingly deprive Mr. Zehm of his constitutional rights,' City Attorney Howard

Delaney said. But he added, 'I have not necessarily seen everything the grand jury has.'

The day prior to the press conference Mayor Verner said that she wasn't briefed by federal authorities about the evidence in the case. 'Like the rest of the public, I'll be watching the evidence unfold in the court system.'"

In July, 2009, despite his salary and prior ownership of an expensive home near Hayden Lake, Idaho, United States Magistrate Judge Cynthia Imbrogno declared Officer Thompson indigent, obliging the federal government to pay for his defense. Soon afterward officers of the Spokane Police Department initiated the "Band of Blue" campaign by selling blue wristbands for $10 apiece to raise money for Thompson's out-of-pocket expenses. Officer Jennifer DeRuwe, the Department's spokesperson, said, "I was going to give money whether I had a bracelet or not. It's just one more way to show support and raise money so that as a collective group we are visibly showing support."

According to defense attorney Carl Oreskovich, "The case is going to be a long case with a significant amount of experts. Although the court has appointed me, the funds are not unlimited. Anything raised by fellow police officers is greatly appreciated."

Center for Justice attorney Jeffry Finer said, "It's not surprising that Officer Thompson would be a symbol for his supporters just the way Otto was a symbol of the community he represented. But their support is not the same thing as exoneration."

Breean Beggs, co-counsel with Mr. Finer in the civil suit, indicated that Otto's mother did not begrudge Thompson's support by his fellow officers. He wrote, "Ann Zehm realizes that Officer Thompson's involvement in the homicide of Otto Zehm will cause him distress for the rest of his life. As for financial support, local and federal taxpayers are already financing lawyers for his civil defense and criminal defense. The fact that taxpayer support is rarely offered to victims of police homicides is why Otto's mother has committed to using the recovery in her civil suit to create a fund for families of victims killed by law enforcement."

Soon after the indictment was released, the Department of Justice asked for a stay of the civil suit until the criminal proceeding was concluded. Victor Boutros, Assistant U. S. Attorney in the civil rights division, indicated that such delays are common. The stay of a civil suit until the conclusion of the criminal proceeding serves the dual purposes of protecting the integrity of the criminal case and protecting the rights of the defendants against self-incrimination in one proceeding due to statements made in the other.

Explained to the public in a Spokesman-Review article, "'Discovery,' in a legal context, is a pretrial disclosure of pertinent facts, documents or other evidence." The law requires that the two sides share much more information and evidence in civil suits than it does in criminal cases. The Department of Justice was concerned that the defense attorneys in the civil suit, Rocco Treppiedi and Carl Oreskovich, would use the more liberal discovery process afforded civil litigants to Officer Thompson's advantage in the criminal proceeding.

In support of its request that the civil suit be stayed, the Department of Justice pointed out that Carl Oreskovich had been hired by the City of Spokane to defend "the City of Spokane and its employee(s) in the claim and lawsuit filed by the Estate of Otto Zehm." However, when asked who he represented, Mr. Oreskovich "informed the Department of Justice that he exclusively represented Karl Thompson and he did not, notwithstanding any City resolution to the contrary, represent the City, the Police Department and/or any other Spokane Police Department administrators or officers... Mr. Oreskovich further indicated that he and only he would be representing Mr. Thompson's criminal and civil interests in the Otto Zehm incident." Yet only one month before, Rocco Treppiedi had told the Department of Justice that Thompson was being represented in the civil suit by the City and "did not have separate criminal counsel." Treppiedi indicated that he had continued to work on the civil suit on behalf of the City and Officer Thompson.

The Department of Justice was aware that Treppiedi was sharing information gleaned through discovery with Carl Oreskovich, his coworker in the civil case, which was not contested. Oreskovich sat in on Treppiedi's meetings with other involved officers, and the two filed documents jointly. Furthermore, the Department of Justice alleged that Oreskovich told Assistant U. S. Attorney Timothy Durkin that he intended to "have available the full cadre of liberal civil discovery processes to defend Mr. Thompson on the Plaintiffs' and conceivably, the United States' claims of excessive force."

The impact of this collusion was compounded by the extraordinary steps Treppiedi took while defending the City in the civil suit. According to a Department of Justice filing, "From October 2008 through June 2009, it became apparent to the Department of Justice that Assistant City Attorney Rocco Treppiedi was briefing and preparing most of the Spokane Police Department and/or the City of Spokane witnesses called to testify before the Grand Jury. It was also learned that Mr. Treppiedi had debriefed witnesses that appeared before the grand jury. In addition, the Department of Justice learned that Assistant City Attorney Treppiedi was conducting an 'investigation' that appeared to actually 'shadow' the investigative activities of the Grand Jury. For instance, in addition to preparing and/or debriefing the majority of Spokane Police Department witnesses, Mr. Treppiedi also conducted post-grand jury testimony interviews of one or more non-Spokane Police Department witnesses that recently appeared before the Grand Jury."

In the spring of 2009 Treppiedi attempted to contact Robert Bragg, a consultant and expert witness in the criminal proceeding for the Department of Justice. When Bragg reported it, Assistant U. S. Attorney Timothy Durkin contacted Treppiedi and "requested that he cease and desist all further contact with the Department of Justice's expert." Treppiedi refused, but the matter was resolved when his boss, City Attorney Howard Delaney, indicated the City would "temporarily stay further attempts to engage in ex parte contact with the United States' expert witness until a further review of the issue was performed."

The Department of Justice wrote, "On information and belief, and based on a survey of the Criminal Chiefs and other career United States Assistant Attorneys in the U.S. Attorney's Office who have been conducting grand jury investigations and criminal prosecutions during the past approximate 30 years, this is the first time that the target of a federal criminal and grand jury investigation has been provided seemingly direct access to and direct information about traditionally confidential grand jury proceedings by counsel purporting to also represent the interests of a fellow law enforcement agency." The Department of Justice concluded its request to stay the civil suit with this statement: "Based on assertions and arguments made by Assistant City Attorney Treppiedi at the time of the party's September 10, 2009 conference call, and based on the foregoing history of interaction between Assistant City Attorney Treppiedi and the Department of Justice, the United States fully expects Mr. Treppiedi and the City Attorney's Office will also make full use of the liberal civil discovery processes to try to defend Officer Karl Thompson, who is the City's principal 'civil liability client,' and the other named Defendants as well."

In September, 2009, in response to the Department of Justice's request to stay the civil suit, the City of Spokane produced statements it called "depositions" from 14 Spokane Police Department officers and the City Information Technology Manager who had handled the FBI's requests for records. The statements were offered in support of the City's request that the civil suit be completed in as timely a manner as possible. Nine of the statements alleged improper conduct by FBI agents and Assistant U. S. Attorneys ranging from unreasonableness to coerced grand jury testimony.

In particular, Detective Burbridge's statement caught the public's attention. "In May 2009, I received a grand jury subpoena for this incident. I had both the City Attorney and a private attorney contact the U.S. Attorney's Office to find out if I was a target or a witness. I was assured I was a witness only. My scheduled testimony was delayed and I was re-subpoenaed in June 2009.

"I arrived in the waiting area of the U.S. Attorney's Office one half hour early, as was requested by U.S. Attorney Tim Durkin. Mr. Durkin came out and introduced himself. He then requested that I accompany him to a conference room so he could introduce me to several people. I declined. This made Mr. Durkin very mad. He raised his voice, crooked his finger at me and ordered me to come with him. I told Mr. Durkin I was not a child and asked him not to crook his finger at me. I told him that he had no authority to order me anywhere, especially since I was just a witness. Mr. Durkin stepped back, took a deep breath and apologized. Mr. Durkin said that he had someone important he wanted to introduce me to and asked if I would please come with him. I agreed. Spokane Police Officer S. McIntyre witnessed everything that happened in the waiting area...

"Mr. Durkin then spent ten minutes telling me how multiple witnesses had given the FBI statements that were substantially different than what my reports said. Mr. Durkin told me if I went upstairs and testified to the accuracy of my reports, there was 'a high likelihood you will be indicted for perjury' and sent to prison for ten years.

"I told everyone present to 'pound sand' and I would be testifying to the accuracy of my reports."

Other officers made nearly identical allegations pertaining to Durkin's behavior, stating they were asked to come to the grand jury proceedings early, taken into a room with the head FBI agent on the case and others, and threatened with a perjury charge if they did not testify as expected.

Three who didn't file "depositions" at the time, Officers Uberuaga, McIntyre, and Moses, had given evidence to the grand jury that was unfavorable to Officer Thompson but changed their testimony later. Those changes favored Officer Thompson, and two of the three officers subsequently alleged coercion at the time of their first grand jury appearance. Neither former Assistant Police Chief Nicks nor Detective Ferguson made a similar allegation.

Opposing a stay of the civil suit, attorneys for the defendants claimed, "The U.S.A's arguments are based on a list of perceived problems which are not based on fact, and are not relevant under the law. The U.S.A's allegations demonstrate its overreaching desire to not only manage the prosecution of *U.S.A. v. Karl Thompson,* but the entire civil case and each of the civil litigants herein. The U.S.A's concerns are baseless, and its motions to stay should be denied because it fails to establish the substantial prejudice required by Ninth Circuit case law."

Their arguments began with a response to the Department of Justice's account of the history of the case, addressing first the matter of Carl Oreskovich's representation and the accusation of unethical collusion. They explained that a few days after Mr. Oreskovich was hired by the city, Officer Thompson asked him "to represent him with respect to a grand jury investigation convened to investigate his conduct arising out of the March 18, 2006 incident." Oreskovich agreed then to represent Thompson in the potential criminal proceeding. But he also acknowledged that he "would not be able to represent any other defendant named in the civil case." As he had been hired to assist the City Attorney's Office in the civil suit, the City Attorney's Office was allowed to delegate Thompson's defense to him, agreeing that Mr. Oreskovich would represent Officer Thompson in the criminal case, and his involvement in the civil case would be limited to work done on Officer Thompson's behalf. It was further claimed that these facts had been known all along to the Department of Justice.

Then the defendant's attorneys addressed the accusation of a shadow grand jury investigation by stating that they were obligated to investigate potential liability risks to the city and had begun investigating the incident the night it occurred. It was claimed that any investigation they did while the Department of Justice was also investigating stemmed from their continuing obligation to represent the City of Spokane and all of its employees. They explained that the duties of the City Attorney's Office require that it "confer with all City employees who have received subpoenas to testify in trials, depositions, hearings, and official proceedings of various nature that are related to their job duties with the City." They indicated the intent of the meetings with city employees is to answer their questions about what will happen and what they have to do. The City Attorney's office provides "a description of the nature of the proceeding, such witnesses are routinely advised to always be prepared, be professional, make sure they understand the questions that are asked, and to answer each question truthfully." It was added that these meetings are protected by attorney-client privilege.

They continued the response to allegations of impropriety regarding the grand jury by defending the legality of their actions. "The U.S.A. argues that the City Attorney's Office has provided 'traditionally' confidential grand jury testimonial information to Karl Thompson. First and foremost, the grand jury witnesses are not bound by the secrecy provisions of Fed. R. Crim. P. 6(e)(2)... The Advisory Committee Notes to Rule 6(e), when adopted in 1944, specifically state: The rule does not impose any obligation of secrecy on witnesses. Perhaps that is why the U.S.A. did not allege that learning testimonial information from witnesses is unlawful or improper... The U.S.A.'s brief only complains that the City Attorney's Office might be violating an undefined, unenforceable 'tradition.' Second, no testimonial disclosures have been made (despite the fact that such disclosures can be made lawfully)."

The defendants' attorneys stated, "The Ninth Circuit has adopted a multi-factor balancing test to determine when a stay of civil proceedings in the face of parallel criminal

101

proceedings is warranted... In determining whether a stay is warranted, the trial court must consider:

1) the extent to which the Fifth Amendment rights are implicated;
2) the interest of the plaintiff in proceeding expeditiously with the litigation or any particular aspect thereof, and the potential prejudice delay would cause to the plaintiff;
3) the burden that any particular aspect of the proceedings may impose on the defendant;
4) the convenience of the court in the use of judicial resources;
5) the interest of non-parties; and
6) the interest of the public in the pending civil and criminal cases."

It was claimed that each factor was either not an issue or should be interpreted in their favor. Furthermore, the right of the Department of Justice to be involved in the civil trial was challenged. "It appears that the U.S.A. automatically presumes that it is a party or has standing in this private civil lawsuit simply because it has a criminal prosecution of one of the multiple defendants in this private civil lawsuit. The U.S.A. does not have standing in this civil lawsuit or any basis to intervene as a matter of right. Courts have denied intervention requested by the U.S.A. where the reason cited for the requested intervention was based upon parallel grand jury and/or criminal prosecution of one or more of the civil litigants."

The defendants' attorneys concluded with the accusation that the motion to stay the civil suit was "based on supposition and inflammatory rhetoric" and claimed that the defendants had been publicly shamed and want the chance to clear their names.

Presiding in the civil suit was Federal District Court Judge Lonny R. Suko. An article published by The Spokesman-Review on October 22, 2009, reported his decision concerning the requested stay. "U.S. District Judge Lonny Suko said he had to balance the rights of Zehm's family members to get information they need with Officer Karl Thompson's right to use the Fifth Amendment to avoid self-incrimination and federal prosecutors' concerns over evidence from a grand jury investigation." He ruled that Officer Thompson's rights were sufficiently protected by the Fifth Amendment and that the civil suit needed to wait until the criminal proceeding was concluded. He also ruled that Officer Thompson was to have access to the grand jury information but could not share it with any other party in the civil suit.

The newspaper quoted the succinct response to Suko's rulings from the U. S. Attorney's Office. "'Such delays are common,' said Victor Boutros. 'Protecting the integrity of the criminal case is paramount.'"

The article also conveyed the judge's response to the complaint of a shadow investigation. "Suko said he wasn't going to rule on complaints by federal attorneys that city attorneys had engaged in inappropriate conduct in talking about grand jury testimony with Spokane police officers, or sworn statements that city attorneys filed to defend their actions. 'It's a side issue,' the judge said, 'and not related to the request to delay evidence-gathering for the civil trial.'"

*

On May 15, 2010, the Spokesman-Review reported that Spokane attorney Rob Cossey indicated he "represents three or four officers as a federal grand jury continues to gather information in the (Zehm) case. He confirmed that one of his clients has received what's known as a target letter, which essentially informs the person that federal officials intend to charge him or her with a crime. 'The person is right square in the sights of the U.S. Attorney's Office. I can't tell you the name of the person,' Cossey said. 'It's more definite than a target letter.'"

CHAPTER NINE

The trial of *U.S.A. v. Karl Thompson* was set to begin on June 7, 2010. The wrangling between the prosecution and defense teams began months in advance of the trial date, and Federal District Judge Frederick Judge Van Sickle's rulings framed the factual basis of the charges the jury would deliberate.

In March, 2010, Carl Oreskovich requested that the facts pertaining to Zehm's 1990 arrest and subsequent hospitalization be admissible at trial. According to the Spokesman-Review, he based this request on a newly-revealed theory that Otto Zehm was suffering from excited delirium before his March 18, 2006, confrontation with police, "making it a pre-existing mental condition that therefore justified the level of force used to detain him... Whenever Mr. Zehm has gone off his medications, he has shown the same or similar types of characteristics. Our theory of the case is the use of force is justified based on the circumstances facing Officer Thompson." The judge's denial of this request relied on a matter of law Rocco Treppiedi had asserted in his June, 2006, correspondence with the Center for Justice, that Officer Thompson must be judged only on what he knew at the time of the incident. That became the justification for many of the evidentiary rulings in the pretrial period, this one favoring the prosecution.

Oreskovich also offered an astonishing argument for dismissal of the charge that Thompson lied to investigators. Recounted in a Spokesman-Review article on April 21, 2010, "Spokane police Officer Karl F. Thompson Jr., accused of lying to investigators over the fatal confrontation with Otto Zehm, unsuccessfully sought to get the charge dismissed Tuesday, arguing that he never 'swore to tell the truth' during his interview with detectives. Although his defense lawyer, Carl Oreskovich, later insisted that Thompson told the truth during the interview, the distinction was drawn during a hearing in U.S. District Court as part of an effort to get the lying charge thrown out on a legal technicality. Oreskovich said the charge should be dismissed because Thompson didn't swear to tell the truth in the recorded interview, and that it was someone else who prepared a transcript of the conversation with detectives. U.S. District Court Judge Fred Van Sickle, however, didn't buy it. 'This is part of an investigation that was conducted. It was recorded clearly at the consent of Officer Thompson,' Van Sickle said. 'To state this is somehow created by a third party strikes me as putting form over substance.'"

The prosecution asked to present evidence that Thompson's divorce was a fraudulent transfer under Idaho law. Reported by the Spokesman-Review: "According to Durkin, 'If Thompson puts his character at issue, then the jury is entitled to hear the facts of Thompson's divorce and fraudulent transfer because they directly implicate his character for truthfulness.' But Oreskovich, who has filed a motion seeking to exclude any mention of the divorce, denied his client engaged in a fraudulent transfer to his ex-wife. 'I'm not going to get into the circumstances of Karl Thompson's divorce, but I will say there is no evidence whatsoever that supports Mr. Durkin's unsubstantiated allegations.'" Evidence pertaining to the alleged fraudulent transfer was not permitted at trial.

The prosecution asked to present a "three-dimensional, computer-animated re-creation of the Zip Trip store and the confrontation between Zehm and Thompson, which was captured by four surveillance cameras." Oreskovich argued that the computer animation showed three-dimensional images derived from two-dimensional camera footage, and the animation was excluded.

A particularly contentious point concerned a piece of evidence Detective Ferguson was expected to testify to be among the "many glaring missteps and omissions" in her investigation. The item was a short note handwritten by one of the paramedics which included the statement that Officer Thompson told Officer Moses that he had hit Zehm in the head, neck, and upper torso with his baton.

The defense argued, "The United States fails to point out that Michael Stussi, the AMR responder who drafted the AMR Patient Care Report, has no recollection as to whether Officer Moses told him that Mr. Zehm had been struck in the head, neck, and upper torso... In fact, Mr. Stussi is entirely unclear as to how he learned that Mr. Zehm had allegedly been struck in the head, neck, and upper torso and subsequently entered that information into the AMR Patient Care Report... Even more surprising is the fact that the United States has failed to mention that Officer Timothy Moses has recently met with the government, correcting his grand jury testimony that Officer Thompson told him that he hit Mr. Zehm in the head." Nevertheless, the AMR report was ruled admissible.

*

Shortly before the trial was to begin, the Department of Justice voiced its concerns about the conflict of interest in Thompson's representation by Treppiedi and Oreskovich, claiming the timing of the challenge was because they had been waiting for the defense counsel to address the issue. Thompson's counsel, however, claimed the allegation was nothing more than an attempt to disrupt the defense right before the trial.

The conflict of interest concerns pertaining to Rocco Treppiedi had been enumerated in filings related to the stay of the civil suit. The Department of Justice emphasized that Treppiedi represented every defendant in the civil action, which allowed him to conduct his shadow investigation and ensured that a conflict of interest issue would arise. "Mr. Treppiedi asserted that since he continued to represent the criminal target Mr. Thompson that he felt he had an ethical obligation to provide any and all information that he acquired to Mr. Thompson and/or to Officer Thompson's private counsel." It was pointed out that while Treppiedi was investigating the grand jury and working in Officer Thompson's interest, some of the individuals he represented in the civil suit were giving testimony to the grand jury that was unfavorable to Thompson. Statements from Assistant Chief Nicks, Detective Ferguson, Officer Uberuaga, Officer Moses, and others documented the claim.

According to the Department of Justice, Oreskovich and Treppiedi had both stated that Oreskovich started to work solely on Thompson's case on March 13, 2009. However, from the time of his hiring in October, 2008, until that date he had worked for the City of Spokane and all of its employees. The Department of Justice wrote, "In connection with this 'joint representation of the City of Spokane and all of its employees,' Mr. Oreskovich and seemingly other members of his firm participated in both pre-grand jury and post-grand jury interviews of a number of SPD police officers who appeared before the grand jury."

Oreskovich's reply to the conflict of interest allegation was concise and dismissive. He stated that he and he alone had represented Officer Thompson from a very early point in the case and had worked with Treppiedi as a representative of Thompson's interests. In his words: "Mr. Oreskovich's association with the City of Spokane has been for the limited purpose of representing Officer Thompson. Mr. Oreskovich has never claimed to globally represent all officers and Spokane Police Department employees." He also provided a waiver of potential conflict of interest from Karl Thompson.

A few days before Judge Van Sickle ruled on the conflict of interest issue, the City terminated the City Attorney's representation of Officer Thompson in the civil suit, prompting the Spokesman-Review to request an interview with City Attorney Howard Delaney. City spokeswoman Marlene Feist responded to the request, "This decision was made to simplify case management for the city's lean Legal Department and could change as the civil case proceeds."

Having received statements from a number of co-defendants in the civil suit that they had never been represented by Oreskovich in any capacity, Judge Van Sickle ruled that Mr. Oreskovich had not had an attorney-client relationship with any defendant other than Officer Thompson. After two hearings in which the judge thoroughly questioned Thompson about his understanding of his waiver of the right to conflict-free representation, he stated, "To the extent a potential conflict may be deemed to exist, Thompson has knowingly, voluntarily, and intelligently waived his Sixth Amendment right to conflict-free counsel. The Court, in its discretion, finds no basis to override that waiver."

Less than a week before the trial was to begin, the Department of Justice asked to include in its opening statement that Zehm was innocent of any crime. "The fact that Zehm had committed no crime and had no idea that an officer was coming for him casts enormous doubt on the credibility of Thompson's story. The jury simply cannot effectively evaluate Thompson's claim that Zehm was gearing up for a fight with Thompson from the moment Thompson entered the store without knowing the undisputed fact that Zehm had committed no crime and thus had no reason to believe a law enforcement officer was looking for him at all, much less target him. Hiding that information from the jury would radically undermine the jury's truth-seeking function and invite the jury to draw sinister inferences about Zehm's guilt that both sides know to be false.

"It is undisputed that Thompson never explained to Zehm why Thompson was there or why he needed to talk to Zehm. It is undisputed that Thompson never said he needed to ask Zehm some questions about what happened at the ATM – in fact, he never mentioned the ATM at all. And it is undisputed that Zehm had committed no crime and therefore would have no reason to think a police officer was going to approach, confront or attack him. Without this information, the jury is in no position to meaningfully judge Thompson's claim that Zehm displayed no 'confusion' or 'fear' when a police officer he did not know was for some unknown reason rushing at him with a baton raised." The Department of Justice asked to present supporting evidence, including Alison Smith's verification that nothing was stolen, bank records, and testimony that Zehm's last words were, "All I wanted was a Snickers."

On the first day of trial Judge Van Sickle announced his decision. According to the Spokesman-Review, "U.S. District Court Judge Fred Van Sickle ruled that attorneys for both sides could not introduce evidence about Zehm's mental illness, items found in Zehm's pockets, or essentially anything that Thompson didn't know before the confrontation on March 18, 2006. 'Evidence considering matters not known (by Thompson) may not be admitted in the government's case in chief,' Van Sickle said."

When mention of Zehm's innocence was excluded, Assistant U. S. Attorney Victor Boutros objected and requested a short delay, after which he announced that his superiors in Washington, D.C., approved his request to appeal that ruling to the 9th U.S. Circuit Court of Appeals. 'The government believes this evidence is so significant...that it needs to seek review,' Boutros said."

U.S.A. v. Karl Thompson would not proceed until the appellate court's decision was received.

*

Three months after the criminal trial was suspended, a new conflict between Rocco Treppiedi and Breean Beggs became public. Treppiedi had written to Beggs concerning legal advice Beggs had volunteered to Spokane City Council members regarding proposed changes to strengthen the city ordinance governing police oversight. According to the Spokesman-Review, "Treppiedi's letter, sent in June as the city was finalizing the new ordinance, argues that Beggs' discussions with the City Council about the changes to police oversight were done on behalf of the Zehm estate. 'Your direct advice to the council members has been contrary to the advice provided by this office.'

"But Beggs said he never talked about the Zehm case with council members and...that changes to the ombudsman rules have no effect on the lawsuit... He was asked by City Council members to help craft a stronger ombudsman ordinance that could withstand a challenge from the Spokane Police Guild, the union representing police officers. He even participated in a meeting with city attorneys and City Council members about changes. No city attorney in the room expressed concern about his presence, Beggs said.

"In his letter, Treppiedi threatened to file a complaint with the Washington State Bar Association if Beggs did not cease contact with city leaders about the ombudsman ordinance."

In response Beggs contacted Michael Piccolo who, like Treppiedi, was an Assistant City Attorney. "I am writing to you in your capacity as the assigned attorney for Spokane City Council Members. I am in receipt of a letter from Assistant City Attorney Rocco Treppiedi requesting that I not have any further communication with Council Members regarding the proposed changes to the Municipal Code provisions relating to police oversight... Mr. Treppiedi's attempts to reduce my participation in the debate on appropriate police oversight [are] without support in the law and appear to violate both my constitutional rights and the rights of Council Members... As I read the law, I have the right to discuss the Zehm case directly with City Council Members in their official capacity since they are not named parties in this litigation and have no individual authority to bind the City to a settlement. In this instance, I believe they will confirm that my communications with them on improving police oversight did not involve the Zehm litigation... This is not the first time that members of the

City's executive branch have attempted to use the City's legal department to forestall reforms by the legislative branch..."

Beggs also contacted Michael Kipling of the Kipling Law Group in Seattle, Washington, who reviewed the matter in detail and corresponded with Howard Delaney, City Attorney for Spokane. "This is written on behalf of the ACLU of Washington. We have reviewed correspondence among Rocco Treppiedi and Mike Piccolo, Assistant City Attorneys, and Breean Beggs, of the law firm of Paukert & Troppmann (formerly of the Center for Justice in Spokane). In this correspondence, Mr. Treppiedi attempts to prevent Mr. Beggs from communicating with members of the Spokane City Council on matters such as police accountability and oversight.

"The ACLU-WA is very concerned about this conduct because we believe Mr. Beggs has a constitutional right to communicate with elected officials, under both the U.S. and Washington Constitutions, regarding issues of general policy such as these. The City Attorney's attempt to interfere with Mr. Beggs' constitutional right to petition his representatives is improper and should stop immediately.

"Mr. Treppiedi argues incorrectly that Washington's Rules of Professional Conduct applicable to lawyers (RPC 4.2) prohibit contact between Mr. Beggs and City Council members because Mr. Beggs represents a client who is suing the City and further because the lawsuit might implicate issues of accountability and oversight of the police. I understand that there is a factual dispute as to whether that characterization of the lawsuit is accurate, but for these purposes there is no need to resolve that dispute. There can be no dispute that accountability and oversight are matters of general policy and of legitimate public concern. As such, citizens such as Mr. Beggs have an absolute right to communicate with elected officials regarding such issues and there is no justification for lawyers from the City to use RPC 4.2 to restrict that right... The fact that Mr. Beggs may also represent a client with similar interests in a pending lawsuit does not deprive Mr. Beggs of his constitutional right to petition the government. Nor is it appropriate for the City's lawyers to circumvent this authority by advising City Council members not to speak with Mr. Beggs unless a City Attorney is present.

"On behalf of the ACLU-WA, I ask that you...instruct Mr. Treppiedi and the other attorneys in your office that they should immediately stop any efforts to preclude communications between Mr. Beggs (or any other person) and City Council members. I also ask that you inform the members of the City Council of your position and confirm in writing to Mr. Beggs that he has the right to communicate with City Council members on any matters of public interest, including matters pertaining to police accountability and oversight."

Soon after Kipling's letter was received, the City's support of Treppiedi's position and his threat of a bar complaint was reported by the Spokesman-Review. "City Attorney Howard Delaney said his office is taking the ACLU letter 'under advisement. I don't view the factual scenario similarly to the way Breean couches it,' Delaney said.

"In an interview...Mayor Mary Verner said she agreed with Treppiedi's action. 'There wasn't any concern about (Beggs) exercising his right to petition his elected official... It was that he had simultaneous roles going and there was a blurring of which role he was engaged in at any given time.'"

*

On March 24, 2011, the 9th Circuit Court of Appeals upheld Judge Van Sickle's ruling in *U.S.A v. Karl Thompson.* The trial was scheduled to resume on October 11, 2011. Each side continued to try to bolster its case.

CHAPTER TEN

Assistant Chief Jim Nicks had been one of the first city officials to acknowledge concern about the conclusions of the Police Department's internal investigation. His testimony to the grand jury in 2008 was a key factor in the indictment of Karl Thompson the following year on charges of using unreasonable force in the Zehm encounter and lying to investigators afterward. It wasn't until March, 2010, that the public learned that Nicks would testify for the prosecution. In August, 2011, a summary of the testimony he was expected to give during the criminal trial was released to the public:

"Thompson's stated reasons for using an impact weapon on Zehm are not supported by objective evidence. Officer Thompson's baton strikes were not within SPD policy, were unnecessary, were not appropriate and were unreasonable under the circumstances. Thompson's immediate baton strikes to the retreating, non-assaultive Zehm did not serve a legitimate law enforcement purpose (i.e., Terry stop detention of a non-threatening suspect) and no reasonable officer would have perceived Zehm's response to Officer Thompson's presence as assaultive. I have not reached this assessment lightly and in fact have peer reviewed my analysis, assessment and conclusions with Chief Anne Kirkpatrick. She concurs with the assessment that unnecessary and unreasonable force was deployed by the responding officer against Mr. Zehm."

Delivering a prepared statement, Mayor Verner said, "Assistant Chief Nicks' affidavit is consistent with what U.S. Attorney Durkin indicated the Assistant Chief would testify to in a legal filing in April, 2010. As we did then, we are evaluating this information in light of the case the City is involved in-the separate civil case."

When Breean Beggs and Jeffry Finer filed a $2.9 million civil claim against the City of Spokane and a number of its employees in March, 2009, city attorneys responded with a lengthy denial of responsibility and blamed Otto

Zehm for his death. After Chief Nicks' expected testimony was released, Beggs indicated it was clear that city officials already knew or should have known about his grand jury testimony before their response to the civil suit was written. "I'm waiting for them to explain to us why they thought it was better not to reveal what they knew about the case from the beginning. All this information is going to come out. So why not get it out so the public has all the facts and so the case can get resolved?" He concluded, "Nicks speaks for the city. The only remaining thing left for the civil case is the nature and the extent of the damages."

The stay of the civil suit halted the discovery process but did not prevent the parties involved from settling. On August 17, 2011, one week after the release of Nicks' opinion that Thompson violated Spokane Police Department policy during the confrontation with Zehm, the Spokesman-Review published an article describing a new press release from the city. "Spokane Mayor Mary Verner announced Tuesday that she is seeking 'all courses of action' to resolve the civil case surrounding the city's handling of the fatal 2006 confrontation between Spokane police and mentally ill janitor Otto Zehm. Verner said media attention over the past week has brought 'raw emotions and ongoing frustration from our community, made worse by the complexity of legal processes surrounding the matter... Admittedly, these steps are part of a complex process, but we have to ensure that we are doing everything possible to secure the confidence of our citizens. I have a responsibility to maintain trust in our Police Department and to work in good faith to reach a fair resolution in the civil case.'"

A short while later the Spokesman-Review reported, "Breean Beggs...said last week that he hasn't heard from the city since Verner announced that she is seeking to resolve the civil case for the sake of the city and Ann Zehm. 'I'm waiting,' said Beggs, who sent the city a letter seeking to restart negotiations some two weeks before Verner's announcement. 'We've had no phone calls or letters.' Beggs, however, said he wasn't concerned, and noted that Delaney recently was on vacation. 'They seem to take their time. I don't know what's going on,' Beggs said. 'We don't know what the plan is. I haven't got that press release.'"

Oreskovich and his law partner, Steven Lamberson, filed a motion seeking to exclude the testimony of Assistant Chief Nicks' from the criminal trial on June 4, 2010, the day they questioned him about the full extent of his grand jury testimony. After the August, 2011, release of the summary of Nicks' expected testimony, Oreskovich said, "My recollection was he told us during the course of the interview that he didn't consider himself an expert on use of force. If he doesn't qualify as an expert, then his opinion is irrelevant."

The Spokesman-Review reported, "Van Sickle said he will allow Nicks to testify, but he can't offer testimony on whether Thompson violated department policy. That testimony is 'irrelevant and becomes confusing for the jurors,' Van Sickle said. 'It's not something that needs to be addressed or should be addressed by Nicks or any other witness.'" He also ruled that the jury could not be told of Zehm's schizophrenia, cognitive delay, or any other information not directly related to the incident.

In September, 2011, the "mystery officer" targeted by the grand jury was identified as Sandra McIntyre. Attorney Rob Cossey stated he believed the pressure on Officer McIntyre was intended to compel her testimony in the Thompson trial. He claimed she would "tell the truth, regardless."

Shortly before the trial was to resume, Oreskovich requested it be moved from Spokane. "Due to the recent politicizing and barrage of media coverage, I am compelled to bring a motion to change venue at this time because the coverage has resulted in presumed prejudice making it impossible for Officer Thompson to receive a fair trial in this venue."

In support of the motion Oreskovich released an account of local media coverage. According to him, "A total of over 1,000 newspaper articles and news stories have been published or broadcast about the confrontation between Officer Thompson and Otto Zehm. More than 650 news broadcasts alone covered the events. Many of these news stories contained evidence that had been deemed inadmissible, with the vast majority of them referring to Zehm as 'the mentally disabled janitor.'"

The prosecution based its objection to moving the trial on the fact that, unlike the defense, it had refused to comment on the case to the media. "[The] defendant's multiple counsel (both private and within the City Attorney's Office), his supervisors, co-workers, political supporters, and friends have all actively participated in, have promoted and have solicited media interviews, statements, stories, reports, and even news conferences. The United States further submits that the defense's active participation and conduct stops the defendant and his counsel from now crying wolf about perceived negative media reports at this 11th hour stage in these criminal case proceedings."

Judge Van Sickle ruled on the issue on October 4, 2011. The Spokesman-Review reported, "While Van Sickle said he's not persuaded that the publicity has created 'actual' or 'perceived' bias against Thompson, he decided to move the trial nonetheless. 'There has been a great deal of publicity in the community,' Van Sickle said. 'Yakima is not that far away.'"

Shortly afterward Assistant U.S. Attorney Durkin submitted a motion asking Judge Van Sickle to reconsider that decision. "Presently, the United States anticipates calling approximately 60 witnesses... The Defense has subpoenaed no less than 57 witnesses that they expect to appear in court for examination and testimony... Approximately 90% of these identified witnesses are local residents of Spokane and its nearby areas. All of these witnesses will be significantly and adversely impacted by the Court's election of a venue that is more than 200 miles from these witnesses' residences, families, and places of employment. The U.S. Marshal's Service and the District's apparently limited Criminal Justice Act fund will have to pay for this additional, substantial cost created by the Court's change of venue selection."

Jeffry Finer submitted a statement in support of Durkin's motion on behalf of the Zehm family. "The barriers to the Zehm family are both financial and logistical. Age and illness make the trip infeasible for the immediate family except, at most, for a token opportunity." In a statement to the Spokesman-Review he said the family members "don't have the means to travel to Yakima for a trial they had hoped to attend daily... The phrase I heard is, 'We are shut out.'"

Oreskovich's callous response to the family's predicament was, "The best option for all parties involved is to move the trial from the Spokane area to protect Officer Thompson's constitutional right to a fair trial... While Defendant is mindful that the change of venue may make it more difficult for Otto Zehm's family and friends to attend the trial, nothing is actually prohibiting them from doing so."

Judge Van Sickle resolved the matter by having video cameras placed in the Yakima courtroom to relay the trial proceedings to the courthouse in Spokane where the Zehm family could observe the proceedings daily.

*

The election cycle brought another mayoral contest to Spokane in 2011, and the city's legal tactics in the Zehm case played a prominent role in the campaign. The August primaries showed that Mayor Verner had a nearly 2-to-1 lead over her opponent, David Condon, who outlined his position on the Zehm matter on September 6, 2011:

"The City of Spokane has mishandled the Otto Zehm case from the very beginning. As mayor, Mary Verner has wasted taxpayer money and slowed the course of justice by her defense of the city bureaucracy and the mismanagement of this case. A quarter of a million dollars and thousands of hours have been wasted while the bureaucracy churned away, trying to obscure the process. The indictment of a Spokane police officer by a federal grand jury was an indictment of Spokane's city government itself. Who is to blame? Prosecutors, police officers, and city attorneys all contributed to this terrible situation. Ultimately, Mayor Verner is to blame for failing to put on the brakes. We elect a strong mayor because someone must ultimately take responsibility for the actions of city employees. A federal trial will begin soon to decide if a Spokane police officer is guilty of using unreasonable force on Otto Zehm. A jury will decide. But we already know that Mary Verner and the bureaucrats at city hall are guilty of wasting time and hundreds of thousands of dollars in a vain effort to keep the facts from coming out. The mayor needs to show leadership and stop hiding her head in the sand. She cannot look at everything through a lawyer's narrow legal perspective. According to the news reports, I believe Treppiedi should be dismissed immediately. When I'm mayor, I will insist we have a strong and independent police ombudsman even if it means re-opening contract negotiations with the guild."

With a hefty lead in the polls, Mayor Verner issued a scathing reply that was published by the Spokesman-Review. "'Condon clearly has not checked the facts,' says Mayor Verner, 'He is a newcomer to this issue and to city government. This is a complex case with many parties and to further victimize the Zehm family by attempting to elevate himself was thoughtless,' Mayor Verner says. 'The city is not a party in the federal criminal trial and has been under a court-ordered stay in the civil matter for over two years.

'Why a former aide to Congress would issue a news release disrespecting the jurisdiction of the federal court is puzzling,' says Mayor Verner. 'A federal judge ordered that there be no further action in the Zehm civil case until the criminal case is concluded. A federal judge has also determined that Assistant City Attorney Rocky Treppiedi's actions in the case have been appropriate.'"

During the fall campaign Condon criticized the mayor's handling of the Zehm case frequently and severely. An act that marked the start of what the Spokesman-Review called Verner's "worst few weeks as mayor," she released a statement concerning the use of the Zehm tragedy for political gain. While he had contributed money to the Verner campaign, Breean Beggs stated, "Zehm family members do not feel exploited or victimized by Condon or other city candidates who have discussed the case. Beggs said that's because they feel that police oversight, training, procedures and other issues surrounding the case are legitimate issues that should be considered by those seeking city office."

In a late September press conference, Mayor Verner announced that she and the City Council intended to "complete a thorough internal and external review of all aspects of this matter" as soon as all legal issues were resolved. In fact, the city had an open contract with police consultant Mike Worley to perform that review as soon as the investigation concluded, which antedated her tenure as mayor. Introducing a "fact sheet" at the press conference, she said, "With the criminal case on the eve of trial, it is inappropriate for me or the council members to get into legal details or strategies, so we're not going to take questions. However, we have provided to the press and will provide to any member of the public a sheet of frequently asked questions."

Titled, "Zehm Issue Frequently Asked Questions (FAQs)," the fact sheet delineated the criminal charges against Officer Thompson, the date of the upcoming criminal trial, and the reasons the civil suit has not been resolved. It was stated that a huge volume of information about these cases is available to the public. One question and answer in the FAQ attracted the attention of the Department of Justice.

"Why didn't City elected officials meet with the U.S. Attorney in 2009?"

117

"Assistant U.S. Attorney Tim Durkin did request to meet with the Mayor, Council President, and Police Chief to discuss potential conflict of interest questions. It is highly unusual for an attorney to meet with another attorney's clients. However, City Attorney Howard Delaney and Assistant City Attorney Rocky Treppiedi did meet with the U.S. Attorney's Office as a result of this request. They met with the U.S. Attorney for Eastern Washington at the time, Jim McDevitt, along with Mr. Durkin and other representatives of the U.S. Attorney's Office. The City responded to the concerns in a court filing two years ago. The court found no issues of conflict or impropriety on the part of the City."

Just days after the FAQ was distributed, the Department of Justice filed a response in federal court. Referring to the document as the "Failed FAQs," the Spokesman-Review summarized the filing, "Two items in the FAQ drew the greatest interest from federal prosecutors. In one, the city responds to criticism that it ignored requests by the Justice Department to meet with the mayor, the police chief, and council president to express concerns over potential interference in its criminal investigation of the Zehm fatality. The city claims its legal staff met with federal officials instead, which Durkin contends is false. In fact, Durkin said, city attorneys never even 'communicated response to that meeting request.' In the other, Durkin noted that no court has 'yet considered, reviewed, and/or addressed' the actions of any city attorney related to the Zehm matter.'"

Mayor Verner's "worst few weeks" culminated with an evening newscast that showed her being chased down the street by news crews, sticking her hand at the camera and refusing to answer questions.

The criminal trial of Karl Thompson took place in the weeks immediately preceding the November election. Intense media coverage kept the City's handling of the Zehm matter in the spotlight and Mayor Verner on the defensive. Her lead eroded first in the polls and ultimately, within her own party. David Condon won the election handily.

*

The day after the ballot count was completed, Mayor Verner announced that she would request a "patterns and practices" investigation of the Spokane Police Department, which is a lengthy investigation conducted by the United States Department of Justice. Through that process the Department of Justice is given the power to override any local or union objections in court and force the police department to implement the current best practices in law enforcement. By this time, however, the public had stopped paying attention to Verner's calls for integrity and change and looked instead to Mayor-elect Condon to fulfill his campaign promises.

CHAPTER ELEVEN

Karl Thompson's criminal trial began on October 11, 2011, in the William O. Douglas Federal Building in Yakima, Washington. Before jury selection started that morning, Judge Van Sickle addressed a number of issues with the attorneys. First, clothing that was obviously supportive of Otto Zehm or Karl Thompson, like OTTO buttons and police uniforms, was banned from the courtroom. He reviewed the instructions the jury would receive, including how the jury was to evaluate the evidence and witness testimony and the criteria that had to be met in order to convict Thompson of either charge. A request from the defense to preclude the prosecution from mentioning Officer Moses in its opening statement because the officer planned to plead the Fifth Amendment and refuse to answer questions was denied. Finally, the judge dealt with the matter of the toxicology screening by asking each side to submit brief arguments that addressed allowing into evidence the fact that Otto Zehm had not been under the influence of illegal substances.

A pool of potential jurors had been summoned from across eastern Washington, and selection was completed the first morning. After eight men and four women jurors and three alternates from varied ethnic backgrounds and careers were chosen, the trial began in earnest.

Assistant U. S. Attorney Victor Boutros gave the prosecution's opening statement. Fortyish and a little pudgy with a small bald spot at the back of his head, his eloquence and obvious grasp of a complex set of facts commanded the attention of everyone in the courtroom. "This is a case about a police officer who chose to strike first and ask questions later. It's a case about a fellow citizen who walked into a convenience store to buy soda pop," to which Carl Oreskovich immediately objected. Judge Van Sickle stated, "Objection is sustained. That is not pertinent. It is not admissible, Counsel, and the Court has previously ruled. Counsel both understand and all should understand the Court has made a number of pretrial rulings and those are adhered to. They apply. And they apply to opening statements as well... That portion of the opening statement is stricken, and the jury is instructed to disregard it."

Boutros continued, "The evidence in this case will establish that on the early evening of March 18, 2006, Otto Zehm went to a Zip Trip convenience store. Mr. Zehm frequently goes to the Zip Trip convenience stores to buy soda and snacks."

Oreskovich interrupted, "Your Honor, Your Honor? Just, again, this is not what this case is about. This court has ruled, and I'm objecting to this."

Judge Van Sickle replied, "Objection is sustained, Counsel. I previously ruled this area is not involved in this cause, it's not relevant, and the jury is instructed to disregard it. And please recall that any statements of counsel or arguments of counsel are never evidence. Disregard that as evidence or even considering as evidence."

Boutros resumed his statement, "Just before Mr. Zehm went to the Zip Trip that night, he walked over to a nearby ATM. At the time, two teenagers were using the machine while sitting in their car. After the teenagers pulled away, Mr. Zehm went up to the machine and then continued on to the Zip Trip."

Oreskovich objected again, "This has been ruled upon. This is has been ruled upon in terms of the government's motion...as to what occurred there, Your Honor, and, again, I'm objecting to it."

The judge ruled, "Objection sustained. Please proceed."

Then Boutros turned to the Computer Assisted Dispatch and the circumstances of the 911 call. "Even the defendant admitted that, based on the call, he didn't have probable cause to believe that the man at the ATM had committed any crime. Nevertheless, the defendant chose to rush into the Zip Trip and attack Mr. Zehm rather than wait another 20 seconds for the originally assigned officer to join them so they could talk to Mr. Zehm together. Contrary to his training, the defendant did not calmly approach Mr. Zehm, stop, and tell him that he needed to ask a few questions about what he was doing at the ATM. In fact, the defendant never explained to Mr. Zehm why he was there nor even asked Mr. Zehm a single question. He had decided to strike first and ask questions later."

Boutros told the jury that eyewitnesses will tell them that Zehm looked surprised even as the first blow came down on him and that many of them, including the young woman who made the 911 call, were "horrified to see the defendant immediately and repeatedly striking Mr. Zehm, who had done nothing to provoke the officer. And they were shocked at how suddenly the defendant attacked him." He provided additional details of the encounter between Officer Thompson and Zehm before addressing the second count of the indictment, that Karl Thompson had lied during an investigation within the FBI's jurisdiction. He stated that Thompson told Officer Timothy Moses that he had hit the suspect in the head because the suspect had attacked him first with a pop bottle, information that Moses relayed to the responding paramedics who included it in their pre-hospital care report.

Boutros indicated that while Thompson was talking to Moses, Officer Sandra McIntyre was in the store reviewing the video surveillance tapes. "Officer McIntyre was not only one of the defendant's fellow officers but one of his closest friends. She will tell you that she and the defendant had an almost father-daughter relationship. Zip Trip employee Angela Wiggins was operating the playback of the store security video for her. Miss Wiggins will tell you that as Officer McIntyre saw the video of the defendant's first baton strikes, her demeanor suddenly changed. Officer McIntyre appeared shocked and exclaimed, 'He didn't lunge with the pop bottle!'

"The evidence will show that after Officer McIntyre viewed the security video and spoke to the defendant, the defendant decided to shift gears... Unlike other officers on the scene, the defendant did not write a report shortly after the incident about what had occurred on scene. Instead, the defendant had four days to think of something to say before he provided a tape-recorded interview to another member of his very own police force, Detective Terry Ferguson... By that time the defendant knew that Mr. Zehm was dead and couldn't contradict him. So in that statement he made up what the evidence will show are lies about Mr. Zehm. The story he told was audio recorded and transcribed, and the defendant reviewed and signed the transcription a few days later."

Constrained by the time allotted for opening statements, Boutros enumerated only six of the 12 lies the prosecution claimed Thompson told, a list they would refer to repeatedly as 'the dirty dozen.' He stated in closing, "The evidence will show that Mr. Zehm never understood why the defendant attacked him. We, you, may never know why, either. But your job is to find out what the defendant did, not why he did it. And the evidence in this case will bring what the defendant did that night out of the darkness and into the light."

Fiftyish, dark-haired, exceptionally tall, soft-spoken and not particularly eloquent, Carl Oreskovich began the defense's opening statement, "It is not a case of 20/20 hindsight, but it is a case that I will explain to you momentarily about an officer who relied upon information that was given to him through radio dispatcher, information that was given to him by a computer assisted dispatch, or a mobile computer screen, that took himself off...a lunch break because the suspect was fleeing from an ATM machine near an area that the officer was...because he knew he was the closest one to the area, put himself on service, responded to the location, and was the first person to come in contact with a fleeing criminal suspect.

"This is a case about a good police officer who tried to recall things out of his memory that he had perceived during a very violent encounter, trying to do his best to answer some questions without viewing a videotape, without refreshing his recollection, and now being criticized because while he was under very difficult, intense circumstances, didn't perceive everything right, as shown in a videotape that, frankly, he knew was in a convenience store before he even entered it... The evidence will teach us, and you'll have the opportunity through the witnesses you will hear, about the training and experience of a police officer in terms of how they assess risk, how they arrive to a particular scene, what they are taught to look for. And the evidence will show you that these things that you and I may realize or think aren't weapons, don't have the potential to be weapons, that in a certain context can, in fact, be a weapon.

"So, one of the things that you're going to learn is that police officers on a daily basis deal with risk. And police officers on a daily basis deal with threat assessment. And trained police officers, who are experienced police officers, have the ability to see things that perhaps you and I would not see because it is not our training and experience. The evidence will show, ladies and gentlemen, that we as citizens ask our police officers to go out and protect us. And when we ask them to do that, we give them certain tools: we give them a Taser, we give them a hand gun, we give them what's called pepper spray-OC spray, and we give them a baton. And the Court will tell you under the circumstances when that force can be used. And you will learn in this particular case that Mr. Thompson's use of force was appropriate...

"One of the Court's earlier instructions to you are the things that you look at...the bad purpose. Let me talk to you a bit about Karl Thompson. Let me talk to you about the man that you are going to judge. The evidence will show, ladies and gentlemen, that Karl Thompson is a very respected, veteran police officer. As he sits here today, he's 64 years old. At the time of this event, he was 58 years old. He was...a patrol officer, and he had a long and distinguished police career... Never graduated from high school, got a G.E.D. After he got out of the military, was a veteran. And then in 1969, he became employed with the Los Angeles Sheriff's Department, the LAPD, and spent 10 years as a police officer in Los Angeles where he was a patrol officer, where he became a hostage negotiator, where he became a member of the SWAT team. The evidence will show that his training and experience is of...a man that has been shot at, who's had partners stabbed, who understands the realities through what he has lived of what occurs to a police officer on a day-to-day basis unexpectedly. The evidence will show you that after 10 years with the LAPD that Mr. Thompson moved up to Kootenai County, up to the Coeur d'Alene, Idaho area, where he set up his own business...working as a private investigator doing arson investigations, but that he missed police work. That was his calling.

"And after a period of time he began to work with the Idaho State Patrol as a detective, and then with the Kootenai County Sheriff's Office – that's Coeur d'Alene, Kootenai County – where he was a captain, and as a captain, had the responsibility for all kinds of persons in patrol; that Mr. Thompson was one of the officers who was instrumental in setting up the SWAT Team in Kootenai County; that Mr. Thompson was one of the officers who was instrumental in managing the marine division, the rescue division. The evidence will show that this is a very articulate, well-thinking, well-taught, police officer.

"In the mid-'90s, in about 1996, Mr. Thompson ran for Kootenai County sheriff and lost. And after his loss, he had to leave the department. And in 1997, he came to the Spokane Police Department where he had to go through the training academy, and...he was the number one in his class and, in fact, he gave the commencement address to all the other police officers.

"The evidence will show, Your Honor, ladies and gentlemen of the jury, that the cruel irony of this case is that the very same quick decision-making that this officer is accused of committing a crime, is exactly the same quick decision-making that he employed in 2002 when he pulled, from the Monroe Street Bridge in Spokane, Washington, a suicide jumper back from his death and was awarded the life-saving award...the very same quick, experienced police thinking. In late 2005 in Spokane, we had a vacancy in the police chief's position. And the evidence will show that there were various people who made applications for it. One is a Mr. Nicks that you will hear about. The evidence will further show that the patrol officers, the rank and file of the Spokane Police Department, many of them drafted a petition for...Karl Thompson to be appointed as the Spokane Police Department Chief. And the evidence will show that this is a highly respected, honored police officer who was doing his duty on March 18th, 2006."

Then Oreskovich returned to Thompson's involvement with the call. He told the jury that Officer Thompson had been on his break, eating hamburgers and writing reports, when he heard a call over his shoulder radio. He heard that he was close to the area and, "being a good, responsible police officer, then went out into his car to look at the CAD. Thompson checked back in to work and headed to the area. While en route, he heard Zehm's description and heard the dispatcher confirm that the suspect had taken the money. When he drove up to the Zip Trip in his marked police car, Zehm watched him before going into a store... Under those circumstances he made a decision. He made a decision as a police officer, he will tell you, because he observed that there were citizens, including two young girls, inside the store at the counter. And so Officer Thompson quickly, and you'll see it on the video, pulled his car up, jumped out of his car, and quickly ran inside, quickly moved inside of the Zip Trip store to stop the suspect.

"The evidence will show you that, under these circumstances...a police officer has a right to use a certain amount of force...and that then as he entered the Zip Trip that he lost sight of Mr. Zehm... He knew, as he entered the Zip Trip, a couple of different things:

- One, he didn't know if Mr. Zehm was armed. After all, Mr. Zehm had a big, heavy jacket on...

- Two, the officer will tell you within a Zip Trip store, that there are all kinds of objects that can be used as weapons. Either weapons to poke or hit or, ladies and gentlemen, that can be used to distract.

"The evidence will show you that there is a certain amount of time that an officer has, that there is a reaction gap, and that there is an advantage, and the trainers will tell you about the advantage that each of us has, not to react to somebody, but to act before.

"And the evidence will show you that as Officer Thompson came around the corner and spotted Mr. Zehm and began issuing commands to him that Mr. Zehm turned with a pop bottle. Now, it's a pop bottle. But it is a two-liter pop bottle that the evidence will show, by all trainers, could be used as a weapon to blunt and to reach for a weapon. And Mr. Thompson made very quick decisions, very quick commands. And when Mr. Zehm didn't drop the pop bottle, Officer Thompson struck him with a baton and...a struggle ensued, a very violent struggle. And you're going to see portions of it. You're going to see portions of it on a video camera from the Zip Trip. There are four different camera angles.

"Unfortunately, the video doesn't give us all that we need to have because it doesn't capture all of the conduct that occurred between the two. You will see...that the video is blocked in places by shelving. You will learn from the persons who operate the video that the video camera only records at three or four frames a second, so...there is conduct that can occur that doesn't get captured. You'll learn from the experts that movie frames that we're used to operate at 30 frames a second.

"And so you will see bits and pieces of a video. And I'm here to tell you you're going to see violence in it. You're going to see baton strikes in it. And you're going to see an officer using his Taser to someone who kept struggling, that wouldn't comply with his orders.

"Unfortunately, the video doesn't have an audio. It doesn't tell us what was occurring at the time, but you'll hear witnesses' testimony as to what they observed. And the video will not show us what occurred from the officer's vision, what the officer saw. He will have to tell you that, and he will.

126

"But what you will learn after looking at this video is that there was a struggle; that there was indeed kicking, that there was indeed some fist swinging, some punching. Now, Officer Thompson got it wrong when he later told them, some four days later, when it occurred. But you're going to see that it, in fact, did occur...

"Now, Officer Thompson will admit to you, and admitted in his statement, that this was not a situation where he was authorized to strike the head, and that he didn't strike the head in any way intentionally. But the evidence will show, ladies and gentlemen, the uncontroverted evidence...that there were not strikes to the head. Because we know, despite what witnesses may or may not have seen, unfortunately, that Mr. Zehm was hospitalized, he was treated at a hospital, and that he was assessed by various doctors...

"Mr. Zehm was examined very closely by a trauma team at the hospital. And the evidence will show there was no evidence of any type of injury to his brain or to his head. No baton strikes. No lacerations. No bleeding. And that the areas where there were baton, or where there were contusions and hematomas, were consistent with what Officer Thompson described with strikes that were by Officer Braun. You will hear medical evidence that Mr. Zehm had some little markings, scabbing on his face, but they were not caused by baton strikes. More likely they were caused by a struggle that occurred in a convenience store in forty and a half inch aisles, aisles that are very narrow, and coming into contact with items that were within the shelving of the store. And you'll have the opportunity to see all of this in terms of the pictures.

"We know that when the second officer arrived, Officer Braun...that Mr. Zehm was struggling with Officer Thompson, that when Officer Braun arrived and he saw the struggle, that he began to use his baton and using what is called a power jab, jabbed Mr. Zehm. And that didn't work-he couldn't stop the struggle, and that he used his Taser to taser Mr. Zehm who is fighting back.

"But, ladies and gentlemen, the point about all this is that this was a very violent struggle that went on. And Officer Braun will tell you about punches by Mr. Zehm and kicks by Mr. Zehm. Now, afterward, after other officers arrived and ultimately, Mr. Zehm was brought under control, Officer Thompson immediately left the area, immediately

127

left the store and went outside. He's 58 years old and exhausted. But he came in periodically. And one of the things that you'll see is that he was so shook up by what happened that he was asking officers, 'Where's my baton at? I don't know where it's at...' when someone pointed to him and said, 'Well, it's hanging on your holster here.' And that, ultimately...it was Officer Thompson who told persons, 'Well, secure the video. Get the pop bottle. Get the Taser.' It was Officer Thompson who was telling others to secure the evidence...

"The evidence will show that Officer Thompson gave a voluntary statement, and that when he gave a voluntary statement, he was offered the opportunity to view the videotape before he gave the statement. And he said, 'I don't want to. I want to tell you what I remember happened that night. I want to tell you as to what I perceived... Now, unfortunately, ladies and gentlemen, he got some of this out-of-order. Unfortunately, in his mind when he said he came to a stop, the video evidence will show he didn't come to a stop. But it will show punching and kicking. Maybe not in the same order that Officer Thompson described it to you, but it will be there. And, now, Officer Thompson, the government says, lied. You will see evidence, ladies and gentlemen, that when the government wanted to use videotape...wanted to use it with some lay witnesses to interview witnesses and didn't quite like what they said, they used videotape to refresh their memories. Officer Thompson didn't want to have that type of circumstance. He just wanted to tell it the way he remembered it. And, unfortunately, now he gets called a liar...

"Ladies and gentlemen, in the end the evidence will show that this police officer was acting not with bad purpose, but with the purpose that he was charged with, to investigate and protect citizens. And the evidence will show...that this man, this honorable man, veteran police officer, is innocent of these crimes."

As soon as the lawyers got to speak to the judge outside the presence of the jury that day, Oreskovich brought a motion to dismiss the case because of "willful prosecutorial misconduct in the opening statements." He argued, "We are here trying to get a good, fair trial. We'll accept what the result is. But it is the government's duty, not only our duty, not only the Court's duty, to make sure that Mr. Thompson gets a fair trial and to live up to ethical standards and to make sure due process is delivered to my client. They're not here to do that... This is blatant, willful misconduct on three occasions in an opening statement...not once, not misunderstanding, but with warning by the Court."

Assistant U.S. Attorney Aine Ahmed responded, "Everything he said about the ATM is...right on the CAD report... Now, at some point, Your Honor, with all due respect, we have to have a way to question Mr. Thompson's statement. We have to have a way to do that. And his statement that he was intending to use it as a bottle (sic), that's come into evidence. You can use it as a weapon. We have to be able to rebut that. We have to prove that that is nonsense. And I think the video depicts that, but I think it's more important that witnesses come in here and say, 'He bought pop all the time.' I have to show what Mr. Zehm was thinking, too. And I can't show that if he's dead..."

Judge Van Sickle ruled that the mention of Zehm shopping at the Zip Trip rather than evading arrest was not "willful prosecutorial misconduct." He stated that those references in Boutros's opening statement were not grounds for a mistrial, much less for dismissal of the case. He reminded Oreskovich that the jury had been instructed to listen to the evidence rather than the lawyers' opinions and concluded that his instructions that those references be stricken from the record and ignored by the jurors should be a sufficient remedy.

The following day the judge ruled that the prosecution could present evidence that Zehm was not under the influence of illegal drugs at the time of the incident only if the defense referred to Zehm possibly being intoxicated.

CHAPTER TWELVE

The prosecution began its case with the brief testimony of several individuals. An FBI agent showed photographs he had taken of a police baton next to a set of calipers. Officer Randy Lesser, the Taser trainer for the Spokane Police Department, described the weapon and explained its use. A Zip Trip employee recounted making the copy of the security video used by the Spokane Police Department, and an FBI analyst testified about "cleaning up and processing" the video.

Then FBI Special Agent Lisa Jangaard testified. "In this investigation my responsibilities included collecting and analyzing all of the evidence from the Spokane Police Department...all of the investigative materials and all of the physical evidence. I conducted multiple eyewitness and fact witness interviews. I spent multiple hours analyzing video, and I collected medical records and other records which were reviewed and analyzed." She identified Officer Thompson's baton and pointed out key details from the security video, including the location of various witnesses to the encounter and Officers Thompson and Moses talking privately afterward. Her testimony concluded with the introduction of the audio recording of Thompson's interview by Detective Ferguson, which was played in its entirety for the jury.

Through questions to these witnesses Oreskovich introduced the concept of "compression artifacts," glitches in the video induced by the digital recording process. Both the video analyst and Agent Jaangard attested that in the images of Officer Thompson's first baton strike, a compression artifact was present that made it impossible to verify that Thompson's hand was holding the baton.

The first expert witness called by the prosecution was Robert Bragg, the Washington State Justice Training Commission Academy Program manager of fitness-in-force training. He stated, "I'm in charge of developing and delivering...both the basic law enforcement curriculum...as well as...training for in-service officers who come to the academy, become instructors, and then go back to their agencies and train there." He was responsible for programs including arrest, control, and defensive tactics, neck restraints, and the use of OC pepper spray and impact weapons like batons. At the time he testified, he was the chairman of a professional law enforcement trainers association. He had created training batons and developed the current training regimen. In fact, it was he who had designed the baton Officer Thompson carried.

Bragg stated that Officer Thompson had been trained to hold the baton at the bottom of the handle and strike limbs and nonlethal targets with a horizontal swinging motion to maximize the force, lessening the possibility of striking a lethal area and the number of strikes needed. When asked about threat assessment, Bragg indicated that law enforcement officers are trained to verbalize if at all possible before escalating to the use of force and to continue to verbalize during encounters. "They're told that if you perceive someone looking or some type of setting up, these threatening gestures...you even ask them, 'You thinking about hitting me? You look like you're getting ready to hit me.' So you can interrupt that cycle. They might think they're being sneaky. You just told them, 'I know what you're thinking about-don't do it.'"

Then Bragg addressed law enforcement training to call for backup. "It's one of the...key factors where officers have been killed-one of the things we call 'tombstone courage,' that...it's 'not a big deal, I can take care of it all myself; forget about backup.' We strongly encourage the use of backup. Wait!"

When the prosecution asked for his opinion of Officer Thompson's use of force during the Zehm encounter relative to his training, Bragg responded that Thompson would have failed had the incident been a training scenario because he justified the strikes with a "boxing stance" that did not exist, used vertical strikes, choked up on the handle of his baton, created his own emergency to justify the use of force, applied lethal force, closed distance when concerned about a close-range weapon, and "spanked" Zehm with his baton in the center aisle. He added, "If the context didn't require the officer to use physical force, then any physical force used is...outside of what we teach and legitimate law enforcement ends or means."

131

On cross-examination by Oreskovich, Bragg acknowledged that enough erroneous information had been transmitted by radio dispatch and CAD to justify the conclusion that a robbery may have occurred. Bragg was asked if he could see situations the way the police officers do. He responded, "Well, I don't need to be a law enforcement officer. I train law enforcement officers to see those kinds of things, so, no, I haven't done it as a law enforcement officer, but as a trainer of them, yes."

Oreskovich asked, "There are courses at the academy that officers are required to take that provide them guidance as to the legal and constitutional principles that help determine the proper use of force?"

Bragg's response was, "Correct. As I said, that's the one that I teach, I developed. I wrote the course."

The next witness, Richard Gill, was an expert in both photogrammetrics and human factors. Photogrammetrics uses the known dimensions of objects to provide otherwise unavailable data from images. Human factors combines the disciplines of mechanical engineering and psychology to study human behavior. During his career Gill had done research and gathered intelligence for the military, consulted in accident reconstruction, and taught and conducted research in the field of human factors. From that unique perspective he offered a number of observations and conclusions pertaining to the behavior of Otto Zehm and Officer Thompson just before and during the encounter:

- Thompson watched as Zehm left an unconstrained and dark area to enter a well-lit, enclosed space.

- Zehm walked past an easy exit from the store.

- Zehm's mannerisms did not change at any time while he was recorded prior to the encounter.

- While the average adult walking speed is 3.5 miles per hour, Zehm's walking speed was 2.4 miles per hour.

- Thompson braked his patrol car abruptly, causing the nose of the car to bounce.

- Thompson's walking speed from his car to the door was 7.5 miles per hour and inside the store, 6.7 miles per hour.

- Zehm's only opportunity to see Thompson approaching was for approximately 2.5 seconds while outside the store as Thompson drove into the parking area. Zehm did not look in Thompson's direction between then and when he turned and backed away from the officer.

- Thompson made the decision to pull out his baton before he entered the store.

- When confronted, Zehm did not lunge, stop, or adopt a set, firm, resolute stance.

- Thompson continued moving forward from the moment of confrontation until he made the first baton strike.

- Thompson offered no verbal exchange as asking a single question and getting a response is not possible in the less than three seconds between the confrontation and Thompson's first strike.

- Video surveillance recorded 13 baton strikes by Thompson.

- The surveillance footage of the first strike shows that what appears to be Thompson's baton is not an artifact.

No matter brought up on cross-examination seriously challenged Gill's conclusions.

The medical evidence was presented next. First to testify was Dr. Sally Aiken, the Medical Examiner of Spokane County. The autopsy of Otto Zehm was one of 7,000 she had performed during her career. She presented photograph after photograph graphically documenting the findings described in her report. Oreskovich objected repeatedly to the number of photographs, and Judge Van Sickle instructed the prosecution twice that the presentation had become repetitive. But several important points were established:

- Zehm had multiple tram track pattern injuries, which are parallel bruises with a gap of approximately 3/8 of an inch in between that result from blows by a baton. She identified one such injury on his right eyebrow.

- Few of the tram track pattern bruises had been recorded by the Emergency Department physicians who treated him.

- There were two large bruises in the deepest layer of the scalp, one above Zehm's left ear and the other, right at the top of his head. Although she did not classify them as baton injuries, she indicated they could not be attributed to Zehm's hair being pulled or a fall. She explained, "If you imagine wearing a hat around your head, where the brim fits, when you fall you tend to strike the hat brim... Part of the injury on the left side of the scalp could be in the vicinity of the hat brim line... The one on top of the head is not...and would not be typical of a fall."

Then a highly qualified physician with diverse professional experience testified. Dr. Harry Smith held a Doctor of Medicine degree as well as a Ph.D. in nuclear engineering. He had practiced emergency medicine for nine years and was board-certified in flight surgery, nuclear medicine, and radiology. He had consulted concerning injury causation throughout his career, including in the Rodney King case.

Dr. Smith was shown autopsy photographs of the bruises found in the deepest layer of Zehm's scalp. He described the findings to the jury and then correlated them with abnormalities he demonstrated on the two CT scans of Zehm's head, one taken on the night of March 18th and the second, the following day. He also discussed an abnormality in the soft tissue of the right side of Zehm's neck depicted by the CT scan of that area, which had been examined only externally at autopsy.

The galea aponeurotica is a helmet-shaped band of fibrous tissue lying deep to the skin and superficial tissues of the scalp. It is separated from the skull by a thin layer of soft tissue and blood vessels. Blunt force against the head can cause bleeding from the blood vessels between this fibrous tissue and the skull, producing a thin collection of blood called a "subgaleal hematoma."

In the autopsy photographs Dr. Smith identified four different subgaleal hematomas, one on each side in the parietal areas, which form the back half of the top of the head, one in the vicinity of the right temple, and one deep to the right eyebrow. Whereas Dr. Aiken had not attributed the parietal hematomas to baton strikes definitively, Dr. Smith did. He stated they were not consistent with a fall and that no force other than baton strikes was observed or described that could have produced them.

On cross-examination by Stephen Lamberson, Dr. Smith stated that a subgaleal hematoma results from blunt force that does not necessarily produce laceration or bruising of the overlying skin and scalp, so the lack of outward physical signs of injury to those areas reported by the treating physicians did not invalidate his conclusions. He also testified that the pattern of bruising at the right eyebrow was consistent with "mechanically produced blows." He refused to agree that the hematoma near the right temple was possibly due to a fall impacting the "hat brim" area,

134

describing that term as vague as to the exact area of the head it designates.

Dr. Aiken had photographed a bruise on the right side of Zehm's neck that she attributed to the insertion of an intravenous catheter into the right jugular vein. However, Dr. Smith pointed out soft tissue swelling on the CT scan of Zehm's neck that was located within the right sternocleidomastoid muscle, a large muscle on the right side of the neck that rotates the head to the left. As the CT images demonstrated separation of the area of swelling from the catheter insertion site, he concluded a hematoma was present in the muscle that most likely resulted from a baton strike, also.

Then ten witnesses to the encounter were called to testify. There was some variation in the description of events corresponding to the location of the witness and the time at which each began paying attention to the altercation. For example, the reports of the number of baton strikes varied from two to ten. However, there was consensus among these observers concerning several important details:

- Zehm had walked in slowly and calmly.

- Officer Thompson had rushed in to confront Zehm.

- Zehm had not spoken or acted aggressively before being struck by the officer.

- All the baton strikes had been vertical; none were horizontal.

- While reports of the location of the first strike were inconsistent, most said it impacted either Zehm's head or shoulder.

Greg Lakarish had watched the encounter closely from start to finish. He reported seeing five blows in quick succession, two to the side of Zehm's head, one on the crown, one on a collarbone as Zehm backed up and fell backwards, and one on the knee while he was lying on the ground. He had heard a command from Thompson nearly simultaneous to the first baton strike.

Other witness gave different reports about the time they heard a command from Thompson. Leroy Colvin said he heard commands but did not know if they were given before the first baton strike. Michael Dahl didn't see the first 10 seconds or so of the altercation but reported hearing a command before he witnessed a strike. The Balows, who had seen the beginning of the encounter in their rear view mirrors, reported the officer paused momentarily and said something before striking. Three witnesses gave clearly erroneous reports, two stating that Zehm's back was still turned when Thompson first struck him and one, that the altercation began in the center aisle.

Several of the witnesses testified that the statements they gave to police officers had been altered in the reports of their interviews. Kristina Turner was adamant that she never told the officers she heard Thompson say, "Drop the pop!" Dustin Balam said he never told the officers he wasn't paying attention to the altercation, and Britni Brashiers indicated that she had not said that Zehm was aggressive.

During the cross-examination of these witnesses, Oreskovich asked each if he or she had special police training in small signs of aggression. At one point he asked if it would be a surprise that Zehm was wanted for a robbery. The judged ordered the question stricken from the record but later ruled it permissible to ask police officers how they would interpret the available information and approach a robbery suspect.

The defense's questioning of these witnesses lead to heated arguments concerning Oreskovich's "theory of the defense," which he summarized as, "Officer Thompson...a 30-year police officer, doesn't respond to this incident in a vacuum. He has information that indicates that this is a possible robbery. There's not necessarily a weapon displayed in the CAD report or in the dispatch information, but it's strong arm robbery, it's theft by fear and intimidation." Continuing this argument later, he said, "One of the...issues under the Graham analysis in terms of whether or not an officer's force is reasonable is the severity of the crime. And what the government wants to do is to strike any reference whatsoever to anyone responding to the potential of a robbery attempt when Officer Thompson said... 'I thought I was investigating a theft or a premature robbery.'"

The prosecution argued vehemently against this line of questioning of these witnesses and the limitations imposed by Judge Van Sickle on their ability to provide evidence of Zehm's innocence... "Lay witnesses are being asked about possible robberies. They don't have any reason to know this stuff... But (the defense is) trying to get this in, because they kept doing this with every witness, to taint Mr. Zehm, who didn't do anything wrong. They are just tainting him, that's all they're doing...and it's simply not true."

The contentiousness resurfaced later when the prosecution argued to the judge, "No one can speak for Mr. Zehm right now... I'm not talking about what happened at Washington Trust (Bank). We all know that Mr. Zehm was found with a paycheck in his pocket and a deposit slip in his hand when he died. That's a fact, and I can't prove...anything about his innocence. So what can I show? What was his intent? What was in his mind? What was in his mind when Officer Thompson struck him with the baton?

"Officer Thompson states that (Zehm) planned to use (the bottle) as a weapon. I have to be able to counter that... I would be confident that this Court, if Mr. Zehm was alive, would allow him to...come and testify, even if innocence wasn't an issue. 'I didn't use that as a weapon. I bought pop all the time there.' And if it was impeached, we would certainly be allowed to bring a witness in to state, 'Yes, he bought pop all the time there, specifically 2-liter bottles.' So I think that this Court should allow that testimony in... The jury can determine how much weight to give it."

Judge Van Sickle ruled that both sides could present evidence that attempted to show Zehm's state of mind but did not touch on guilt or innocence. In this regard the prosecution was allowed to question Officer Erin Raleigh, one of the responding back-up officers, and Zeth Mayfield, a Zip Trip employee who was not at work when the incident occurred.

Officer Raleigh said he did not see an officer strike Zehm on the head during the dog pile and verified that Zehm's last words were, "All I wanted was a Snickers." Oreskovich had the officer describe how long and hard Zehm resisted the effort to subdue him.

Zeth Mayfield had been working for only two months at the Zip Trip where the altercation occurred and had never seen Zehm in that store. But he had worked for five years at two nearby Zip Trip stores that Zehm had visited "every or every other day" since 2002. He said that Zehm arrived either on foot or by bus and bought "soda, snacks, anything...he needed for groceries-milk, eggs..." When asked specifically, Mayfield indicated that Zehm bought "2-liter bottles of soda, mainly Pepsi products...every other day."

CHAPTER THIRTEEN

The remaining prosecution witnesses gave evidence pertaining to the false statement allegation that formed the basis of Count Two of the indictment. Officer Ty Johnson stated that during his conversation with Karl Thompson on the night of the incident, Thompson said that Zehm had attacked him with the pop bottle. Precluded from addressing Thompson's violation of the Spokane Police Department's use of force policy, former Acting Chief Nicks testified only that Officer Thompson had approached him shortly before the June, 2010, trial date and said, "I would just like to remind you that sometime after the event happened, I tried to correct you or I corrected you on the lunge issue." Nicks said he did not recall anyone, including Thompson, ever correcting that statement.

Paramedic Michael Stussi and EMT Aaron Jamarillo had been part of the AMR team that responded to the call from the Zip Trip. They were shown surveillance footage of the conversation they had with Officer Moses that captured the officer demonstrating and one of them mimicking a vertical baton swing. Both testified that Officer Moses told them that Thompson had hit Zehm in the head, neck, and upper torso with his baton, which they entered into their reports. They indicated they relayed that information to an Emergency Department physician at Deaconess Medical Center in the presence of a group of police officers; none suggested then that the statement was incorrect.

*

Officer Timothy Moses had appeared before the grand jury in January and June, 2009. During the June appearance he stated that he and Officer Thompson were friends as well as fellow officers. He testified then that when Officer Thompson "vented" to him outside the Zip Trip immediately after the incident, he said the suspect had lunged at him and that he had hit him about the head, neck, and torso with his baton. Moses acknowledged that he relayed the location of

138

the strikes to AMR personnel at the scene and that surveillance footage of his conversation with two of them captured him gesturing baton strikes with his right hand. However, in April, 2010, he went to the U.S. Attorney's Office and claimed that his testimony to the grand jury 10 months earlier had not been accurate. He said then that his grand jury testimony had resulted from six or more hours of discussions with U.S. Attorneys and FBI agents during which he was told repeatedly that he would be charged with obstruction of justice if he answered questions by saying, "I don't recall," "I don't remember," or "I'm not sure." As a result, Judge Van Sickle allowed the prosecution to examine Officer Moses as an adverse witness, permitting Boutros to challenge his testimony and ask him leading questions.

Victor Boutros asked Officer Moses, "Now, you had a conversation with two AMR personnel on the night of the incident, correct?"

Moses answered, "Yes, I remember them coming into the store as I was standing there by the magazine rack."

"And the AMR personnel wanted to know how Mr. Zehm had been injured, correct?"

"Frankly, I don't remember exactly what he asked me. I have no idea. It's five and a half years ago. I wish I could tell you."

"Now you testified before the grand jury in this matter, is that correct?"

"Twice, that's correct."

"And the second time that you testified was on June 16th, 2009, correct?"

"Yes."

"And when you went before the grand jury, you took an oath, is that right?"

"I did."

"And you testified based on your memory, correct?"

"Yes."

Referring to a transcript of Moses' June, 2009, grand jury testimony, Boutros continued, "Were you asked the following questions and did you give the following answers, 'Question: And you had a conversation with these two AMR personnel on the night of the incident, is that right? Answer: That's correct. Question: And AMR wanted to know how Mr. Zehm had been injured, correct? Answer: That's true, yes.' Did I read that right?"

Moses replied, "Um-hum."

Boutros asked, "And you wanted to provide accurate information to AMR so they could effectively treat Mr. Zehm's injuries, correct?"

"I don't think I had that information at the time they came in the store."

"Well, sir, my question to you is, did you want to provide accurate information to AMR so that they could effectively treat Mr. Zehm's injuries?"

Moses answered, "If they had asked me that question, I certainly would have."

Boutros asked a short while later, "And you had no incentive to tell AMR anything but the truth that night, correct?"

"I had no incentive to talk to AMR at all, actually."

"My question is, you had no incentive to tell AMR anything but the truth, correct."

Moses answered, "That's correct. I don't lie, no."

Boutros continued, "And your intention was to tell them exactly what you knew about how Zehm had been injured, correct?"

"That's what I'm trying to explain to you. I don't recall having that information at the time AMR came in the store."

"And the information you provided AMR you received from the defendant, correct?"

"No, I don't recall that."

Boutros referred again to the June, 2009, grand jury transcript and asked, "Were you asked the following question and did you give the following answer, 'Question: And the information that you provided to AMR personnel you received from Officer Thompson, correct? Answer: Yes.'"

Moses acknowledged, "You did ask that and I answered affirmatively."

"Thank you. And you told AMR personnel that Zehm had been struck in the head, neck, and upper torso with a baton, correct?"

"I don't recall saying those to any AMR employee."

"And in the grand jury you were asked the following question and gave the following answer, 'Question: You told AMR personnel that Zehm had been struck in the head, neck, and upper torso with a baton, correct? Answer: Yes.' Did I read that right?"

Moses answered, "Yes. You did ask that question and I did answer affirmatively."

Proceeding in this manner, Boutros elicited further conflicts between Moses' June, 2009, grand jury appearance and his current testimony. Moses denied that he gave AMR personnel information about Zehm's injuries and that Officer Thompson had given him information before Zehm was transported to the hospital. He denied that the movements of his right hand up and down during a conversation with AMR personnel were gestures of baton strikes, stating, "I don't know what I was doing it for. I was probably just talking." He also denied that Thompson told him that Zehm had "lunged" at him, claiming instead, "I'm the one that coined that word."

Boutros established that Officer Moses had a meeting with Carl Oreskovish during which he reviewed a transcript of his June, 2009, grand jury testimony and that he was questioned about it and shown a portion of the Zip Trip video depicting him having a conversation with Officer Thompson inside the store after Zehm had been placed in the ambulance. Moses acknowledged it was soon after that meeting that he went to the U.S. Attorney's Office and recanted his June, 2009, testimony. He stated then that he had no recollection of having a conversation with AMR personnel on the night of the incident or of Officer Thompson telling him he had struck Zehm in the head. Furthermore, he believed the word, "lunge," had been his way of describing the beginning of the encounter and not Thompson's.

Boutros questioned, "Your explanation for why you no longer recalled so much of what you testified to during your June, 2009, grand jury was that several days after giving your sworn testimony...you became concerned that your recollection relating to all the above events was different from your prior testimony. Is that correct?"

"I don't know if I used the word, 'different,' but I was not having any clear memory, any sustainable clear recollection of the things I testified to in June. That was after seven hours with you guys."

"And what you told the U.S. Attorney's Office was that several days after that June testimony, you realized that your recollection was different than what you had testified to in the grand jury, is that correct?"

"That's correct. And to this day I don't have those recollections."

"And during that grand jury were you asked the following question and did you give the following answer, 'Question: If you realize that you had provided misleading, false, or incomplete information to this grand jury, do you agree to immediately contact FBI Special Agent Lisa Jangaard and inform her of that? Answer: I will.' Did I read that right?"

"Yeah, you read it right."

"But the first time that you provided any information apart from the word, "lunge," being your summary of what the defendant said, was over ten months after your June, 2009, grand jury and just weeks after you met with Mr. Oreskovich, is that accurate?"

Officer Moses answered, "Yes, I guess so."

On cross-examination Oreskovich established that after Officer Moses recanted his June, 2009, testimony, he received a third grand jury subpoena pertaining to obstruction of justice and that he was testifying at present under a grant of immunity. Then he reviewed with Officer Moses some of the police procedures employed and that he had been in charge of the crime scene before turning to the matter of his grand jury testimony. Regarding his January, 2009, testimony, Oreskovich asked, "Is it fair to say that you had a conversation with Karl Thompson at the Zip Trip store concerning what occurred?"

"Yes, I did."

"You understood...that Mr. Thompson had described an event where Mr. Zehm had a 2-liter bottle, isn't that right?"

"Yes. "

"And you can't tell us whether or not Mr. Thompson told you that Mr. Zehm came at him with the bottle or that Mr. Thompson thought Mr. Zehm was going to come at him with the bottle...can you?"

"No."

"You made a conclusion based upon what you heard that in some capacity Otto Zehm lunged at Officer Thompson, right?"

"I used the word, 'lunge'."

"That was your word that you chose to characterize what Karl Thompson said?"

"That's right."

"Knowing then and knowing now...you can't tell us specifically what he said."

142

"No, not word for word, no. Not verbatim, absolutely not."

"And you testified to that previously, sir, in January of 2009, didn't you?"

"I did."

Then Oreskovich turned to Moses' June, 2009, grand jury testimony. He established that when Officer Moses arrived at the U.S. Attorney's Office on the morning he was to testify, he was taken into a room where he was joined at various times by several different FBI agents and Mr. Boutros. "It included (Agent) Meador...someone that you thought was your friend... At the beginning you were there solely with Mr. Meador?"

"Yup, that's right."

"Mr. Meador was telling you that there was new information...that officers were going to get into trouble, correct?"

"Yes."

"And your friend told you that you needed to tell information to (Agent) Harrill... Then Mr. Harrill joined you in a room, didn't he?"

"That's right."

"And...you were shown bits and pieces of the videotape, right?"

"I was, yes, sir."

"And did you have any recollection prior to that time of having any discussion with the American Medical Response team?"

"I had no recollection at all."

"And what the government did in this particular case, they showed you a video, right, bits and pieces?"

"Bits and pieces."

"They also showed you animation, correct?"

"Yes, they did."

"And the animation that they showed you was a kind of a graphic re-creation by the Government as to what they say happened in this case, right?"

"Basically it was a cartoon, yes."

"Demonstrating what the Government thought occurred, right?"

"You're right. That's right."

"And they told you...answers like 'I don't know, I don't recall,' that ain't going to work here, right?"

"That's what Special Agent Harrill told me. He made that very, very clear-I was not to say anything like that."

"And you knew, sir, that if you didn't comply with what the Government wanted you to say, that you were going to have problems, didn't you?"

"They made that very clear, you're absolutely right."

"And they showed you the video...and this animation, and they got you to say that Karl Thompson told you that the reason that he used force (was) because Otto Zehm lunged, is that right?"

"They got me to agree to that, you're right."

"But that's not what happened, is it?"

"Not to my knowledge. I have no recall of that whatsoever."

"So they showed you the AMR report and then they showed you the portions of the video when you're talking to AMR and they told you, you were the one that provided that."

"You're right. That's right."

"And you agreed with them?"

"Yes, I did."

"Why?"

"I was a little bit scared. I...trusted the FBI to tell me the truth. I didn't know any better. I had no recall of that. So I sat there for six hours, basically being interrogated, and them, um, I'm going to stop short of saying 'manipulated,' because I still trust law enforcement, but I was definitely, my memory's definitely, without a doubt, influenced by those six hours of meetings."

"You went into the grand jury and said what the FBI wanted you to say?"

"I agreed to everything Mr. Boutros asked me. You're right."

"Your memory wasn't refreshed on that day, on June 16th, 2009, was it?"

"I wouldn't use the word, 'refreshed.' I would say, 'influenced.'"

"And in fact, the difference between your grand jury testimony in June of 2009 and that you gave in January, 2009, was the wire brushing you got that morning, wasn't it?"

"That's correct."

"You were bothered by it to the point that you contacted Mr. Meador?"

144

"Yes."

"Where did you meet him?"

"There's a, City of Spokane has a very large fueling depot...right next to a railroad track out middle of town."

"Well, why would you meet him at a railroad track in the middle of town?"

"Frankly, I didn't trust him at that point... I was going to talk to him next to a railroad track where there was a lot of noise that would interrupt any kind of recording device he might have."

"Did you talk to him about the way you were treated on June 16th, 2009?"

"I did. That's why he contacted me. He had heard through another member of the hostage team that I was a bit angry about the occurrences that day, and he called me up and wanted to clear the air..."

"You were the one that told Jim Nicks, the Assistant Chief, about the word 'lunge,' correct?"

"Yes, sir, that's right."

"And you told that to Agent Meador that day, didn't you?"

"I did."

"You told him that the word, 'lunge,' was your word, it wasn't Karl Thompson's word?"

"No, it was mine. I was very emphatic about that... I own that word."

"How is it that someone like you, a veteran police officer, can go into a meeting with the FBI and then into the grand jury and give testimony that you know they want that's different from your recollection?"

"I trusted them at the time."

"Well, you trusted them at the time. Why in the world would you do it?"

"I was scared. They, um, had, um, pressured me all day long to give that testimony, and they threatened me with obstruction of justice charges. The quote that Mr. Meador gave me, 'That train has left. You better save yourself.'"

"All right. Let's get this out, let's get it clear. At our request you came to my office, didn't you, sir?"

"Yes, sir, I did."

"April 9th of 2010, is that right?"

"Yes, sir."

"You were given the opportunity to read your grand jury testimony?"

"Yes, sir."

"By yourself, in the library of a law office, weren't you?"

"Yes, that's correct."

"You were also given the opportunity to view portions of the video?"

"Yes."

"Did you think that the grand jury testimony...was improper?"

"Improper? Yes, sir, it was."

"You took steps then, sir, to contact a lawyer?"

"I did, immediately."

"And you took steps then again, sir, to have discussions with the FBI, this time with a lawyer?"

"That's correct."

"And that was within some 11 days, correct?"

"Yes, sir."

"After June 16th, 2009, you didn't go back and contact Mr. Boutros, did you?"

"No."

"Why not?"

"I didn't trust any of them..."

"Officer Thompson never told you that he struck Otto Zehm in the head with a baton, did he?"

"No."

"You knew, sir, that if you were charged with obstruction of justice, you wouldn't work in law enforcement again, would you?"

"No... I know exactly what obstruction of justice means."

Then Boutros asked Officer Moses, "And each time you testified before the grand jury...you were told that you can talk to an attorney if you want to, is that correct?"

Moses ultimately replied, "You did afford me the chance to an attorney."

"And you told me that your testimony in June was based on your memory, is that correct?"

"Yeah, I did."

Oreskovich countered, "But before the grand jury, you were told 'I don't know, I don't recall' answers aren't going to be accepted. Isn't that what you were told?"

"Yes, sir...almost word for word."

146

"And they showed you a video and they would show you an animation and then they would get you to say what they wanted you to say, isn't that right?"

"Yes, sir, it is."

"And Mr. Boutros was part of it, right?"

"Yes, sir, he was."

Concluding, Boutros asked, "Well, what you were told in the grand jury and what you were told by the FBI is, if you say, 'I don't know the answer to the question' but you really do, that's being untruthful, correct?"

"That would be, yeah, if that was the case."

"And you knew that to be true as a law enforcement officer for 20-something years, is that correct?"

"Yeah."

"Thanks."

CHAPTER FOURTEEN

On the evening of March 18, 2006, Zip Trip employee Leroy Colvin had contacted his supervisor, Angela Wiggins, to come to the store to play back the video footage of the encounter for the police. She testified that soon after she arrived, she went into a back room and replayed the footage of the incident on the store's video equipment for Officer Sandra McIntyre. Ms. Wiggins said Officer McIntyre made notes about the video while having her "stop and back up...we would go forward again and then stop, back up...pretty standard."

Ms. Wiggins indicated she was asked by Officer McIntyre to play the specific footage demonstrating Zehm entering the store and then, of Officer Thompson entering. She described a change in Officer McIntyre's demeanor as the replay proceeded. "Just her tone started to be a little more stern, um, a little louder, a little more persistent as to what she was wanting... The officer wanted the video backed up to when Otto Zehm first noticed Officer Thompson...and to slow it down and clarify it, if possible." After the struggle moved to the center aisle, Ms. Wiggins heard Officer McIntyre count to seven. "As she was counting along with the video, it was the baton strikes, each time the officer was hitting Otto Zehm with the baton."

Wiggins indicated that Sergeant Joseph Walker joined them later in the back room. Mr. Boutros asked, "Were there any particular portions of the video that you were asked to play back for both Officer McIntyre and Sergeant Walker?"

"It would have been the baton strikes and when Otto Zehm first noticed Officer Thompson."

"Did Officer McIntyre say anything to you as this portion of the video was playing where...Mr. Zehm first noticed Officer Thompson approaching?"

"She...just made the comment that he didn't lunge."

"Do you remember that clearly?"

"I remember that clearly because I didn't understand what she was talking about."

148

"Was there any mention of the pop bottle?"

"After the initial comment and we...backed up the video for her to show again in slow motion, she made the comment... 'See, he didn't lunge with the soda bottle.' And that was the point that I realized what she was talking about with the first comment of him not lunging."

"And what made you realize that? What made it clear for you?"

"When she said, 'He didn't lunge with the soda bottle,' because at first I...wasn't paying attention to what was in his hands...or what was really transpiring."

"And you said that there was a second portion of the video besides the initial approach by the defendant that you showed to Officer McIntyre and Sergeant Walker, is that correct?"

"It would be...the baton strikes."

On cross-examination Oreskovich established that the report Ms. Wiggins completed for her employer's insurance company approximately one week after the incident did not contain any reference to comments made by the police officers. Neither did she describe those comments in her interview with Special Agent Jangaard five months later or in a telephone interview three years later. "And it was not until now, the third time that you met with the FBI and the U.S. Attorney. Where did you see the video? When you watched it a couple of times with the FBI, where did you see it?"

"The district attorney's headquarters."

"So we know you gave them a statement in person in August of 2006...and we know you gave them grand jury testimony in September of 2009... So would those have been the two occasions that you watched the video with them, ma'am?"

"Yeah, I watched it...with them both times."

"And on the first occasion when you watched the video with them...in August of 2006, you didn't tell them anything about any conversations, correct, ma'am?"

"Um, obviously not, no."

"And when you watched the video with them the second time, before the grand jury, they actually pointed out to you these officers, right?"

"No, I pointed out the officers that were in the back office with me."

"I see."

"And they had me pick them out from pictures, so I knew what their names were."

"And they asked you questions about whether or not there were comments about 'lunge,' correct?"

"No."

"Oh, they didn't? You just volunteered that to them now...after seeing them three times and seeing the video?"

"Things tend to come back to you as you watch it more and more and you're putting things together. You're a little nervous when things like this first happen."

"But you had the opportunity to watch the video with them in August of 2006, right?"

"Yes, I did."

"And you had the opportunity to tell them then, comments that you're testifying here before this jury, right?"

"Yes."

"And you didn't?"

"I-no, I did not."

Boutros countered, "I'm going to ask you some questions about what Mr. Oreskovich talked to you about regarding your May 26th, 2009, testimony to the FBI. And he asked you about this comment that, when asked if you recalled discussion concerning baton strikes amongst the officers in the video, 'Wiggins replied that while she did not recall specific discussion concerning the use of a baton, a reference to the baton may have been made after the second responding officer arrived on the scene.' Is that correct?"

"Correct."

"Did the FBI or the U.S. Attorney's Office or anybody in the Federal Government specifically ask you about a lunge before you mentioned that to us?"

"No."

*

Then Officer Sandra McIntyre was called to testify. She acknowledged having a longstanding personal and professional relationship with Officer Thompson, whom she regarded as a "father figure." She indicated that through her work as a police officer she had become a "trained observer," had learned to distinguish what is important to put in a police report, and knew to include everything that's important in her reports.

Boutros asked, "You were the first officer to look at the tape that night?"

"Yes, I was the first officer."

"You asked the Zip Trip employee operating the playback of the video to replay certain parts for you that night, correct?"

"That is correct, um-hum."

"And that was because you wanted to see the content of the video, correct?"

"No, that's not correct. I wanted to make sure that the copy was being made of that videotape."

"Do you see the date there on this document... Is that September 23, 2009?

"Yes."

"And this is the verbatim report of the proceedings of the testimony of Sandra McIntyre before the grand jury, is that correct?"

"Yes, that is correct."

"And in that grand jury you took an oath to tell the truth, correct."

"That is correct."

"And did you tell the truth?"

"Yes, I did."

"And during that grand jury you were asked the following questions and gave the following answers, 'Question: When you were looking at specific portions of the video and asking it to be replayed, that was not to preserve evidence; that was because you wanted to see the content of the video. True? Answer: True. Question: Okay, that had nothing to do with saving the tape? It had to do with seeing the content of the video? Answer: Right.' Is that correct?"

"Yes, that is correct."

"And while you were watching the video, you had a notebook with you, is that correct?"

"Yes."

"You recorded time stamps from the security video, correct?"

"That's correct."

"And you later shredded that notebook, correct?"

"Well, that's what we do. As soon as we complete a notebook, we shred the notebook. Yes."

"So all of your notes related to this incident have been destroyed, is that correct?"

151

"That is correct. That's normally what we do. It's not just this incident."

"And as you were watching the videotape on the screen, you began to count out loud the baton strikes that you saw, correct?"

"I don't recall doing that."

"Don't recall one way or the other?"

"I don't recall... I don't recall doing that. I...I could have done that. I do not recall doing that. I don't investigate another officer, so I know my responsibility was to get the tape and to make sure that that was there for major crimes."

"And based on what you saw on the video that night, you didn't see anything to suggest Zehm was being aggressive, correct?"

"I...I did not. Um, during the portion of the video that I saw, I didn't completely see the whole video. My concern was truly just to get the videotape for the sergeant."

"And you didn't see Zehm doing anything aggressive with the pop bottle, correct?"

"I did not."

"And it was clear to you, based on your review of the tape, that Mr. Zehm never lunged at the defendant, correct?"

"That's correct."

"And while you were watching the portion of the video showing the defendant's initial baton strikes, you exclaimed aloud, 'He didn't lunge at him with the pop bottle,' correct?"

"That is not correct. I did not say that word."

'You're saying you did not say the word, 'lunge'?"

"No, I did not."

"You made a note in your head at least and you could have said it out loud that Otto Zehm did not lunge at the defendant, correct?"

"I...I would not have made a note of that. There was...obviously, that did not occur."

"And in your grand jury were you asked the following question and did you give the following answer: 'You made a note in your head at least and could have said it out loud that Otto Zehm did not lunge at Officer Thompson, correct? Answer: Correct.' Is that right?

"That is correct."

"And after you looked at the video in the back room, you went and you spoke with the defendant, correct?"

"Yes, I did."

"And you told the defendant that the video showed that Mr. Zehm never lunged at him, correct/"

"No, I did not talk to the defendant about the video."

"Well, you agree that you may have told the defendant that he had a problem with the lunge account because it was not supported by the video, correct?"

"No, I did not."

"Were you asked the following question and did you give the following answer, 'Question: Did you ever tell Thompson that he had a problem with the lunge account because it was not supported by the video? Answer: I don't know. Question: You might have? Answer: I could have. I have no idea.' Is that accurate?"

"I did answer it that way, but in the same respect, I, um, didn't say that to him, because I had not heard the word 'lunge' that night at all."

"So, you claim that you never heard that Mr. Zehm lunged at the defendant with a pop bottle on the night of the incident, is that true?"

"That is true."

"And your claim is that you never heard anyone say that Zehm lunged at the defendant or anything similar or equivalent to that prior to hearing the press briefing by Chief Nicks, true?"

"That is true."

"You never heard anybody say that Zehm came at the defendant and that that's what prompted use of force...on the night of the incident, correct?"

"Correct."

"Now, you testified that you know for sure that you didn't exclaim in the back room that Mr. Zehm didn't shoot at the defendant, correct?"

"That is correct."

"Because you never heard any allegation that he had, correct?"

"Correct-didn't hear that."

"And you know for sure that you didn't exclaim, 'Hey, Mr. Zehm didn't stab the defendant,' correct?"

"That's correct."

"Yet you say that you may have explained that Mr. Zehm didn't lunge at the defendant, you may have exclaimed that, without ever having heard in the first place that there was any allegation that Mr. Zehm lunged at him at all, true?"

"I did not say that he, that Mr. Zehm lunged at Officer Thompson. No, I did not say that."

"In grand jury were you asked the following question and did you give the following answer, 'Question: Could you have said that Otto Zehm did not lunge at Officer Thompson without ever having heard in the first place that there was any allegation that Zehm had lunged at all? Answer: I could have said that.' Did I read that right?"

"You did read that right."

"Would you agree that if you had known at the time you wrote your report that the lunge justification wasn't true, that would have been very material to you, is that correct?"

"Yes. If I heard anything that was dramatic according to the incident, I would have written that in my report. My duty was truly to make sure that there was a copy of the tape. Um, I knew that the major crimes detectives were coming in, I knew that they were going to be taking over it, and their expertise is to review the tape, and to review the whole tape and not portions of the tape like myself."

Boutros established that on the night of the incident Officer McIntyre received an Email from Corporal Tom Lee stating that there was a lunge by Mr. Zehm that had prompted the use of force. She indicated that she received it as it had been sent to all police officers but would not necessarily have read it that night.

Boutros asked, "In any case, within 24 hours of the incident, you learned that the Acting Chief of Police said there was a lunge, right?"

"That is correct-on a press release."

"That Mr. Zehm had lunged at the defendant and that was what prompted the defendant's use of force that night, correct?"

"That is correct."

"And you knew based on your review of the video that there was no lunge, right?"

"I did know that."

"But after learning the core justification for the defendant's use of force was not true, you didn't do anything, right? You didn't tell anybody, correct?"

"No. I wasn't at work. It wasn't my job to correct that. That was the chief's press release, and major crimes was with him. Major crimes are the ones who took over the whole investigation."

"But you only said that that night. You never told anybody about the lunge justification being false after that time, correct?"

"That is correct."

"Did you previously testify that after you looked at the video in the back room you went and spoke with the defendant that night?"

"Yes, I did... I didn't speak to him about what was on the tape. I asked Officer Thompson if he was okay, and that was my concern. What occurred there, not my concern."

"So is it your testimony that immediately after watching the video, you went out and spoke with Officer Thompson and you had seen the content of the video, correct?"

"Yeah, well, I saw portions of the video. I didn't see the whole video."

"You saw portions including the initial baton strikes, correct?"

"The initial baton strikes, yes, but I didn't know about the rest of what occurred there."

"You saw the portion that showed that there was no lunge, correct?"

"That is correct."

"And you went outside and had a conversation with the defendant immediately afterwards, correct?"

"Yes, I did."

"And your testimony now is that you didn't mention anything to him about the video, is that correct?"

"I didn't mention anything to him about what was on the video."

"And you met with the city attorney prior to testifying before the grand jury, correct?"

"Yes, I did. I don't recall which grand jury."

"And after you spoke with him, you came to the grand jury and you testified that you didn't recall to many of the questions that you were asked, is that correct?"

"That is correct."

"And that was true even when you did have a recollection of events to the question that was asked, is that correct?"

"To a certain point. I wanted to expand and explain some answers, which I didn't feel like I was given a chance to."

"Did you answer questions in grand jury, 'I don't recall,' when you had a recollection but it wasn't one hundred per cent?"

"Yes. Um-hum."

"Have you ever heard officers suggest that it's sometimes helpful to say, 'I don't recall,' to avoid disclosing something that you would rather not disclose?"

"I have heard that be stated. It's not something that I would do. I tell the truth-that's what I do."

On cross-examination Oreskovich first established that when the critical incident protocol was employed, Officer McIntyre's role became keeping the crime scene log and preserving evidence. Then he established that she had testified before the grand jury in January, June, and September, 2009, and had met with FBI agents before each of the last two grand jury appearances and again in May, 2010. He asked, "The second time you were brought in to the grand jury, in June of 2009...you had a meeting with FBI agents, did you not?"

"Yes, I did."

"Prior to your grand jury testimony, correct?"

"That's correct."

"And were you advised that you could be charged with obstruction of justice, you better say what we think you know?"

"Yes, I was."

"Were you frightened by that, ma'am?"

"Very much so."

"Do you have any children?"

"Yes, I do."

"How many?"

"I have two."

"What ages?"

Officer McIntyre started crying and said, "Forgive me for a minute."

"That's all right."

"19 and 14."

"Are you all right?"

"Yes, sir."

"Okay... You were brought in a third time...on a grand jury subpoena, correct?"

"Yes, I was."

"And you had one more meeting with the FBI and with Mr. Boutros, isn't that fair to say?"

"Yes, I did."

"Mr. Durkin was present during that meeting, was he not?"

"Yes, he was."

"And you were advised that you were a subject now of a grand jury investigation, weren't you?"

"Yes, I was."

"You were told they were going to show you some videotape...and weren't you told that depending upon the outcome of your testimony, that could get you charged with a crime?"

"That is correct."

"Did you feel like you were being pressured by the Government to say things?"

"Yes, I did. I was told, 'Now's the time to save yourself.' I've told the truth...so how are you going to save yourself when you've told the truth?"

"And after that grand jury testimony, the Government sent you a letter and said, 'You are now a target of an investigation, and here's a proposed indictment against you,' isn't that what they did?"

"That's correct."

"And said, 'If you want to come back in and talk to us, you can,' isn't that fair to say?"

"Um-hum. Yes."

"And you did, didn't you?"

"Yes."

"You are here testifying, ma'am, aren't you, in the face of a threat by a government charge to indict you."

"Yes, I am."

Concerning her meeting with FBI agents in May, 2010, Oreskovich asked, "And there was a comment made...that McIntyre is now of the opinion that Officer Thompson overreacted at the Zip Trip. Do you remember that question being asked of you?"

"Yes, sir...that's not the opinion I hold. It's the opinion that I held back in 2010. When you look at the incident, the video that continues to run daily in the news, yeah, it looks horrible. It looks bad. But my personal opinion? I wasn't there in the beginning. I don't know what started this. Only Officer Thompson knows that."

Then Boutros asked additional questions. "Officer McIntyre, you testified that you weren't allowed to explain answers in grand jury, is that correct?"

"That's correct."

"But you actually were given an opportunity repeatedly to add anything you wanted, isn't that true?"

"I was given an opportunity, but under the things that were going on and the intimidation, I did not feel like I could do that."

"Well, you were asked, were you not...'Question: How have you been treated by the individuals conducting this investigation on behalf of the Department of Justice? Answer: Good.' Is that accurate?"

"No. That's how I answered it."

"So, you're saying it is not accurate what you said?"

"Yes, it is accurate what I said."

"And did we also say to you, 'Hey, if you realize that you provided inaccurate, false, or incomplete information to the grand jury, do you agree to immediately contact Special Agent of the FBI Lisa Jangaard to alert her as to that? And you said: Absolutely.' Is that correct?"

"Yes, I did."

"And you were also asked: 'Based on you testimony that you've provided today, and during your prior grand jury sessions, is there anything that you want to change about your testimony, any corrections you want to make? This is the time. Answer: No.' Is that correct?"

"That's correct."

"Now, you also said you felt intimidated...and that you provided information that wasn't accurate based on that intimidation, is that true?"

"I felt like I was intimidated. I provided you the truth."

"Isn't it true that the people in the Federal Government that spoke to you just asked you to tell the truth?"

"Yes."

"They never told you what to say?"

"They did not tell me what to say."

"And in fact, when you met with the U.S. Attorney's Office on May 18th of 2010, you acknowledged that you had chosen to provide short answers to questions...and that you answered that you did not recall to lots of questions posed to you during those grand jury sessions, correct?"

"That's correct."

"And you apologized for that, true?"

"That is true."

"And you also explained that you answered, 'I don't recall,' to many questions even when you did have a recollection...correct?"

"That's correct. I felt like I couldn't explain things."

Then Oreskovich asked, "Mr. Boutros met with you on September 23rd, 2009, before this grand jury testimony...and told you that you were the subject of a grand jury investigation, correct?"

"Several people in the room did, yes."

"You felt they were leaning on you, didn't you?"

"Absolutely."

"They wanted you to give them testimony that was favorable to them, didn't they?"

"That's exactly how I felt."

"And so, when you get into the grand jury under oath, and they're asking you questions, 'At any time since this incident, has anyone attempted to persuade you to provide false, misleading, or incomplete information,' you're really not in a position to tell them, 'Yes,' are you?"

"No, I'm not, not at all."

"Because you know that if you don't answer the question the way they want it answered, you're going to get charged with a crime, is that fair to say?"

"Yes, it is."

"Isn't that what they tried to do to you, ma'am?"

"Yes."

"You were intimidated, weren't you?"

"Yes, I was."

"It wasn't too difficult before the grand jury to scare you, scare the hell out of you, and then get you to admit what they wanted in front of the grand jury, was it?"

"No."

The prosecution completed the presentation of its case with the recall of Special Agent Jangaard, who testified briefly.

CHAPTER FIFTEEN

Immediately after the prosecution rested its case, Oreskovich addressed the Court, "At this time I would move, pursuant to Rule 29 under the Federal Rules of Criminal Procedure, for the dismissal first of count one of the indictment, the violation of Mr. Zehm's civil rights by Officer Thompson."

Oreskovich claimed that the prosecution failed to establish that Officer Thompson had acted willfully or with bad purpose and that his use of force was objectively unreasonable. He recounted the defendant signing back in for duty where he heard about the 911 call, checking the CAD report, and listening to the radio traffic indicating that a man scared two young women, took their money, appeared to be high, and ran from the scene. He said the only reason the defendant went to the Zip Trip was for a law enforcement purpose and characterized the video evidence and eyewitness testimony as "all over the board." He pointed out that the defendant indicated in his statement that he perceived he was going to be assaulted with the 2-liter bottle and that no trained police officer had testified that the defendant's perceptions were in any way improper. Regarding evidence of possible head strikes and the neck injury, he stated there is no indication that those injuries were delivered intentionally or that the defendant acted willfully when he engaged in the use of force. "It's clear that after baton strikes occurred, that Mr. Zehm resisted, it's clear he was assaulting, it's clear he didn't comply with commands. Where is the evidence that this officer, who is simply responding to a call, who puts himself into service, acted with any bad purpose whatsoever?"

Boutros responded for the prosecution, "The government has established through the testimony of Mr. Bragg that at almost each stage of the proceeding the defendant violated his training...that the defendant knew and was trained in how to respond and nevertheless violated that training... Multiple eyewitnesses said that Mr. Zehm acted surprised as the defendant approached him. Virtually every witness said that Mr. Zehm was not acting aggressively at any time, that he acted defensively, that he used the pop bottle to protect his face and head from blows... There's video evidence that shows that Mr. Zehm never moves forward toward the officer...but is retreating the whole time... And multiple eyewitnesses as well as a human factors expert, Dr. Gill, (testified) that even if the defendant had given commands, he never gave Mr. Zehm time to respond... That alone is evidence of unreasonableness.

"You also heard evidence from virtually every eyewitness that the defendant used overhand vertical baton strikes. You heard evidence from Mr. Bragg that those are trained to be avoided except when deadly force is justified. There's no dispute...that deadly force was at no point justified in this case. You also heard the recorded interview of the defendant as he offered his justification for the use of his Taser, that Mr. Zehm was punching at him. You heard the training from Mr. Bragg is that, unless Mr. Zehm is being assaultive, the defendant is not permitted to use his Taser. But you saw video evidence as well as eyewitness testimony that Mr. Zehm didn't even have free hands to punch with because he was holding the pop bottle over his face...defensively to protect his face from the additional blows.

"In the defendant's statement he described his justification for the next series of baton strikes, that Mr. Zehm jumped up, adopted a boxing stance, and began to throw punches...that he did, in fact, punch the defendant at that time. You have heard from every single witness that has testified about that issue that Mr. Zehm never returned to his feet, adopted a boxing stance, and began punching. So, that justification...is also false...and evidence of unreasonableness."

Boutros referred to the defendant's statements in his recorded interview that intentional strikes to the head are deadly force and that deadly force was not justified in this case. Then he reviewed the eyewitness and medical testimony indicating baton strikes to Zehm's head and neck had occurred. "That, too, is evidence of objectively unreasonable force.

"With regard to willfulness, we know that the typical way you show willfulness in cases like this are that the defendant had received training that he understood and had applied, and he consciously violated that training. That takes us back to the testimony of Mr. Bragg who described that training in great detail and the testimony of the eyewitnesses who described the ways in which the defendant violated what he knew to be his training that night.

"The second way that we establish willfulness is by showing that the defendant lied or covered up his conduct afterwards because, if your use of force was reasonable, there's no reason to lie about it afterwards. Your Honor, perhaps one of the strongest pieces of evidence of willfulness is the AMR report. In that report Mr. Stussi repeatedly wrote that Mr. Zehm had been struck in the head, neck, and upper torso with a police baton, and he identified the source of that information as Officer Moses. We also heard exactly similar testimony from Mr. Jamarillo, who was Mr. Stussi's partner at AMR, who testified to the same thing and described in detail the conversation that they had with Mr. Moses during which Mr. Moses disclosed to them the manner of the baton strikes, that they were vertical, and that there were baton strikes to the head, neck, and upper torso.

"We also heard from Mr. Moses himself and his grand jury came in as substantive evidence of the offenses in this case. And during that grand jury he described in great detail the conversations that he had with Mr. Jamarillo and with Mr. Stussi and the information he provided to them, that he had described strikes to the head, neck, and upper torso. And in grand jury he clearly identified the source of that information as the defendant himself.

"The defendant's own admission that night that he had struck Mr. Zehm in the head, neck, and upper torso shows that he knew that very night that he had used deadly force, that he had struck him in the head and neck despite his training that that was not authorized. Yet he nevertheless, four days later, did his recorded interview and denied using deadly force. If the force were justified, there would be no reason to offer up those lies.

"So, Your Honor, there is ample evidence in this case of both objectively unreasonable force used by the defendant at each stage of his 13 baton strikes and his Taser. And there's also ample evidence that the defendant acted willfully, that he violated his training, and that he lied afterwards to create false justifications for what he had done. For those reasons, Your Honor, the government submits that you should deny the Rule 29."

Judge Van Sickle prefaced his decision with an explanation of Rule 29. "After the government closes its evidence or after the close of all the evidence, the Court, on the defendant's motion, must enter a judgment of acquittal of any offense for which the evidence is insufficient to sustain a conviction. The rule under the law also is that the Court must consider the evidence presented...and all inferences in a light most favorable to the non-moving party."

Then he declared, "I've had the opportunity to review the evidence that has been presented by way of videotapes, the several witnesses that have testified, both eyewitnesses and expert witnesses who presented evidence in the case of the United States, the prosecution. Considering the evidence...and all inferences to be considered in a light most favorable to the non-moving party, the prosecution, the Court does find that there has been presented sufficient evidence, both as it relates to the issues involving objective unreasonableness and willfulness, that a reasonable juror could make a determination contrary to the moving party, the defendant, Officer Thompson. Thus the motion for judgment of acquittal as to count one is denied."

*

The defense team began the presentation of evidence on behalf of Officer Thompson with the testimony of Dr. James Nania, an emergency physician for 30 years and for the last 25, Medical Director of the Emergency Department at Deaconess Medical Center in Spokane.

Dr. Nania indicated he had full confidence in the documentation of Dr. Scott Edminster, who had spent four hours evaluating and treating Otto Zehm at the Deaconess Emergency Department on the night of March 18, 2006. He also indicated that he had reviewed the statements of at least six of the witnesses to the incident at the Zip Trip, the reports of the other physicians who treated Zehm after his admission to the Deaconess Intensive Care Unit, and the autopsy report of Dr. Aiken. He discounted the eyewitness descriptions of baton strikes to the head. "The bottom line is, whatever people think they saw...is there evidence of it medically? That, you've got to look at what was hit. And if you look at what was allegedly hit, you're going to find the ultimate evidence, and it's not there."

He claimed he'd treated thousands of blunt head injuries. As neither the treating physicians nor Dr. Aiken had documented the presence of external signs of scalp trauma, he was of the opinion that baton strikes to Zehm's head had not happened. In regard to the marks at Zehm's right eyebrow he commented, "They're really little marks, so it's a little hard, but the one that looks more brown and kind of irregular, it looks like a scrape or a minor abrasion. The other one is just a little ditzle of a bruise. They could have happened a hundred different ways in this altercation, but it isn't a pattern that suggests a strike from a baton."

On cross-examination Boutros asked, "Are you claiming you know the instrument that caused the injuries to Mr. Zehm's head?"

"No."

"Okay. Now, I want to be sure that I understand what you would expect to see from a baton injury. You're saying that a baton strike to the head can cause a skull fracture, but not that it always does. Is that correct?"

"Yes."

"You're saying that a baton strike to the head can cause intracranial bleeding, but not that it always does. Is that correct?"

"Yes."

"You're saying that a baton strike to the head can cause a laceration, but not that it always does. Is that correct?"

"Yes."

"So a baton strike to the head could take place and there be no skull fracture, correct?"

"Yes."

"No laceration?"

"Yes."

"No intracranial bleeding? Is that correct?"

"And whether those particular injuries occurred depends on a whole bunch of different factors, is that true?"

"Well, not that many factors."

"Well, the thickness of the skull?"

"A little bit."

"The mass or weight of the object?"

"Yes."

"The speed or rotational velocity of the portion of the object that makes contact with the head?"

"Yes."

"Would you agree that a sharper object is more likely to cause a laceration than a blunter object?"

"Again, that would depend on those other factors you cited, yes."

"Would it affect your opinion if you learned that the baton used by the defendant in this case was specifically designed by a use-of-force expert to specifically minimize the risk of laceration?"

"No."

"And why is that?"

"Well, I've held that baton. It's still going to cause a heck of a lump."

"Would it affect your opinion if Dr. Aiken provided sworn testimony that she did find injuries on Mr. Zehm's head that were most likely caused by a baton strike?"

"Well, I would still have to have my own opinion, and I got to see the autopsy results as well. I've dealt with a lot of injuries to the head."

"Were you provided with the grand jury testimony of Dr. Aiken in this case?"

"I believe so."

"Do you recall that Dr. Aiken did find injuries on Mr. Zehm's head that were likely caused with a baton strike?"

Dr. Nania answered, "Well, I think what I remember is she did not find them or identify them at the time of the autopsy, which was probably most important to me. I think subsequently, and it would depend so much on what question was asked, she may have said, 'possible,' or something like that. That's what I remember, something like that. So again, I won't be strong about second-guessing eyewitnesses or another medical professional. My opinion is I significantly relied on my experience and the evidence I have observed medically."

The prosecution argued that the next defense witness, Dr. William Lewinski, should be excluded because the methodology employed in his memory and attention research relevant to his anticipated testimony lacked "the most basic concepts of experimental design, namely a control group, statistical analysis of any kind, hypothesis testing, sample size, and proper coding of data," invalidating the conclusions. The argument did not succeed.

Dr. Lewinski held a Ph.D. in psychology, had worked mainly as a police psychologist, and had conducted studies tracking eye movements during mock shootout scenarios and testing the participating officers' memory of the event afterward. He stated he found that well-trained police officers tend to focus very intently on what the suspect is doing, especially with the hands, and their recall of timeline, details of the surroundings, and even of their own actions are fragmented. "The officers had a narrow external focus of attention, meaning they couldn't tell us often where they were at, where their partner was at, what their partner was doing...as this incident was unfolding and they were responding. But they could tell us what that gun looked like."

On cross-examination Durkin attacked Dr. Lewinski's credentials. He'd received his Ph.D. through a correspondence program at a time when Police Psychology was not a field of study recognized by the American Psychological Association, and none of his research studies had been published in peer-reviewed journals. Then Durkin pointed out that his "scientific" studies had no control group or generally accepted model that allowed for statistical analysis of the results. Dr. Lewinski countered, "The data was so robust that we didn't have to do statistical analysis. When you get results like 10 and 12 times a number in one category as opposed to another, that's considered robust data in and of itself."

Then the defense called Dr. Daniel Davis, a forensic pathologist and death investigator for Lane County, Oregon. He had authored a chapter in the Encyclopedia of Forensic and Legal Medicine on pattern injuries and had regularly given presentations about pattern injuries in child abuse. He stated that the subgaleal hematomas "probably represent bland impact injuries to the head without overlying evidence of any type of instrument impression or feature that we can associate with any kind of instrument. These are characteristic for someone who bangs their head against a bland, flat surface like a wall or a floor...although I do want to offer that the possibility exists these could actually be traction injuries, for instance, from grabbing a big fist full of hair and pulling real hard. And that wouldn't leave any kind of skin bruising, either." Neither did he believe that the two marks on Zehm's eyebrow resulted from a baton injury.

Dr. Davis stated that the neck damage found was due to the intravenous catheter insertion as Dr. Aiken had concluded and claimed that the CT scan finding described by Dr. Gill was not a hematoma because Zehm was rotated slightly in the scanner, creating an asymmetry between the sides that made the right sternocleidomastoid muscle look swollen.

Prosecutor Durkin questioned Dr. Davis about the ability of Emergency Department staff to correctly identify the nature and extent of injuries. Dr. Davis acknowledged, "Their focus is not extensive injury description like we would do as forensic pathologists... They're pretty busy trying to take care of a person, keep them alive, resuscitate them if necessary."

Durkin asked, "Did you review (Dr. Aiken's) testimony relative to the likelihood of a grabbing of the hair to cause a subgaleal hematoma?"

"Yes, I read about that."

"And if I understood your direct testimony, you're saying that the mere grabbing of the hair can cause the subgaleal hematoma's that are reflected on Mr. Zehm's scalp?"

"I don't know about the mere grabbing of the hair, but clearly getting a fist full of hair and yanking on it can cause subgaleal hematoma. This is not a hematoma. A hematoma is a big collection of blood like a raised goose egg that somebody might get from some type of trauma... He just has hemorrhage in the subgaleal tissue. And that could be caused from grabbing a large bunch of hair and yanking on it, because that loose tissue between the scalp and the skull, the subgaleal tissues, can bleed from that."

"So, in light of that, Dr. Aiken testified that in order to sustain the injuries that Mr. Zehm had, that there would have had to have been a very significant amount of pulling of the hair and extraction of the hair."

"I don't agree with that."

"And did you read (Dr. Smith's) testimony relative to the hair pull?"

"I don't recall what he said about hair pulling."

"Okay, and he testified that's not common in adults, more likely to be reflected in children."

"Right, I've seen it more often in children."

The only witness to the encounter called by the defense was Pat Conley, who had not seen the initial part of the struggle and was observing from approximately 70 feet away. The first thing he saw was Officer Thompson pulling on Zehm's back or hair and swinging him back and forth. He stated that the police officers who arrived later also were unsuccessful at controlling Zehm, who continued growling, spitting, struggling, and waving his fists. He described Zehm fighting the restraints while police officers repeatedly told him to calm down.

John Cappellano, one of the responding paramedics, had a different impression of Zehm's resistance. "The fighting that I saw him doing...was fighting against the restraints, you know, writhing on the floor, squirming, that kind of thing." He said his partner had seen blood in Zehm's mouth and he had seen spittle flying out, which increased the threat to the officers trying to control him.

A respected videographer, Michael Schott, testified that the ethics of his field require that videographers not look at witness statements or corroborating information and look only for evidence that is proven definitively by the video or still images. He disputed the number of baton strikes in the center aisle, claiming that only six rather than seven were apparent. He also disagreed with Dr. Gill's report concerning the first strike, stating that what was believed to construe Officer Thompson's hand and arm was the combination of a headlight and a video artifact. When asked on cross-examination if it would make any difference in his professional opinion if witnesses and Thompson himself said that it was a baton strike, he answered, "No."

The first of the Spokane Police Department officers to testify was Steven Braun, who initially described the circumstances of the call. He thought a possible robbery had occurred because the people whose money Zehm may have taken were frightened enough to call the police, and Zehm had left the bank going southbound on a northbound one way street, perhaps an attempt at evasion by a criminal familiar with the area. He stated that after entering the store, "I see Zehm on the floor in a seated position and his arms going back and forth in a punching motion and his leg kicking back and forth, and I see that Officer Thompson is next to him... I described it before as flailing, but kind of a thrashing motion where he's just uncontrolled... His hands are...in fists, and his legs are also kicking." He, too, had seen Zehm spitting and had considered Zehm's behavior to be assaultive because his hands were closed, representing a physical threat to anyone near him.

Then Detective Larry Bowman testified. A narcotics investigator and instructor in patrol tactics and the use of firearms, he had trained Officer Thompson in straight baton

168

tactics. When Oreskovich asked him to address what police officers are told about decisions they have to make pertaining to using force to take a person into custody, he answered, "One of the things we tell them in reference to what the person is actually going to do, the first level is...you give them a command, and I'm a police officer and I'm in a uniform. You expect the person to comply with those commands. If the person doesn't comply...there's two things you can do. One, you can close distance, take control of the individual, or two, you want to stay back away... In between is when police officers basically get hurt. That's when they start getting punched in the face...the person could actually start aggressing on them. So the idea behind it is we tell them that they have to make a decision whether they're going to go to cover, to protect themselves from the individual, continue to give commands, and try and get this person to comply...or they're going to go and make contact with the person to take control of them."

Oreskovich asked, "And do you discuss having to make that decision in seconds or very quickly?"

"Yes... The idea behind this is we tell them that you have to control the thinking of the individual you're contacting. You don't want to give him time to make plans on his own of whether he's going to escape or whether he's going to attack the officer."

Concerning the training officers receive pertaining to when to use a baton, Detective Bowman said, "We tell them they have to basically take action first. Once they see the threat, they have to basically deal with the threat, they don't have to wait until they get either kicked, punched in the face, shot, stabbed, hit with an object... It's basically to take action."

Based on his review of the video, Bowman stated that, like he had been trained, Officer Thompson delivered diagonal and not vertical strikes. He felt that if the number and delivery of baton strikes deviated from the manner in which he had been trained, it was because the officer was bent over a prone subject.

Prosecutor Timothy Durkin established that as a baton instructor in the state of Washington, Detective Bowman had gone through the straight baton training course taught by Mr. Bragg. Then he questioned the detective about his review of the video, which had been incomplete and heavily narrated by Detective Ferguson. "You indicated you reviewed Officer

Thompson's movements and baton strikes relative to the training that you provided, correct?'

"That's correct."

"Okay. You also indicated in your report, based on your observation of the video, that the defendant took the initiative in the confrontation and showed initiative. Is that correct?"

"That's correct."

"Okay. But you had no understanding of the underlying call information that purportedly supported taking the initiative in providing that initial confrontation."

"That's correct."

"Now, you agree that the videotape shows a very fast, non-stop approach by Officer Thompson and an attack on the subject, Mr. Zehm."

"I wouldn't use the word, 'attack,' no."

"You would use what word to describe his use of an impact weapon on Mr. Zehm?"

"Officer Thompson approached the subject in an attempt to gain control of him."

"Okay, and in his attempt, his immediate attempt to gain control of Mr. Zehm, he deployed and utilized immediately an impact weapon."

"I couldn't see that in the video."

Durkin asked later, "Now, the training that you provide, it only allows the use of an impact weapon when there is an objectively reasonable factual basis to believe that the subject is either assaultive or about to be assaultive."

"That's the only reason to use an impact weapon."

Durkin reiterated, "That's the training you provide?"

"That's correct," Bowman answered.

"Now, you said that you train the officers to use the least amount of force that is necessary to take that person under control.'

"That's correct."

"And that least amount of force, the very first step of force would be identifying yourself as an officer."

"Your presence, you identify yourself as an officer, so that would be the first step, yes."

"Okay, so your presence. And then there's the verbal part of that, correct?"

"That's correct."

"And that would be identifying yourself as an officer."

"Sometimes."

"And then there would be verbal commands to the subject, correct?"

"That's correct."

"Like directing the subject to do what you want him to do, correct?"

"That's correct."

"And this is all part of the training that you provide in connection with the use of a baton, correct?"

"It's the use of all actions with police officers...not just the use of a baton."

"And when you issue these verbal commands, you train people to allow the subject sufficient time to understand the command."

"Sometimes."

"So you give a command, and then you don't allow them to process it and then respond, is that what you're telling me?"

"I'm saying sometimes you don't have time to do that."

"Okay. But you train...officers to allow the subject sufficient time to understand what you're telling them to do."

"Not all the time, no."

Oreskovich then addressed the issuance of verbal commands with Detective Bowman. "You had mentioned that you train officers to give verbal commands, but not always, or something to that effect. Will you explain, please?"

"Some instances, you don't have time to give a command. The fact is that sometimes you want an element of surprise. The fact that I'm in a full uniform, I drive up in a police car...I walk in there, I want to take control... When I go into whatever incidents, I go into a domestic violence, I go into a store where an individual is arguing with his wife, or I'm in a parking lot that there's something going on, or there's a drug transaction taking place behind this building and I drive around it, I get out, and all of a sudden the people are running from me or they're coming at me... I don't have time to say, 'I'm Officer Bowman, Spokane Police Department. Please, I need to talk to you.' They already know what's happening here. They already know I'm an officer. I have to deal with that.

"Other times I could walk up and go, 'Sir, how are you today? I'm Officer Bowman, Spokane Police Department. I need to talk to you about your doing 30 in a 20 mile-an-hour school zone.' And I identify myself properly. I have lots of time to do that. So it changes depending again on the incident that I'm responding to."

"And is that threat assessment?"

"It is threat assessment."

Then Durkin stated, "Mr. Bowman, even if you're the best trained, most experienced police officer in the world, you still have to have an objectively factual basis to believe the subject poses a threat before you can use an impact weapon."

"I agree with that, yes."

"And a well-trained, very experienced officer's subjective belief must be factually reasonable."

"Correct."

"And you train to use the least amount of force necessary to control the subject, which would include verbal commands."

"That's correct."

Terrance Preuninger was the Spokane Police Department's training officer. At the time of the trial he was the patrol procedures instructor for the Washington State Criminal Justice Training Commission at the Spokane Regional Training Center. One response during Mr. Lamberson's questioning summarized his attitude toward patrol procedures as, "I actually teach a class that we offer to citizens in the community-we call it patrol procedures for civilians. And the whole purpose of the class is to provide a venue where citizens can come and ask us questions... People will see things on the news, they will read things in the newspaper, they will hear stories, and they will wonder, 'Why would the police have done that...' Everything that cadets learn in kindergarten and in Sunday School that make them an outstanding son, daughter, neighbor, parent, those things are not character traits that we want to get rid of. That's what makes them the good guys. But you have to be able to compartmentalize that. If you approach law enforcement situations the same way you approach situations at a neighborhood meeting, your inability to compartmentalize that stuff will directly lead to your being murdered on the job or being hurt or assaulted. And so you have to understand, you have to change the way you look at things."

Lamberson asked, "[In a] use of force situation, Officer, I want to make sure that we're clear, does an officer have to

172

match force with a suspect, or what does an officer do in that regard?"

Officer Preuninger replied, "You don't want to match force. You want to overwhelm their force. You want to use more than they did to control them, which is not just safer for you, it's safer for them. [The] sooner you can end that conflict, the better for you and for them."

"What is your opinion, sir, as to the risk assessment of Officer Thompson entering this store at the time he was contacting Mr. Zehm?"

"I would say that I have a very dangerous situation... I have a suspect who has, at minimum, committed a strong arm robbery, has just walked, has avoided me, has seen me, knows I'm coming, I've lost the element of surprise, and he's walked into a store where there's a bunch of innocent parties and possibly someone else who knows him."

"Sir, do you have an opinion as to whether that rapid advance served a legitimate law enforcement purpose in this case?"

"It served a legitimate law enforcement purpose. It was also probably a good choice tactically."

"Why?"

"...He could not always see the suspect's hands. And so, if he's not going to get compliance from the subject, it would not be smart to stand at a distance from him and just yell at him, not when he is as close as he is to those other innocent parties and/or to other avenues of escape. So, Officer Thompson closed space with him, continuing to give him the opportunity to surrender. The suspect had more than enough time to surrender, chose not to, so Officer Thompson, then by closing space, was able to use force and control him." He said the drawing of his baton as Officer Thompson walked through the door was another good tactical move, since Zehm was wearing a heavy leather jacket that could easily hide a weapon or pad a blow, and the officer couldn't see Zehm's hands while he was approaching. "Every call you go on, you take with you the original dispatch of that call and the other information that's been given to you... In this case, from what I've viewed, it has escalated because of the noncompliance of the suspect, so you have not just the original information, but the subject's actions are validating everything you've been told so far."

Mr. Durkin began the cross-examination of Officer Preuninger by having him verify that the Washington State

Criminal Justice Training Commission had not had a class in two years. Then he asked, "You know the defendant? You know him personally?"

"Yes."

"Okay. You work with him?"

"I never worked with him."

"You worked at the same place with him?"

"Yes."

"Okay. He's a fellow member of the police guild in which you belong?"

"Yes."

"Okay. And he's more than just a mere work acquaintance, isn't he, to you?"

"No."

Then Mr. Durkin asked him to read a document dated January 29, 2006, that stated, "Officer Thompson's professionalism, credentials, law enforcement experience, on the job performance, and demeanor have earned him the respect and admiration of his fellow officers. We also believe these characteristics qualify him for the position. As police chief, we believe that Karl F. Thompson would have the respect of officers, administration, and the public."

After Officer Preuninger identified the document as "a petition to support the candidacy of Karl Thompson...as Chief of Police," Durkin asked, "Is that your signature on that petition at line number 2?"

"It is."

When asked to describe excessive force in policing, Preuninger stated, "The term, 'excessive force,' gets thrown around as a very large umbrella. If I punch someone in the face and I put a number to that punch, I hit them at 90 per cent, and if someone could come down and tell me that, Terry, you only needed to hit that guy at 75 (per cent) and you would have gotten the same result, there are people that would define that strike as excessive force."

As to when it is justified, Preuninger said, "If the officer believed that they were in danger, then that use of force would be authorized."

Durkin asked, "There's got to be a factual basis, a reasonable factual basis supporting the subjective belief?"

Preuninger replied, "No."

"You're aware, are you not, that the subjective beliefs of an officer are irrelevant in terms of determining whether or

174

not the force he used...served a legitimate law enforcement purpose?"

"No," was the reply!

Referring to video of the Zehm encounter, Preuninger acknowledged that he did not see Officer Thompson stop and speak to Zehm before he swung his baton. When asked what evidence justified treating the call as a robbery or attacking Zehm, whom Preuninger had described as taking a "fixed position of aggress," he answered that it was "the totality of the circumstances." He said that conclusion was one a veteran police officer would make, and Thompson's actions showed Tombstone courage that is to be avoided in normal circumstances but was merited in this instance because of the high risk involved in the stop. Concerning whether Officer Thompson knew that the complainants didn't know if Zehm had taken any money, Durkin asked, "Should that stop an officer from...contacting a suspect that's been suspected of robbery?"

"No."

"Why not?"

"Because all they gave was a possibility that he doesn't have the money. They didn't take away any of the other factors that have already happened. All of Thompson's observations are the same. I would still want to talk to that person and initiate contact. And if they resisted that, if they refused my commands, it wouldn't change anything."

Detective Ferguson's testimony was brief. By her count, only three witnesses had described baton strikes to Zehm's head. She had dismissed the statements of two of them, one because of perceived anti-law enforcement bias and the other, because of her youth. It had not occurred to her to interview the AMR personnel who responded to the Zip Trip that night.

Prosecutor Boutros asked, "And your conclusion was that there was no evidence to support that excessive force was used, correct?"

"Yes."

"And that statement was false, right?" The immediate objection by the defense was sustained.

The last person the defense called to testify was Karl Thompson.

175

CHAPTER SIXTEEN

Carl Oreskovich's first substantive question of Officer Thompson was, "Did you ever tell anyone that Mr. Zehm had lunged at you and that was the reason you had used your baton?"

Thompson replied, "No, sir, I did not."

"Did you become aware at some time that Chief Nicks had gotten on the news and had used that description as the reason you had used your baton?"

"Yes, sir."

"When did you become aware?"

"Before my interview when I was on several days of administrative leave."

"And did you learn that by virtue of the news?"

"I did."

"Did you have a telephone conversation with Detective Ferguson to set up your March 22nd, 2006, interview, sir?"

"Yes, sir, I did."

"In the course of the telephone conversation...did you discuss the chief's statement on the news that the justification for your force was that Mr. Zehm lunged at you?"

"I told her that she needed to contact the Chief to correct that statement."

Oreskovich then asked questions that elicited Officer Thompson's educational background, military record, and experience in law enforcement. The jury learned that he had working as a policeman in Los Angeles during the 1970's before moving to Kootenai County, Idaho, in 1979 where he worked as a patrolman for the Sheriff's Department. When he left that department, he started a company with a colleague to investigate insurance fraud and arson. After five and a half years as a private investigator, he spent two years as a major crimes investigator for the Idaho Department of Law Enforcement before joining the administration of the Kootenai County Sheriff's Department. In that department he rose to captain of operations and later, of the jail. In 1996 he ran unsuccessfully for Kootenai County Sheriff, after which he worked as an intense supervision juvenile probation officer for two years. Then he joined the Spokane Police Department where he had been a patrolman, field training officer, hostage negotiator, and member of the dignitary protection team, crowd control unit, and peer assistance team.

Thompson had learned of Zehm's death before giving his recorded interview. Oreskovich asked, "How, if in any way, did that affect you?"

"It was a very powerful raw emotion.."

"Tragic?"

"Yes, absolutely."

"Affect you emotionally?"

"Yes. It was a profound tragedy for his family, his friends, for me. It has extended through my department and the community."

"To this day?"

"I suspect for the rest of my life."

Then he was asked to review the details of his shift on the day of the Zehm encounter and the call that prompted him to interrupt his meal break. Oreskovich asked, "You said what alerted you was radio traffic that the suspect was running... What did you do?"

"I walked out to my car to look at my computer screen... In reviewing the CAD...I learned that a male had approached females in a car who were at an ATM. They had already put their PIN in. They were frightened enough by the male's action...to drive away but still maintain a visual on this person, and then they described him as running from the scene, and he may have taken their money."

"You went to the area of the White Elephant?"

"Yes, because there were updates as I was going to the scene."

""Did you see Mr. Zehm going into the Zip Trip?"

"I did...and with the proximity, I did see him come out of the shadows, look in my direction, then walk into the store."

"And what did you think you were investigating at that point?"

"The last thing I heard before I jumped out of my car was Braun asking radio, confirming did he take her money. 'Affirm.' That was more validation that we had a crime. What I believed I was dealing with was second degree robbery. I knew at least I had a theft... If there's fear and it's significant, we're looking at second degree robbery."

"Tell us what you were thinking."

"When I saw him and he saw me...'Okay, now he knows I'm here.' I'm dealing with a possible robbery suspect, and it's not unusual, when we try and stop and detain people who have been involved in crimes...for them to slow down and try and blend in... That was a consideration when he went in there. But my greatest concern was that there were people inside that store."

"Why did you go in? Why did you go after him?"

"I felt that because he was going inside an occupied building, I was the closest one... I made the decision to try and detain him quickly, and in a lighted building. It was dark outside, we were between the two busiest streets in Spokane...and I have been in foot pursuits when you're running across traffic. Sometimes the greatest danger in a foot pursuit is getting run over by somebody."

"You drew your baton?"

"I did."

"Why did you draw your baton if you thought that there was a theft or a robbery?"

"There was no overt mention of a weapon."

"You went inside the store. Did you lose sight of Mr. Zehm?"

"I did."

"Did you know whether or not Mr. Zehm was armed?"

"No. No, I didn't."

"How was he dressed?"

"Black leather jacket, jeans, I think, black boots..."

"As you approached the store going into it, did you have any thought about weapons being available?"

"Certainly. The fact that someone is wearing a jacket is going to provide available concealment if somebody wants to have a concealed weapon."

"Other than those types of things that might be available on Mr. Zehm's person, did you have any concern entering the Zip Trip as to whether other types of things could be used as weapons?"

"Yes...I knew that just things on the shelves...you've got bottles, you've got cans...the store itself has three sides of glass."

"When did you next catch sight of Mr. Zehm?"

"When I came around the corner."

"We have seen in the video, at some point Mr. Zehm turns, faces you, correct?"

"Yes, sir."

"What, if anything, did you see or do at that point?"

"My recollection and the mental image that I have when I came around the corner is, when he was turning around, and I saw what he was holding and how he was holding it... I recognized it as a 2-liter soda bottle... He had a grip on each end and he had it pulled back against his chest... He had seen me come inside, I have this knowledge of what happened at the ATM, he had the opportunity to flee if he wished, he's chosen not to do that, and he's now facing me in this position."

"Now, we have heard your statement, sir. We watched the video in this courtroom... Are you telling us to the best of your ability what your perception was?"

"Yes, sir, I am."

"There's been some questions raised as to your recall as to whether you came to a stop... What is your recall?"

"My recall is that I did come to a stop... I gave him commands, they were quick, but he gave me quick replies because I was closing distance. But I got acknowledgment from his eyes, I got acknowledgment from his voice and words, and a refusal... I said, 'Drop the bottle, drop it now.' When I said, 'Drop the bottle,' he said, 'Why?' ...When I gave him those commands, I am looking for recognition. I'm looking for compliance... I'm not seeing any submissive gestures. And granted, I'm taking all of this in milliseconds...and I'm going through a checklist of things I need to do. But I'm also closing distance on him because I want to stop him where he's at. I know there are people at the kiosk; I do not want him to go down there. There is nobody between me and him. This is going to be the...best and safest place to try and get him detained."

"You said in your statement that you thought you came to a stop. Do you still have that memory?"

"I do. Now, whether that's a mental pause or physical, I still have that memory, yes."

"All right. You struck him with a baton."

"When I realized he was not going to drop the pop bottle, I thought he was going to come at me... I did strike him with the baton because I wanted to get him down on the floor."

179

"We got a pop bottle. How in the world can a pop bottle be any threat to you?"

"Sir, that's like holding a brick in your hand... You can throw it at me, you can distract me with it, and even if I'm not hurt, if you have had a basketball thrown at your face...typical reaction is you're going to move away... Somebody who is aware of that technique, it gives them time. If he were to have a concealed weapon, especially a firearm, that's enough time to draw, and I would not have even had my weapon out at that point."

"Did you honestly believe that he was going to do something assaultive to you with that?"

"Yes, sir, I did. I certainly did."

"Mr. Zehm went to the ground...correct, sir?"

"Yes."

"You used a Taser."

"I did."

"Why?"

"Because as he was going down, I was going down. I didn't fall on top of him, but I came down and as I did, there were two quick swings at my face."

"Now let's stop. We don't see that in the video anywhere."

"That's right, you don't."

"Is that your recollection, sir?"

"Yes, sir, it is... When I came down and I saw two fists coming at my face and I popped back up, that's when I drew my Taser, because I have very good success with a Taser of being able to control a subject."

"Did he continue to have the pop bottle in his hand after that?"

"When I pulled my Taser, I looked down and he had the pop bottle, yes."

"Were you giving him commands?"

"I was."

"What was it?"

"I said, 'Drop the bottle. Stop resisting. Stop fighting.' Because there was kicking, he was moving around, he was holding that bottle, I have an enhanced concern at this point about if this guy's got a gun, you know, it's getting really dangerous because now we are right in front of the kiosk. We have people around."

"Did you warn him, 'I'm going to tase you?'"

"I did."

"Did you tase him?"

"I did."

"Have you used a Taser in the past?"

"Yes."

"Does it incapacitate somebody when you've seen it in the past?"

"Yes... I've been successful five or six times."

"Did that occur in this case?"

"No."

"What occurred?"

"He continued to move. In fact, he started to get up on his knees as I'm assessing and my thought was, 'Oh, shit, he's getting on his feet.'"

"Well, what's significant about that?"

"It didn't work. That's another tool. I have already used my baton to strike him, I have now used my Taser to try and control him, and neither is getting compliance from him."

"Did you become fearful at all?"

"Yes...there's fear there."

"Now, sir, have you ever said to anybody that Otto Zehm assumed a boxing stance with his sugar foot forward?"

"No, sir, I have not used that phrase."

"Did you have some recollection at some point in time of him boxing you or punching you?"

"Yes."

"Where did you feel punches?"

"In my chest. I also had a contact to my face throughout this, but I don't know if that was his head against my face or his fists. But I definitely know I was hit in the chest."

"At some point in time, do you apply any type of a hair hold?"

"I do."

"Is that something that you're trained to utilize?"

"Yes, it is."

"Officer Braun came at some point, did he not?"

"He did."

"When you and Officer Braun were trying to restrain Mr. Zehm, trying to get him under control, did you give Officer Braun any instructions?"

"I did... I told him, 'Use your baton.'"

"Did you tell him to use the Taser?"

"After the baton didn't work, I said, 'Try and get a choke on him.' That didn't work--he was unable to do that. And then I said, 'Use your Taser.'"

181

"Were you and Officer Braun able to get Mr. Zehm under control by yourselves?"

"The best we could do was to pin him with our body weight."

"And you called for a Code 6... What's a Code 6?"

"Code 6 means basically, 'Help! We need help now!'"

"And did other officers respond?"

"They did, within a couple of minutes... When they got handcuffs on him, I knew my job was done at that point, plus I was totally spent. I was out of gas."

"What did you do?"

"I stood up, I may have briefly told the officers what had happened to me, but I went outside. I needed to get some air... I drank some water. I tried to start breathing normally and deeply..."

"Did you go back into the store?"

"I did. I think I was in and out maybe several times."

"Did officers check on you, see if you were all right?"

"Yes."

"All right. Did you have a discussion with Mr. Moses?"

"I did."

"What discussion did you have with him/'

"He asked me where I hit Mr. Zehm."

"What did you say?"

"I said I hit him wherever I could, except the head."

"Did you hit him in the head?"

"I don't believe I hit him in the head. I never directed a strike to the head. But in that type of fight, with moving bodies, I've been in fights where, unintentionally, the suspect has been hit in the head. I don't believe that happened, but it's possible."

"Sir, you have had training as a hostage negotiator."

"Yes..."

"And as a hostage negotiator, you talk to people, don't you?"

"Absolutely."

"And why didn't you use your skill as a hostage negotiator here?"

"I've been both a SWAT officer and I'm still a hostage negotiator. Probably 98 percent of the time we use our communication skills to be able to resolve situations. The remaining time, you have to know when to be decisive... It is critical that you know how to use action, to use force when you need to."

"Did you think this was one of those times?"

"There's no question it was."

"What were you trying to do, sir, just so we understand?"

"I was trying to control and detain Mr. Zehm so that we could complete the investigation that started with that call."

"Other than commands, did you say anything else to him? Did you cuss at him?"

"No."

"Did you kick him?"

"No."

"Did you punch him?"

"No."

"When you gave your statement, sir, to Miss Ferguson on March 22nd, 2006, why didn't you look at the video?"

"I did not want it to influence my memory. My testimony, I wanted it to be from my memory."

"But you knew there was video?"

"Yes, I knew it when I went into the store that night."

"A minute ago you were talking about striking Mr. Zehm... Did you strike Mr. Zehm for any purpose other than a legitimate law enforcement purpose?"

"Absolutely not."

"There have been issues raised here in this courtroom as to whether or not you talked to Sandra McIntyre that night about the contents of the video. Did you?"

"I talked to her, but not about the video."

"Before this happened, in January of 2006, did you put your name in for police chief?"

"I did have an application in for chief, yes."

"For the City of Spokane, there was a vacancy?"

"Yes."

"Why did you do that?"

"I was asked to do it by fellow officers who actually circulated a petition. I accepted that because, number one, it was an honor to be asked by them. And frequently in administration, I think the field officers are overlooked... They are the ones who provide the services to the citizens."

"Did you ask these officers to come forward and sign a petition on your behalf?"

"No."

"And specifically as part of this...you see that it reads, 'Officer Thompson's professionalism, credentials, law enforcement experience, on-the-job performance, and

183

demeanor have earned him the respect and admiration of his fellow officers.' Do you see that?"

"Yes, sir."

"When you were interviewed by Detective Ferguson, were you giving your best memory, Officer?"

"Yes."

"Did you make up some story in the course of the interview to justify...what occurred here?"

"Absolutely not."

"Did you intend in any way, were you acting for any other purpose in the Zip Trip other than for a law enforcement purpose?"

"No. I was doing my job, my duty, trying to protect people."

CHAPTER SEVENTEEN

Officer Thompson was cross-examined by Timothy Durkin, who initially presented him with the Spokane Police Department's training manual and asked, "Law enforcement officers, they're trained to know what the law is, correct?"

Thompson replied, "Yes," and then verified he had been taught what robbery, theft, and Third Degree Assault constitute.

"You're also taught that a subject, where an officer uses excessive force, has the right to resist."

Thompson answered, "It is my understanding he does not have the right to use violence, use force against an officer, on a Terry stop," which is the brief detention of a person on reasonable suspicion of involvement in criminal activity when probable cause to arrest is lacking.

"If an officer uses excessive force during a Terry stop, a citizen has the right to resist with proportionate force to avoid injury or death... You've been trained in that?"

"I probably have been."

"You just don't recall it at this moment?"

"Not specifically, no."

"Okay. Did you recall it the night of March 18, 2006?"

"Not specifically, no."

"Now, you're taught, trained in the area of Terry stops, correct?"

"Yes, sir."

"And you're taught, are you not, that a Terry stop is an investigative stop."

"That's correct."

"And you're taught that a citizen, when contacted on an investigative stop, has the right to tell the officer, 'No.'"

"Correct."

"Okay, and then you're taught that you can use reasonable force to temporarily detain that subject for further questioning if you have reasonable suspicion that a crime may have been committed."

"Yes...and have, has been, is, or will be committed."

"Okay, but it's just a reasonable suspicion that a crime is being or may have been committed, correct?"

"Correct."

"Now, misdemeanor theft, you're taught that the elements of misdemeanor theft, what they are, correct?"

"Yes."

"And misdemeanor theft is the taking of money that is not your own under the amount of $1,500."

"$2,250."

"You have an understanding based on your training that the amount of money for a...gross misdemeanor theft has to be...under what amount?"

"What I'm certain about, you mentioned the $1,500 figure... That is a felony amount."

"So, below $1,500 is a gross misdemeanor amount?"

"That's why I carry a small digest just like we have here on the desk, and I refer to that for the dollar figure."

"Okay, and how much money in 2006 could you get out of an ATM?"

"I didn't know, sir. I didn't use an ATM then."

"You had no training in what the limitations are in an ATM in 2006?"

"No, I did not."

"Okay. So, you just assumed that it could be felony theft of more than 1,500 bucks in 2006 from an ATM?"

"I assumed that it could be theft or a second degree robbery."

"Okay, but you didn't describe it as a second degree robbery in your recorded statement, did you?"

"My word was 'premature robbery attempt'."

"And it wasn't 'premature robbery attempt'. It was 'a premature possible robbery'."

"That's correct."

"Now, you've provided significantly more details today about your subjective recall of the events of March 18th, 2006, than you did back on March 22nd, 2006, is that correct?"

"I answered the questions of the interview. That's what I was responding to. I have answered the questions posed here."

"And you provided a lot more detail here today than you did back in 2006, March 22nd."

"I...I'm not sure I could agree with that. I had an extensive interview."

"And in fact, you had an extensive pre-interview, correct?"

"Yes."

"Approximately two and a half hours before you had your second interview?"

"I don't remember the exact time, but it may have been several hours."

"And that was four days after the incident."

"Yes."

"And would you agree with me that your recollection of the events as they occurred was probably more accurate back on March 22nd, 2006, than they are today?"

"They were certainly more vivid and...much more emotional."

"You haven't given any statement, public statement or corrected statement, about the interview information you provided on March 22nd, 2006, until your testimony here today, have you?"

"That's correct."

"And that's five years and seven months by my short calculation, is that about right?"

"Yes, sir."

Referring to the Police Department's training manual, Durkin asked, "Are you familiar if the ethical standards are reflected in...canons?"

Thompson answered, "Yes."

"And these canons, do they reflect that officers are to ascribe to the highest level of integrity and honesty?"

"Yes."

Durkin then presented him with a document and asked, "Could this document be part of your training file?"

"It could have been."

"In the course of your training, are you taught that violations of civil rights are within the jurisdiction of the FBI?"

"Sure."

Officer Thompson was asked to read a segment of his recorded interview, "Ferguson: Why did you run into the building? Thompson: I was already formulating, uh, plans as I normally do and as we're trained to do, that if the suspect had seen me, I knew from the layout of the business that he had at least two other exits, um, one facing Division and one facing, uh, I believe it's Spofford on the south side. So I had to be prepared, number one, if he had seen me, if he was going to flee from me and we were going to have a foot pursuit, So that's the reason initially I was trying to close distance by catching up to him inside the store."

Durkin asked, "Now in your recorded statement, unlike today, you didn't say that you were running into the store to save two little girls from being kidnapped?"

"Well, I was aware, I was aware of bystanders...and they were part of the formulation."

"Did you say you were worried about them being kidnapped on March 22, 2006?"

"Well, that's an extension of my concern for them, certainly, from my experience."

"It is your extension that you're making here today. You didn't make it back in 2006, did you?"

"I'm answering your questions, sir. I was answering Detective Ferguson's questions then."

"You indicated that the reason you initially tried to close was to prevent him from fleeing."

"That is correct."

"And you saw him enter the store."

"Yes."

"And you saw him walk through the store."

"Yes...and I lost sight of him."

"And you lost sight of him but regained sight of him, didn't you?"

"Yes."

"Rather quickly?"

"Yes."

"And he was not fleeing?"

"No."

Durkin then inquired about the representation provided to Officer Thompson after the incident and for his interview. "Guild representation was there to make sure that you were not unfairly, according to the guild's contract with the City of Spokane, questioned that very night about what had happened, correct?"

"Among other things, sir."

"Is that one of them?"

"Yes, sir."

"Okay. And the other thing is that, pursuant to the contract that the guild has, you, unlike ordinary citizens, were granted...a minimum of 48 hours before you could be interviewed."

"Yes, sir."

"And in this case, it was almost 96 hours."

"Yes, sir."

Returning to the recorded interview, Durkin next had the officer read, "When I stopped and, as I said, I believe I was about four feet from him, uh, the baton would have been in a... cocked position...that if I do have to strike with the baton, it is ready to go."

Durkin asked, "And when you give verbal commands, that's very, very important in terms of your continuum of force, isn't it?"

"If you're allowed to, if the situation allows you to give commands, yes."

"Okay. And you say you gave commands in this instance."

"Quickly, but yes, I did."

"Yeah. And you say the subject responded quickly as well."

"That's correct, he did."

"And the commands you gave, according to your statement, were, 'Drop the pop!'"

"No...I said, 'Drop the bottle,' or, 'Drop it now!' And then I said, 'Do it now!'"

"Okay...you said that Mr. Zehm had turned towards you and was holding that pop in a position of aggress...a very common term in describing a subject that's taking a position where they could be aggressive towards you... Is that an accurate description of what you provided in your March 22nd statement?"

"Yes, yes, it is."

"And you said that while the subject was holding that, he looked at you and said, 'Why?'"

"Yes."

"You received that response, cognitively processed it, and then responded as well by saying, 'Drop it now!'"

"'Do it now!' Yes."

"Okay."

"'Drop it now!'"

"And you articulated, and in describing the subject, Mr. Zehm, as then saying, 'No.'"

"Correct. Except this took place within a couple of seconds."

"You stated you're familiar with reaction time, correct?"

"Yes."

189

"And you described it as being approximately .75 seconds."

"It is."

"So when you ran up on Mr. Zehm and you had a position of ready strike and you initiated your verbal command, that's when the clock starts ticking, correct?"

"No, sir...I don't believe so."

"That's not part of the two seconds...of this verbal exchange that you had with Mr. Zehm?"

"Can I explain?"

"Go ahead."

"In my statement I think I said that I came up to within four feet, gave him commands, his refusals, and then I made the strike. I think that is one of the time distortion errors that I made in my report because, after when I did see the videotape, I recognized that my training is that when we see a threat, we immediately address it. If you can do it verbally, that's what you start doing. And everything I did here, because of the time compression, was based on experience and training. This happened so quickly that you're not thinking your way through it. This was not a conversation. These were commands, refusals. I already had schemas knowing what options I had."

"Did you tell the SPD investigators that this was a time distortion, you know, 'I made something wrong, I think I miscalculated in terms of describing...the conversations and commands that I gave to the subject, Mr. Zehm'?"

"I was trying to be as precise and accurate as possible with the questions asked of me. I made some errors in there as far as accuracy and from watching the video in this court, I've recognized that."

"Would you agree with me, Mr. Thompson, that every one of your errors seems to help justify the immediate use of force that you deployed on Mr. Zehm?"

"I don't agree with how you're presenting that. No, I don't."

Special Agent Jaangard played portions of the videotape and Durkin asked, "Could you please tell me in that sequence where you see Otto Zehm turn around and see you coming through the door for him?"

"I never said that, sir."

"You never said that he turned around and saw you coming in the door?"

"I believe my testimony was when he was outside, he looked in my direction."

"So it is your testimony here today that you never described Otto Zehm as having looked and turned around to see you as you were coming through the door of the Zip Trip?"

"I don't believe so."

Agent Jangaard displayed a portion of the officer's recorded statement and Durkin asked, "Do you recognize that portion of your statement of March 22nd, 2006?"

"Yes, I do."

"And did you describe Otto Zehm as having turned around and looked at you as you were coming in the door just before he grabbed something?"

"Yes, sir, and that's in error."

"Could you describe for me where those verbal commands are that you stopped to a distance of four feet and exchanged with the subject, Mr. Zehm?"

"After reviewing the video...as soon as I saw him when he turned around with that bottle is when I would have started giving commands."

"You would agree with me that in that photograph...Mr. Zehm is looking in a southerly direction away from you, correct?"

"He does appear to be looking south."

"And you haven't turned the end of the aisle yet, have you?"

"No."

"However, we can see, can we not, your baton in a ready strike position on your right?"

"In a ready position, ready position, yes."

"And if we could continue on, then... That photograph shows him turning toward you...and would you agree with me that you are rounding the corner?"

"Yes."

"And this is when you started barking your commands?"

"When he turned around with the bottle, when I recognized the position of the bottle, is when I started."

"Okay. Let's talk about recognition for a second, since you're familiar with perception-reaction time. You indicated three-quarters of a second is your average perception-reaction time, is that correct?"

"That was my understanding, yes."

After displaying more photographs, Durkin asked, "Does that reflect the first baton strike that you delivered to Mr. Zehm?"

"I believe frame 71 accurately depicts the first strike."

"Impact of the first strike?"

"Yes."

"Would you agree with me that Mr. Zehm is moving backwards the entire time?"

"He is moving backwards."

"Do you recall your description of Mr. Zehm's fixed position and holding a pop bottle in a defiant, resolute, fixed state in a threatening manner towards you?"

"Yes, sir, I do."

"And what you have just seen...is inconsistent with those descriptions."

"No, sir, no, sir, it's not."

"What you see on the video is consistent with the way that you described it in your recorded statement?"

"It's not inconsistent."

"Fair enough." Durkin returned to the recorded statement and asked, "This is a discussion after your first baton strike, correct?"

"Yes."

"Could you read that for the jury?"

"Sure. 'Thompson: He immediately pivoted to his right. He didn't drop the bottle...and he was turning away from me. I grabbed the back, probably the collar of his jacket which was the easiest thing to grab, and pulled myself in closer, and at this point he is...pivoting and moving to the right... I delivered another strike to his right leg."

Durkin returned to the video and asked, "Do you see the long black cylindrical object?"

"Vertical, is that what you're referring to? Yes, I do see that."

"And now we see Mr. Zehm on the floor in front of the kiosk, would you agree with me?"

"Yes."

"He's on the floor, but he's still facing up towards you, correct?"

"I believe so."

"He was facing you when you hit him the first time, and now he's facing you when he's on the ground a second later, correct?"

"That's correct."

"Do you see a Pepsi-looking object in the hands of Mr. Zehm there, just to the right of your baton?"

After viewing several images Thompson answered, "Yeah, I, I think that's probably the bottle, yeah."

"And Mr. Zehm seems to be holding that bottle in a fairly steady position. He's moving it back and forth, but he's not jousting with it, is he?"

"He was moving the bottle."

"He was moving the bottle, but he wasn't jousting it towards you?"

"He was moving it more laterally."

The video was advanced, and Durkin asked, "Now you're over the top of him, right? Is this the straddle position you described earlier?"

"I believe so."

"Could you describe for me where you fell on top of Mr. Zehm and he threw two punches at you?"

"I never said I fell on him."

"You said you went down on top of him?"

"I said I went down, but I did not say I fell on him."

"Your testimony earlier is that when Mr. Zehm went down, you went down on top of him and he took two punches at you."

"That's correct."

"Where...are those two punches that you described Mr. Zehm throwing at you in an assaultive manner?"

"It's likely there."

Durkin presented another camera angle of this exact time and asked, "Do you see the pop bottle, Mr. Thompson?"

"I see what I think may be a pop bottle."

"Okay. And do you see the hands of Mr. Zehm on both sides of that pop bottle?"

"Yes, sir, I do."

"Now you're standing over Mr. Zehm, correct? You're straddling him?"

"Yes, sir."

"Okay. Why don't we stop right there... Where are the two punches that you described being thrown by Mr. Zehm at your face that caused you to jump back away from him?"

"You can't see his upper torso completely and it's not...displayed in the frame."

The video was advanced and Durkin asked, "And now you're about to pull your Taser, correct, to fire the probes from a distance you described of three feet?"

"Approximately three feet."

"And under your training, you're not allowed to fire a Taser at anybody that is not actively assaultive or about to be assaultive."

"That's a general rule."

"That's a generally accurate rule?"

"Yes, sir, yes, sir, it is."

"And holding a pop bottle in front of...one's head, are you telling the ladies and gentlemen of the jury that you interpreted that to be assaultive?"

"Yes, sir, one of many actions that...this is a continuum. It is not isolated. Actions have occurred in the totality of everything that is happening."

"The reasons why, one of the reasons why you pulled the Taser was your description of Mr. Zehm as taking two punches at your face immediately before?"

"Yes, sir, that is correct."

"Now, Officer Thompson, describe for me in the videotape where you fell down on Mr. Zehm, or went down on top of him, excuse me."

A section of the videotape was replayed, and Thompson indicated, "That's the down position that I believe I was describing."

"That's the down position? You would agree with me that you're standing straddling Mr. Zehm, correct?"

"Correct."

"Let's take a look at the time stamp... You were straddling Mr. Zehm from 1826:16 until 1826:32, correct?"

"Okay."

"And you're a seasoned officer, correct?"

"Yes."

"You've got 42 years of experience."

"Yes."

"You thought this gentleman...was a premature robbery attempt suspect."

"Certainly could be, and that's how I was approaching this."

"And you thought he may still be armed. He was wearing a long black leather coat."

"He could be, yes."

"And you stood over him with the most vulnerable part of your body exposed for 16 seconds?"

"That's correct."

194

"A seasoned, professional officer would not do that, would they, if they thought that person presented a true threat to their self?"

"A good officer would do everything they reasonably could to protect other people in that store. Maintaining that close proximity was the best way to do that."

"And you described him after your first baton strike as having pivoted, do you recall that description?"

"I do, yes."

"And having pivoted away from you, and you grabbing the back of his leather jacket."

"I do."

"And you described the second baton strike as, since he's facing away from you, as being delivered to the right upper thigh, correct?"

"That's correct."

Referring to two different camera angles of the first part of the encounter, Durkin asked, "But could you show me where Mr. Zehm pivots, turns away from you, and you deliver a baton strike to his thigh?"

"No, sir, it's covered...there's areas that are covered in there. It's not on the videotape."

"What happened would have had to happen within one second."

"Believe me, it was quick."

"Okay. Between camera one where we see the baton going up, Mr. Zehm backing away from you, until camera four where he's on the ground is approximately one second."

"Again, I'll take your word for it."

"And in that one second it doesn't appear that Mr. Zehm turns away from you at all, does it, according to the camera angles?"

"The cameras do not give continuous full coverage throughout the store, and that was one of my surprises... In fact, one of the sergeants there later on while I was still at the store, I said, because he had gone back and he was reviewing the video, and I said, 'Does it show him punching me?' And he said, 'No.' And I said, 'Oh, shit.' I didn't know all of the coverages there, but I was confident that this was going to fully document what had happened there. What I have learned since then is that there is not full coverage. There are areas that are blocked in there, that you cannot see everything."

"You would agree with me that cameras one and four do not show...you delivering a thigh strike, correct."

"Correct."

"You would agree that camera one does capture the baton in an elevated position."

"Correct."

"Okay. And the width of the aisle is approximately forty and one-half inches, correct?"

"I...you know, within four feet?"

"Okay, shorter than four feet. Like three and a half feet, correct?"

"Um, I believe so."

"Okay. And that's a very tight area as you described previously."

"It is."

"You previously stated that you delivered nothing but diagonal baton strikes to Mr. Zehm that night."

"That was my recollection, yes."

"And so you took a baton strike grabbing Mr. Zehm's top of the back of his leather coat and delivered a diagonal strike to his right thigh in a forty and one-half inch aisle with a 29-inch baton?"

"I did."

"All right. You would agree that cameras number one and four do not show you thrashing into the shelves with Mr. Zehm."

"That is correct."

"Okay. You would agree with me that cameras one and four do not show you standing, getting away from further boxing blows to your chest by Mr. Zehm while he's on the ground."

"That is correct."

"Mr. Zehm still swinging his fists at you while you activate your Taser is not captured by camera four."

"No, sir, I can't say that."

"You can't say that it isn't captured or you agree with me that camera four does not capture your description of Mr. Zehm?"

"It doesn't capture my description."

"You agree with me that cameras one and four do not capture Mr. Zehm standing there boxing, throwing punches at you in that aisle as you're coming up towards the kiosk."

"I agree that they did not capture that, yes."

Durkin had Officer Thompson read the segment of his recorded interview in which he described Zehm standing and throwing punches at him for the second time, after the first Taser deployment. Then he presented video of the officer's repeated baton strikes to Zehm while he was on the floor, acknowledged by Officer Thompson, and asked, "Sir, would you agree with me that the description of Mr. Zehm standing and boxing as you described it is not reflected in the security cameras of the Zip Trip."

"The...yes, the shelves block the view."

"So you would agree with me it's not reflected in this security video of the Zip Trip."

"That's correct."

Then Officer Thompson was asked to review a number of photographs taken of him right after the incident. Thompson agreed that the only outward sign of injury seen was a scuff on his left knee. After he identified his two-way radio microphone on the right shoulder of his uniform, Durkin asked, "And we've seen photographs wherein you're delivering baton strikes where that microphone is flopping back and forth, correct?"

"Correct."

"Now, the night of the incident when Sergeant Torok contacted you about possible injuries, you told him you thought that Mr. Zehm might have hit you."

"I was pretty adamant that I was hit. That was not a question in my mind."

"Sir, on the night of the incident, you didn't know what you were hit with, did you?"

"Not correct."

"Okay. It could have been your two-way radio that struck you on the right upper brow, couldn't it have?"

"I know that at least fists unequivocally hit me in the chest. I may have been kicked. As far as the radio, yeah, it's dangling and it could have hit me. But I guarantee you, to the day I die, I know I was hit with fists."

Officer Thompson acknowledged that he learned of the lunge statement by Chief Nicks the day following the incident, well before he gave his recorded statement to Detective Ferguson. Durkin asked, "And yet, at the time of your statement on March 22nd, 2006, there's no discussion whatsoever about the lunge issue."

"It's not in the statement. No, I didn't include it. I responded to the questions that were posed to me... That is the protocol for this type of statement."

"Didn't she offer you the opportunity at the very end, 'Is there anything else that you would like to bring up that I have failed to address?'"

"Yes."

At the end of his cross-examination Durkin said, "You would agree with me, Officer Thompson, that there are material inaccuracies in your statement and report of what occurred on March 18th, 2006."

"Yes, there are some errors."

"And you would agree with me that your assaultive description of Mr. Zehm, in terms of throwing punches, in terms of boxing, is not supported by the...store's security video."

"The answer would be no to that."

Then Oreskovich asked additional questions. "Now you had...told us at various points and times about what your memory is. Is that correct, sir?"

"Yes."

"Do you recall that Mr. Schott said that Mr. Zehm was out of the video for 49 seconds?"

"Yes."

"Were you continuing over that 49-second period to continue to try to control Mr. Zehm?"

"Yes, I was."

"Were you struggling during that time period?"

"Yes."

"Is it possible, Officer Thompson, that you've got some of this out of order?"

"Yes, the sequence, some of the sequences."

"Did you do that intentionally? Were you trying to lie to anybody on March 22nd?"

"No."

"One more time, officer. When you went into the Zip Trip, were you using your force for any reason other than a law enforcement purpose?"

"No."

"When...you were interviewed by the detective voluntarily on March 22nd, were you giving her your best recollection as you knew them?"

"Yes."

CHAPTER EIGHTEEN

The last witness was Joseph Callanan, called by the prosecution to rebut the testimony of Officer Preuninger and Detective Bowman. Mr. Callanan had extensive experience in the field of law enforcement tactics in high risk situations and had authored a number of articles concerning the use of force.

Prosecutor Aine Ahmed asked, "Did you hear Mr. Preuninger talk about the facts he assumed in terms of his methodology as to his opinion that Officer Thompson acted properly in approaching the store?"

"I did. Yes, I did."

"And do you agree with his methodology?"

"The methodology that was apparent in the testimony was that the witness assumed the facts presented by the officer and the department and deselected other facts that were available, and that is not proper methodology for an expert. In this exact case, you have at least two versions of the same event..."

"In terms of Mr. Preuninger's methodology, when you say he assumed facts, can you go into specifics about that?"

"I remember exactly that he testified...that he reviewed the CAD and the broadcast information, and...he put the classification on it of 'robbery.' And that is a huge leap in logic or a great extension of the worst-case scenario and seemingly divorces from a more innocent explanation of something that happened back at the ATM, something yet to be fully resolved. But the idea that it's 'a felony' such as a robbery is, to me, premature."

"Can you tell us why you disagree?"

"It's a serial idea of thought, and that is that the assumption is that it's a robbery. Later that assumption gets to, this is a hostage taker, the people are going to be kidnapped. The point I'm trying to make is that you take some raw information that's not yet tested or verified and you go to the extreme worst-case scenario, and from that you back up and justify what I would say is very poor police procedure... I accept that all of us would agree that the police would stop and detain Mr. Zehm. I do not agree that you would rush Mr. Zehm and forcefully take him into custody without some other things occurring. I draw particular attention to the entry attributed to Officer Thompson and videotaped, to...Officer Braun, who testifies about a safe approach, looking inside, even selecting a different door to protect a weapon. There you have good policemanship. Opening a door, running in within a matter of split seconds, drawing a baton, transferring it to the strong hand, closing on a subject essentially whose back is facing you, is very poor policemanship."

Callanan criticized Officer Thompson for closing distance on a suspect he was worried had a weapon without backup when bystanders were around, misinterpreting the danger of the pop bottle, continuing baton strikes to a subject lying on the ground, and justifying his use of force by subtle body language cues.

When questioned by defense attorney Stephen Lamberson, Callanan agreed that a Terry stop was justified under the circumstances. Then Lamberson asked, "You had a lot more information to evaluate than Officer Thompson had when he entered the store, correct, sir?"

"That's clearly true, sir."

"And you weren't there?"

"No, I wasn't."

"You didn't see Mr. Zehm's face?"

"No."

"You didn't see his eyes?"

"No."

*

All testimony heard, Judge Van Sickle listened to presentations from the attorneys concerning the matters to be mentioned in the closing arguments. He ruled that connecting Zehm's paycheck with the events that occurred at the ATM would not be appropriate but that the pop bottle statement and the candy bar testimony would be allowed. Then he reconvened the jury and said, "Now that you have heard the evidence, it becomes my duty to give you the instructions of the Court as to the law applicable to this case. It is your duty to determine the facts in this case from the evidence produced in court. It is also your duty to accept the

200

law from the Court, regardless of what you personally believe the law is or ought to be. You are to apply the law to the facts and, in this way, decide the case.

"The evidence you are to consider consists of the testimony of the witnesses and the exhibits admitted into evidence. It has been my duty to rule on the admissibility of evidence. You must not concern yourselves with the reasons for these rulings. You will disregard any evidence which either was not admitted or which was stricken by the Court... Counsel's remarks, statements, and arguments are intended to help you understand the evidence and apply the law. They are not evidence, however, and you should disregard any remark, statement or argument that is not supported by the evidence or the law as given to you by the Court."

He explained that Officer Thompson was charged with committing two crimes, each a separate count in the indictment, that he pleaded not guilty, and that he "is presumed innocent of a crime unless and until proven guilty beyond a reasonable doubt, ...doubt based upon reason and common sense and...not purely on speculation. Reasonable doubt may arise from a careful and impartial consideration of all of the evidence or from lack of evidence. It is not required that the government prove guilt beyond all possible doubt. Proof beyond reasonable doubt is doubt which leaves you firmly convinced that the defendant is guilty." He reminded them that they must decide each count separately and that their verdict on one count should not control their verdict on the other. He specified, "There is no allegation that defendant caused or contributed to the death of Otto Zehm. The cause of death is not an issue for you to consider in this case.

"In order for you to find the defendant guilty of Count I, the government must prove beyond a reasonable doubt:

- The defendant was acting under color of law when he committed the acts charged in Count I,

- The defendant deprived Otto Zehm of a right that is established by the Fourth Amendment to the Constitution, namely, the right to be free from objectively unreasonable force,

- The defendant acted willfully, and

- The defendant's conduct resulted in bodily injury to Mr. Zehm.

"A police officer may temporarily stop and briefly question a person whom he reasonably suspects has committed a crime. Reasonable suspicion is formed by specific, articulable facts which, together with objective and reasonable inferences, form the basis for suspecting that a particular person is engaged in criminal activity... When reasonably necessary, a police officer may use force in order to stop a suspect and question him. A police officer violates the Fourth Amendment if he uses objectively unreasonable force during a stop.

"Whether an officer acted in an objectively reasonable manner during an investigatory stop must be judged from the perspective of an objective officer on the scene rather than from the 20/20 vision of hindsight. The issue is whether an officer's actions were objectively reasonable in light of the facts and circumstances that were confronting him, including the severity of the crime the officer was investigating, whether the suspect posed an immediate threat to the safety of the officer or others, and whether the suspect actively resisted the officer's attempt to detain him or attempted to evade detention by fleeing. A person is entitled to defend himself against the immediate use of objectively unreasonable force by a police officer. However, the person may use no more force than appears reasonably necessary under the circumstances.

"'Willfully,' means that the defendant acted voluntarily and intentionally, with the intent not only to act with bad or evil purpose, but specifically to act with the intent to deprive Otto Zehm of a right that is made definitive by the Constitution. To find that the defendant acted willfully, you must find that the defendant not only had a generally bad or evil purpose, but also that the defendant has the specific intent to deprive Mr. Zehm of his Fourth Amendment right to be free from objectively unreasonable force. This does not mean that the government must show that the defendant acted with knowledge of the particular provisions of the Fourth Amendment to the Constitution, or that the defendant was even thinking about the Fourth Amendment when he acted.

"One may be said to act willfully if he acts in open defiance or in reckless disregard of a known and definite constitutional right, in this case, the right to be free from objectively unreasonable force. This specific intent to deprive another of a constitutional right need not be expressed. It may at times be reasonably inferred from the surrounding circumstances of the act. Thus, you may look at the defendant's words, experience, knowledge, acts, and other results in order to decide the issue of willfulness.

"If you find the defendant had that purpose...then the defendant acted willfully. By contrast, if you find the defendant acted through mistake, carelessness, or accident, then he did not act willfully.

"The government alleges a number of the defendant's acts of force were unlawful. In order for you to find the defendant guilty of Count I, you must unanimously agree upon at least one of the specific acts of force alleged by the government, and you must agree that the specific act of force was unlawful as defined by these instructions.

"In order for you to find the defendant guilty of Count II, the government must prove each of the following elements beyond a reasonable doubt:

- The defendant knowingly made a false entry into a record or document, and

- The defendant did so with the intent to impede, obstruct, or influence the investigation of a matter within the jurisdiction of the Federal Bureau of Investigation.

"The use of objectively unreasonable force by police officers is a matter within the jurisdiction of the Federal Bureau of Investigation.

"The government alleges the defendant knowingly made a number of false entries in a record and document. In order for you to find the defendant guilty of Count II, you must unanimously agree upon at least one of the specific entries alleged by the government, and you must unanimously agree that the specific entry was unlawful as defined by these instructions.

"You are here only to determine whether the defendant is guilty or not of the charges in the indictment... It is for you to decide how much weight to give to any evidence. While you are to consider only the evidence in the case, you are not limited to the literal statements of the witnesses. You are permitted to conclude from the facts which you find have been proven, such reasonable inferences as seem justified by reason and common sense.

"You may have to decide which testimony to believe and which testimony not to believe. You may believe everything a witness says, or part of it, or none of it. In considering the testimony of any witness, you may take into account:

- The witness' opportunity and ability to see or hear or know the things testified to,

- The witness' memory,

- The witness' manner while testifying,

- The witness' interest in the outcome of the case, if any,

- The witness' bias or prejudice, if any,

- Whether other evidence contradicted the witness' testimony,

- The reasonableness of the witness' testimony in light of all the evidence,

- Any other factors that bear on believability.

"The weight of the evidence as to a fact does not necessarily depend on the number of witnesses who testify. What is important is how believable the witnesses were and how much weight you think their testimony deserves.

"You have heard testimony from persons who, because of education or experience, are permitted to state opinions and the reasons for their opinions. Opinion testimony should be judged just like any other testimony. You may accept it or reject it, and give it as much weight as you think it deserves considering the witness' education and experience, the reasons given for the opinion, and all other evidence in the case.

"The defendant has testified. You should treat this testimony just as you would the testimony of any other witness.

"The law does not permit jurors to be governed by sympathy, prejudice, or public opinion. The accused, as the public, expect that you will carefully and impartially consider all the evidence, following the law as stated by the Court, and reach a just verdict regardless of the consequences... The punishment provided by law for this crime is for the Court to decide. You may not consider punishment in deciding whether the government has proved its case against the defendant beyond a reasonable doubt.

"Each of you must decide the case for yourself, but you should do so only after a discussion and consideration of the case with other jurors. Remember at all times that you are not partisans. You are judges, judges of the facts. Your sole interest is to seek the truth from the evidence in the case...

"A verdict must represent the considered judgment of each juror. In order to return a verdict with respect to a count, it is necessary that each juror agree thereto. Your verdict with respect to each count must be unanimous..."

Having completed his instructions to the jury, Judge Van Sickle directed Mr. Boutros to begin the closing arguments.

CHAPTER NINETEEN

"As you learned during the course of this case, the victim's name is Otto Zehm, and he was 36 years old... On March 18th, 2006, Mr. Zehm walked into a local Zip Trip as he had many nights before...casually walked over to the soda display and, as he had so many nights before, he picked up a 2-liter plastic bottle of Pepsi.

"But the defendant made sure that March 18th, 2006, would not be a night like any of the others before it. As Mr. Zehm turned toward the candy aisle, his nightly routine was cut short...when he saw the defendant rapidly approaching him with his baton overhead and absorbed multiple blows toward the head by the defendant with his baton. Mr. Zehm suddenly found himself on the floor...with the officer who had just struck him with no explanation standing over him still holding the baton... The only thing between Mr. Zehm's face and the defendant's baton was that 2-liter bottle of Pepsi he had picked up moments before. After the series of sudden, unanticipated, and unexplained baton strikes, Mr. Zehm had every reason to believe that if he discarded the plastic pop bottle he was using to protect his face and head, the defendant would strike him again...

"Mr. Zehm was entitled to defend himself against the immediate use of objectively unreasonable force by a police officer... And you recall from the video that the defendant stood over Mr. Zehm with his legs spread apart for about 15 seconds... Mr. Zehm had the right to resist the defendant's attack on him, but he didn't choose to exercise that right. If he had wanted to deliver a swift kick to the groin and disable the defendant, he could have done so. But he didn't. He lay on the floor with that plastic 2-liter pop bottle covering and protecting his face...

"Your job as jurors now is to take the evidence you've received and decide whether that evidence proves that the defendant is guilty of the charges.

"There are two counts in the indictment... The first is an unreasonable force charge, and the second is an obstruction charge... What the first charge amounts to is that the defendant willfully used unnecessary or unreasonable force against Mr. Zehm at some point that night. The second count...charges the defendant with knowingly making a false entry in a record with the intent to obstruct, impede, and/or influence the proper administration of a matter within the jurisdiction of the FBI. Basically, it alleges that the defendant lied about what happened in his recorded interview on March 22nd, 2006, to keep the truth about his unnecessary or excessive force from being exposed.

"Let's start with the unreasonable force charge... The issue is whether the officer's actions were objectively reasonable in light of the facts and circumstances that were confronting him... There's a couple of factors that the judge asked you to consider under the law. The first is the severity of the crime... You learned about the severity of the crime being investigated and that there was no crime... It was a suspicious circumstances report... The teenagers were not sure whether they canceled their transaction before they pulled away from the ATM and thought the man may have taken their money...The defendant overheard a dispatcher give this information on his police radio, and he pulled up that live report on his computer... The CAD classified this as a suspicious circumstances call... And the evidence in this case showed you that there was no reason to think that this suspicious circumstances call represented an especially tense or dangerous situation. Nothing in the report said that the man at the ATM had done anything violent. Nothing in the report said that he had threatened anyone. Nothing in the report said that he had any weapon...or had threatened to use a weapon.

"In addition, you learned that...errors in the live report were constantly being corrected. Do you remember first the report said that the teenagers left their ATM card in the machine, but it came out later that they had their ATM card after all. First it was reported that the man at the ATM had blond hair. Then it came out that, no, he actually had red hair. First it was reported that the man at the machine had their money. Then it came out that the teenagers were not entirely positive that he had their money after all. The CAD report also showed that two officers had already been assigned to...respond to the Zip Trip.

"This was all the information that the defendant possessed as he approached Mr. Zehm that night.

Nevertheless, the defendant chose to rush into the Zip Trip and attack Mr. Zehm rather than wait another 20 seconds for the originally assigned officer, Officer Braun, to join him so that they could talk to Mr. Zehm together. Contrary to his training, he did not calmly approach Mr. Zehm, stop, and tell him, 'Hey, I need to ask you a few questions about what you were doing at the ATM.' In .fact, the defendant never explained to Mr. Zehm why he was there, nor ever mentioned the ATM to Mr. Zehm at all. He decided to...strike first and ask questions later...

"This is not a murder...a rape...a bank robbery...a guy firing weapons at cops. It's just a suspicious circumstance...that needs an officer to go and figure out what's going on... One other point that is critical for you to understand about the seriousness of the crime...is that in his statement the defendant himself basically tells you it doesn't matter... 'The single reason I hit him with the stick is...I thought I was about to be attacked, and I was going (to) preempt that and try to gain some tactical advantage.' He says the single reason he hit him with the stick was because...he claims that Mr. Zehm was holding the pop bottle and because of his supposed response to the defendant's alleged commands. That's it, not the seriousness of the crime...

"After you look at the severity of the crime that the officer was investigating, you've got to look at whether the suspect posed an immediate threat to the safety of the officer or others and whether the suspect actively resisted the officer's attempt to detain him or to evade detention by fleeing. That's really what the unreasonable force prong amounts to, and I want us to look at that together. Specifically, I want to talk about all the different ways you can find him guilty of Count I.

"If you find that the defendant willfully struck Mr. Zehm in the head, then you can find him guilty of Count I. Everyone in this case has...agreed that deadly force was not authorized...and a willful strike to the head is deadly force. And there's quite a bit of evidence that he hit him in the head. You recall the testimony of the eyewitnesses... You also had the testimony of Dr. Smith...the only radiologist you heard from...and he told you that Dr. Aiken was right about the injuries, the subgaleal hematomas to the head and the brow ridge. And he said, in the clinical context, the cause of those injuries was the baton.

"The...most powerful piece of evidence perhaps, about strikes to the head and neck, is the AMR report... Mike Stussi, the paramedic, and Aaron Jaramillo, his EMT...both told you and even showed you on the video where the conversation occurred with Officer Moses. And they told you...they needed to understand why he was in such bad shape, what caused his injuries. So they asked Officer Moses what had happened as Mr. Zehm was crashing on the floor, and... Officer Moses told them the truth. He said, 'Well, he's been hit in the head, neck, and upper torso with a baton...' And...do you recall in the video he was even using his hand to show vertical strikes?

"The judge talked to you about evaluating credibility. Evaluate their credibility. They have no incentive to lie. They're trying to treat Mr. Zehm, who's in bad shape, and they recorded what they had learned from Mr. Moses in their AMR report that same night.

"You recall that Mr. Moses, when he was in the...secrecy of the Grand Jury, he told the truth, too. He told you he learned from the defendant that Mr. Zehm had been struck in the head, neck, and upper torso during a venting session... And then 10 months later, after the Grand Jury transcript was released to the defense, the defense summoned him to the office and had a conversation with him. And shortly after that conversation he began to say that he didn't recall virtually anything that he testified to in Grand Jury. He couldn't remember it any longer...

"Evaluate his credibility...recall what he said... He described calling the defendant and asking for permission to meet with Special Agent Stanley Meador. But he told you he didn't want to meet with Special Agent Meador unless he could do so by a loud railroad...in case Special Agent Meador was recording him... Why would you be worried about being recorded if you're just telling the truth? And how else do you know that Officer Moses actually told the truth in Grand Jury and not on the stand? Because he was exactly right about the injuries... There were, in fact, blows to the head, neck, and upper torso. That was not a coincidence...because he had a good source, the only source on the scene who knew where those baton strikes had been delivered, the defendant.

"The defendant's story on the stand and Moses' story on the stand make no sense. The defendant says, 'Oh, I just told Moses that I hit him all over, except for the head. How

209

would you go from that to Moses telling the AMR people...he was hit specifically in the head, neck, and upper torso? ...Maybe if it were the other way around, maybe if the defendant said, 'I hit him in the head, neck, and upper torso,' and Moses said, 'Oh, he hit him all over,' maybe that would be believable. But you don't go from the general...to the specific... and magically turn out to be exactly right about those injuries.

"So you know, based on the evidence in this case, that the defendant willfully hit Mr. Zehm in the head... And then four days later he goes and does his official interview and denies it altogether. He says, 'I hit him everywhere except the head.' So, if you find that the defendant willfully hit him in the head or neck, you can find him guilty of Count I. But that's not the only way... If you find the first baton strike that he delivered was unreasonable, then you find him guilty of Count I.

"You know that the first baton strike was unreasonable for lots of reasons. One, you know that it was too fast. He knew from his training that he wasn't supposed to rush up on a suspect and strike someone who's backing away from him... That's why the defendant had to come up with the 'lunge' lie. He knew from his training that he had to have someone being aggressive, not egressive, in order to hit him with a baton. And what does the video show? ...The video evidence proves that what Mr. Zehm was doing was just being egressive. He was doing exactly what your common sense would tell you if a police officer started running at you with a baton held high overhead- he's backpedaling from the strikes.

"And you recall the testimony of the Balows? They actually saw his face just prior to that first strike, and they saw a look of surprise and shock... What did the defendant say? ...Once he knew the 'lunge' lie wasn't going to work, he shifted gears, and he had to come up with something that wouldn't be impeached by the video... He talked about his eyes being fixed, his lips being set, the jaw being clenched, about seeing through his leather jacket that his shoulder muscles were actually tensed... He talked about how he held the pop bottle, that he turned and adopted that aggressive stance with one foot in front of the other, holding the pop bottle horizontally in what he called a loaded position...

"You know that Mr. Zehm had a look of surprise on his face, that he didn't take a fixed position, that he was backing up the whole time. And you also know it's a lie because you recall the defendant said that as he turned toward him, he had a face that displayed no fear or confusion... But do you remember the testimony about...the last conscious words of Mr. Zehm's life? ...His last words were, 'All I wanted was a Snickers.' He was confused until the very end. He never understood why he had been attacked. He was thinking back to what he was doing at the moment of that first baton strike as he turned toward the candy aisle of the store. And yet the defendant would have you believe that this man...somehow showed no signs of fear or confusion as the defendant rushed at him with a baton overhead.

"Zehm was not aggressive. Zehm didn't have the demeanor evidence that the defendant claimed he did... And not a single witness told you that Mr. Zehm barked out the aggressive series of responses that the defendant attributes to him... And Dr. Gill told you that Mr. Zehm didn't even have time to comply with those commands, even if they had been given...

"And so, after delivering that first baton strike...Zehm is already falling onto his butt, what's the purpose of the second baton strike? What legitimate law enforcement purpose does that serve? ...You heard from Mr. Bragg-he knew from his training he's not allowed to use a Taser until the guy's assaultive, and that's why he had to come up with a way to make Mr. Zehm assaultive. So he invented two quick punches... And you saw him changing his story again before your very eyes when he took the witness stand because he realized that the video shows that Mr. Zehm has the pop bottle...all the way to the floor, so he doesn't have free hands to punch with. And so he changed it from two quick punches to, oh, maybe he was just holding...and shaking the pop bottle... His story was changing every time the video impeaches his story. He begins to hide his lies behind the shelf...

"And so now you know the Taser's not okay...because Mr. Zehm isn't assaultive. Mr. Zehm lies on the floor for 15 seconds with the defendant's legs spread over him and doesn't deliver a kick to the groin. The only supposed kick in this case that the defendant has harped on is what happens immediately after Mr. Zehm is tasered, not before... Now you recall from the video what happens next? And you heard from the witnesses, too. Mr. Zehm begins to crawl away from the ongoing attack and never gets back to his feet...

And what does the defendant do? He rains down another series of four baton strikes that we can see... And what does he do to justify it? ...He makes up the story about Zehm jumping to his feet and adopting a boxing stance and starting throwing punches at the defendant... The witnesses spoke with one voice... They never saw Mr. Zehm intentionally punching the defendant, they never saw him intentionally kicking at the defendant, and the way he was using the pop bottle was defensively to protect his face and head from blows. So, if you find strike three, strike four, strike five, or strike six was a willful baton strike that was unreasonable...you find the defendant guilty of Count I.

"Now let's talk about that last series of seven baton blows in eight seconds in the center aisle..." As the video was played, Boutros continued, "His left hand is holding the sleeve of Mr. Zehm, and his right hand is striking down blows one after the other, almost a second at a time, as fast as he can... What happens to Mr. Zehm? What's he supposed to do? What commands is the defendant giving during those strikes? How's he supposed to comply when someone's holding his sleeve with one arm and just beating him with a baton with the other?

"The training is, you deliver a strike and you evaluate. What's going on? Give him a chance. He didn't give him any... It's just like the first strike. There's no real attempt to gain compliance. So now you know that baton strike 7, 8, 9, 10, 11, 12, and 13, if you don't find that any of those is objectively reasonable, and the defendant willfully delivered it, any one of them, you need to find the defendant guilty of Count I.

"So there are, as I count it, at least 14 ways for you to find the defendant guilty of Count I...and there's the additional way of head strikes that we talked about in the beginning...

"Now, what about willfulness? ...Did the defendant act in open defiance or in reckless disregard of Mr. Zehm's right to be free from objectively unreasonable force? ...There's a very important clarification that the judge...explained in the instructions... 'This does not mean that the government must show that the defendant acted with knowledge of the particular provisions of the Fourth Amendment to the Constitution or that the defendant was even thinking about the Fourth Amendment when he acted.' The relevant point is that when he delivered those strikes, when he shot the Taser, was he acting in open defiance or in reckless disregard of Zehm's right to be free from objectively unreasonable force?... In criminal cases you can't crawl into the defendant's head and see exactly what he's thinking. That's why this...instruction's very important. 'It may at times be reasonably inferred from the surrounding circumstances of the act. Thus, you may look at the defendant's words, experience, knowledge, acts, and their results in order to decide the issue of willfulness.'

"The common ways that we prove this are, first, if the defendant violated his training. that's evidence of willfulness...And the second...is if your force is justified, there's no need to lie about it... The only reason you lie about it is because you know it wasn't legit. And that, too, is evidence of willfulness. And in this case, we have both... So you know that...all the baton strikes and the Taser were willful because he created the lies about it afterwards...about the demeanor evidence...about stopping four feet away and having a conversation... about the two punches before the Taser...about jumping up, adopting a boxing stance and started throwing punches. He created each of these lies to justify his force.

"The defense said...Officer Thompson was aware of cameras in the store that day. Yeah, he was. And what did he do after the force? He went to Sandra McIntyre... She talked to you about how she had an almost father-daughter relationship with the defendant. And he goes to Sandra McIntyre and says, 'Go look at the video.' I asked her in Grand Jury, 'Did you tell the defendant that there's a problem with the lunge account because it's not supported by the video?' She said, 'I could have, but I don't recall...' And she...admitted that she answered, 'I don't recall,' to questions even when she did have recall. That's how you know she's not being honest about that. Sandra McIntyre, who initially said, 'Oh, I just was going in just to get the process rolling... I wasn't looking at content,' and then later says, 'Okay, I was looking at content. In fact, I was taking notes about time stamps.' And you heard from Angela Wiggins that she was taking detailed notes. I mean, she was capturing just about every time stamp when Zehm entered, when the defendant enters, first strike, she was counting strikes aloud in the center aisle... She was taking careful notes...and now goes out, has this private conversation with her close friend, the defendant... After that conversation the defendant never tells the lunge lie again... He was gathering information on scene that night about what was on the video... He knew the lunge statement wasn't going to work because Officer McIntyre knew that and had that private conversation with him.

"So the defendant goes in to his interview and tells the story and tells you on the stand that he's so concerned about this lunge allegation that's flying around...Why couldn't he correct it on the scene? ...What happens if he goes up to the chief and says, 'Hey, Chief, there's no lunge.'

"What is the chief going to do? 'I just went on TV and said to the public that...there was a lunge, and there wasn't? Get me in here every single person who told me there was a lunge.' Draws them in. 'Who told you that there was a lunge? What's your source of information that there's a lunge?' And where's the source of information going to be traced back to? The defendant.

"He needed the lunge to justify the first strike, and he didn't have it. So, four days later, he begins to create a story by using 20/20 hindsight... His first draft was the lunge account. That didn't work... So he creates a second draft...all the demeanor evidence that he claims he saw in that two and a half seconds before the first strike, the lips, the jaw, the eyes, the shoulder muscles tensed, the resolute stance. He has to have that because otherwise, he knows it's not justified. And he has to have something that's not going to be impeached by the video, so he creates these very subtle cues. And the defense tells you, well, a really experienced officer can see cues that nobody else can see.... It's almost like...Spidey sense. You remember Spiderman. He had this tingle in his eye and he knows something dangerous is about to happen. And that's essentially what they're doing. They're saying that it gets so subtle that you lose the objective standard altogether because any force can be justified, because if an officer's experienced enough he's going to see things that nobody else can see. And that can't be impeached by eyewitnesses. They're not trained like he is. It can't be impeached by the video... Remember Dr. Lewinski? 'It didn't see what he saw.' It wasn't like a camera right on his head.

"And so the lies get hidden behind the shelf, they get hidden in subtlety, and he moves his draft so that it can't be impeached. But at that point he thinks that Detective Ferguson is going to whitewash this for him. And what happens? She does... She has the AMR report, she has all the statements of the baton strikes to the head, she knows the

214

defendant has said deadly force is not justified, and she writes a report to the prosecutor saying not only don't prosecute, there is no evidence, none, of excessive force. None.

"What he wasn't counting on is that there would be further review, that someone would actually take the time to scrutinize the witness statements, scrutinize the video, and take the time to do a side-by-side comparison like we have done for you in this case, to look at his statement... Under scrutiny...the story he told on March 22nd, 2006, collapsed. No boxing, no punches before the Taser...so he gets on the stand and gives you his third draft, 20/20 hindsight again. 'Well, I got some things out of order, um, and the things I got out of order, they're all hidden behind the shelf. That's why you can't see them on the video. See, there's lots of stuff you can't see on the video. All the stuff you can't see, that's where my justifications are.' That's what he tells you.

"He gets on the stand and he says, 'Um, you know, maybe I didn't stop, I didn't stop, but I mentally stopped. It wasn't a physical stop, it was a mental stop, things slowed down for me, and that's why I stopped.' He says, 'Well, I'm not saying I didn't give those exact commands, but the commands were so, so, so, so fast. So even though it's just two and a half seconds, I did give the commands. But they were just really, really, really, really fast. And the punches right before the Taser, it happened just behind the shelving. You couldn't see it. It was very fast, and then, oh, but he's still holding the pop bottle, so it's not punches, really, it's just him moving the pop bottle...' And he begins to morph his story... But you get to peer behind the shelf because you heard the citizen eyewitnesses who saw it, and they told you it wasn't true.

"So, if you find the defendant acted willfully, and you find that any of those strikes was unreasonable, he's guilty of Count I.

"Now, briefly, I want to touch on Count II... Any of the lies he told, were they with the intent to impede, obstruct, or influence the investigation of excessive force? And here you know that the March 22nd statement was given as part of the investigation into excessive force, which is a matter within the jurisdiction of the FBI... And did he do so with the intent to impede, obstruct, or influence it? Absolutely! That's why he tells those lies. He wants to influence the outcome of that investigation. He wants exactly what happened. He wants

Detective Ferguson to write a report saying no evidence of excessive force whatsoever...

"So, the only remaining question is: Did the defendant knowingly make a false entry in a record or document? And you know...that record or document that we're talking about here is...the recorded interview and the transcript of it that's been signed... Did he make any false statements in that interview?

"What we learned and what the defendant admitted to you on the stand is there wasn't anything in the CAD at the time that told you about the complainant's car... "I saw to the east of the lot a white Dodge Intrepid, which was the same description that was in the CAD as being the complainant's car.' But when you look at the CAD, there is no description. He didn't know that when he went in. That didn't make this a higher risk situation for him... "There's also the statement...'When Zehm turned around and saw me entering, he did not immediately flee. He picked up an object, and it was held in a manner that I realized was in a position that he could use it as a significant weapon against me.' You see what he's doing here? He's saying Zehm turned around and saw the defendant entering the store, and then...reaches for the pop bottle to use as a weapon. The problem is, the store video shows Mr. Zehm never turns and sees him entering. After Mr. Zehm walks in the store, he never looks back toward the defendant as all. He just walks over to the pop stand as he's done so many nights before.

"But the defendant changes his story again, more 20/20 hindsight. 'When I was entering the store, I didn't really mean I was entering the store. What I really meant is that I was turning the corner around the shelf. That's what I meant when I said, 'entering,' and maybe it wasn't the best word of choice.' That's basically what he said. The problem with that is, the whole point of this story is to say he's looking and seeing me and then reaching for the bottle as a weapon. But when he's turned the corner, Zehm already has the bottle... He's already picked up the pop bottle without ever looking back at the defendant. So again, he undercuts his use of force. He's not using the pop bottle as a weapon...

"If you find that he didn't give the commands as he said he did, you can convict him of Count II. If you find he didn't stop, you can convict him of Count II. If you find that he never jumped up and started boxing, you can convict him of Count II. If you find that he never started punching before

216

the Taser, you can convict him of Count II. If you find other statements that I haven't mentioned that you determine are knowingly false, you can convict him of Count II.

"The evidence in this case has proved beyond a reasonable doubt that on the evening of March 18th, 2006, the defendant abused the power entrusted to him as a police officer by carrying out a brutal and unprovoked attack that left Mr. Zehm helpless and beaten in the center aisle. He counted on his police department to whitewash his misconduct, and it did. But now he's in a room where the law will not be ignored. Do not let the defendant escape responsibility for what he's done. Don't let him minimize the fear and terror and panic he inflicted on Mr. Zehm.

"This is a tragic and terrible story, but it is not over yet. You all get to write the last chapter. You all get to hold the defendant accountable for his brutality and lies. You get to show him that no one is above the law. No one gets special treatment...not even police officers. The defendant doesn't get to brutalize Mr. Zehm with impunity and then cover it up. You get the final word...guilty."

CHAPTER TWENTY

Carl Oreskovich began the defense's closing argument, "It's been a privilege representing Karl Thompson. I want to begin by talking to you about some of the things that Mr. Boutros did not tell you... I want to begin with...the concept of reasonable doubt.

"The standard of proof in this particular case is proof beyond a reasonable doubt. What that means is that when you get done deliberating, to convict there cannot be a reason, not one reason for doubt based on the evidence that you have heard here in the courtroom or based upon the lack of evidence that the government has failed to present... There is not one reason, but there is reason after reason for doubt...

"To find the defendant guilty, you have to find that... he acted in an objectively unreasonable...did he use objectively unreasonable force? We dispute that. But that he acted willfully? What is his mental state? Because that is what you have to look at to make the determination... In other words, to convict Karl Thompson of anything that's accused here in the courtroom, the government has to show you that he acted with bad or evil purpose. A bad purpose. An evil purpose. Not that he went in there as a police officer to try to detain someone, not that he used force because he thought he should use force, but that when he went into the Zip Trip store and he utilized his baton, that he was acting with a bad or evil purpose.

"And I ask you...where is the evidence, ladies and gentleman, that this defendant acted with bad or evil purpose? Where is it? He was there to do one thing: be a police officer. He was responding to a call... If you find that the defendant had the purpose, that is, the end at which his act is aimed, to deprive Mr. Zehm of his Fourth Amendment rights...then he acted willfully. Bad purpose, got to act with the intent to violate the right... By contrast, if the defendant acted through mistake, if Karl Thompson was mistaken about what he perceived, if he acted through carelessness, if he acted through accident, he did not act willfully. And if he did not act willfully...the government has failed in its burden of proof...

"So let's begin where we started in this case. Let's begin by looking at the person that is before you. Because when you look at the person that is before you...you could stop right there and you could say to yourself, 'That is a doubt. This is not a man...that is a liar...that creates a web of lies...that goes into an interview and lies...that gets on a witness stand and lies. This is an honorable man, a man who's fought for his country...a good police officer for 42 years...a man that has distinguished himself... He's a man that gained the admiration, the respect of his fellow officers.' Well, in evidence is Exhibit Number 2367. And you recall...that there were a number of police officers, in fact, 51 percent of the patrol officers in the City of Spokane got together when there was a vacancy for police chief...and they said, 'Here's the guy we would like to have be our police chief.' And in his application you see his experience."

Oreskovich reviewed Officer Thompson's military record and prior police work... "Captain of the operations bureau for Kootenai County. I think he told us there was some 50, 60 personnel under his command. Someone who is respected...who is a thinker...who is not rash. Someone who understands and tries to make things better, both for police officers and for the citizens. He told you in 1996 he was a candidate for Kootenai County Sheriff and then, from 1997 to present, a patrol officer with the City of Spokane, a school resource officer, a specialties officer, a hostage negotiator, a fellow that's involved in the dignitary protection, and a man that was awarded, some four years prior to this event, a Lifesaving Award... That's the man they want you to say is a liar, creating a web of lies. Does that sound to you, ladies and gentleman, like that's his background...a man that's going to act with bad intent, bad purpose...going to come in and intentionally, with a bad motive, evil motive, strike somebody? You could stop right there and say to yourself, 'That's a reason for doubt.'

"Now, let's go further... You heard in his statement, this is the second time he's used his baton since he's been a patrol officer here, the second time. You don't hear a history of him being some violent, rogue, rough-type cop. What you see is a history of a good man, an honorable man, who continues through his career to try to do the right thing...

"I want to talk to you about the standards by which we judge him...this 'use of force'... Whether an officer acted in an objectively reasonable manner during an investigatory stop must be judged from the perception of an objective officer on the scene...rather than the 20/20 vision of hindsight. What do you look at? The severity of the crime the officer was investigating, whether the suspect posed an immediate threat to the safety of the officer or others, whether the suspect actively resisted the officer's attempt to detain him or attempted to evade detention by fleeing... An objective officer on the scene... Mr. Bragg has never been an officer on the scene... You've heard the testimony from the officers who go on the scene every day...Officer Preuninger, Officer Bowman, and Officer Thompson... Those are the ones who know what happens in the field...those are the ones, if they're not making the right decision, might not be here tomorrow.

"So...let's talk about whether there's proof... He hears over the radio, information... It was a white male in his forties with long blond hair, wearing a black jacket and jeans, was...messing with an ATM machine, and the complainant thinks he appears to be high, that he's got some sort of money in his hand, and now he's taking off running... And what does our officer do? What does our liar do? He says, 'Boy, this looks kind of serious, he's running now. I'm probably the closest officer...and he went out and read the CAD report...that tells him very similar information...and then Officer Thompson checks himself into service. That is the actions ...of a dedicated, serious police officer...of a man who's doing the job that we want him to do... Even the government's expert, Mr. Callanan, said that showed a high level of commitment to police work and to the safety of the public. Now, you stop there and say to yourself, 'Okay, now where is it, is it somewhere between the COP shop and the Zip Trip that he gets this bad, evil purpose? ...Act willfully? ...You know that didn't happen... He drove up. He heard the radio traffic... It's right after he hears, 'Copy, and just confirm he took the money,' the answer, 'Affirm.'

"You know from the videotape, you know from his testimony that he made a very quick decision at that point... The government experts are going to criticize him because he didn't wait for help. Well, if those are my children standing at the counter, and someone had just taken money and scared someone at an ATM and then ran away and appeared to be high, and as a police officer rolled up, looked at him and made a decision to go into the Zip Trip store, what I want is this man to go there... That's what we ask for, isn't it? Isn't that what we demand of our police officers...to protect people? Respond to the risk? Have the courage? Our 58-year old man doesn't layup at the COP Shop. He does the job we demand of him, and now he gets accused of a crime...of being a liar, creating a web of lies...

"What our officer knew, what he is to be judged by, are the facts and circumstances that he's confronted with. What is his knowledge? What came from the radio...from the CAD? ...Our hostage negotiator, a man that's trained, recognized that there was a risk... This is an officer who knows he's going into a Zip Trip store that has four surveillance cameras...sees that there are witnesses at the counter...approaches from the outside with lights on, a fish bowl... Does that sound to you ...like a guy that's going in with evil intent, going in to hit first, ask questions later? Going in there to deprive someone of their rights? Isn't that a reason for doubt? How much good sense does that make? He drew his baton because he was going to go in there and hit Mr. Zehm? ...You know he didn't have that purpose... He went into the store and as he rounded the corner...he saw Mr. Zehm turn and saw Mr. Zehm with a bottle... All the experts told you, even Mr. Bragg, even Mr. Callanan, that Mr. Zehm holding a bottle like that could be pre-assaultive, could justify the officer's use of force. That's all Karl Thompson did. He saw something in a very brief period of time that caused him to believe that he was about to be assaulted, and he responded with his police-issued weapon, a baton...

"Now, you may say to yourself, 'Gosh, maybe Karl Thompson overreacted. I wish Karl Thompson would have given more time.' We can all say those things in hindsight, but Karl Thompson reacted to what he thought was a threat. He reacted based upon his training and experience, and he acted with legitimate law enforcement purpose... You could conclude he's mistaken, but...that's not willfulness.

"Counsel wants to tell you, 'Well, you can convict him because he used his Taser.' We know...that Officer Thompson...hadn't searched Mr. Zehm. He didn't have him under control. Mr. Zehm wasn't quitting, did not quit resisting and fighting. That right there, in front of all those people where the danger was close...he applied a Taser that did not work... Counsel wants to tell you, 'Well, all the witnesses were the same. Well...I agree. You have heard testimony that Mr. Zehm was swinging his fists...fighting...struggling ...spitting...kicking and squirming...thrashing and yelling, that he was angry, that he was enraged, that he made guttural sounds... They want to say to you, 'Well, Officer Thompson wasn't struck." ...What did Officer Braun tell you? 'I couldn't get him under control. He was kicking and punching. I tasered him at least once and then again and maybe a third time, and it didn't work. I struck him with my baton, thrust strikes. It didn't work.'

"So they want you to believe that because Mr. Thompson got things out of whack, because he didn't repeat it to you exactly what the video shows, that he must be lying. Well, you know and I know that for 49 seconds Mr. Zehm is out of the video, 49 seconds... Maybe Officer Thompson got it wrong in terms of when he got hit, but there sure is all kinds of evidence...of a long, violent fight. There are all kinds of reasons and knowledge that he would have been struck in that type of circumstance...

"Let's talk to you about head strikes. You've heard...argument about Mr. Lakarish, and I think it was Miss Turner who saw head strikes. And you've heard the government's summation of head strike evidence. But think about it. The evidence of subgaleal injuries, the only person that told you those were head strikes was...Dr. Smith. Dr. Aiken didn't tell you those were head strikes. She said that was evidence of blunt force trauma...either the head coming into contact with something blunt or an instrument coming into contact with the head. What did Dr. Davis and Dr. Nania, 30 years of emergency room experience, tell you? 'Those aren't baton strikes... Baton strikes leave a pattern.'

"The only person that said that the subgaleal injuries were related to baton strikes was Dr. Smith. The only one who contradicted...Dr. Aiken, the forensic pathologist. Dr. Smith...also told you that the injuries to the neck was a baton strike... Counsel tells you, 'Well, wait a second. The radiologist saw all this, the only radiologist who looked at it.' That's not true. There was a radiologist at Deaconess, Dr. Terry...who looked at not one CT scan but two CT scans, who said there was no injury to the neck, that there was no injury in the temple area... The only person who is inconsistent with every other medical doctor who has testified is Dr. Smith, the only one.

"One of the great things about coming into courtrooms is common sense, life experience. How many times have you hit your head? ...Dr. Nania and Dr. Davis told you if you get hit with this (baton)...in the head with a hard strike, you're going to have a laceration, a contusion, a big bruise, a bump... And how is it that the government got Dr. Aiken to say that that in some way was a baton strike? Do you remember her testimony? Her autopsy report, when it had baton injuries, said nothing about a head, nothing whatsoever. It talked about chest and legs and other places. Well, the government had a picture taken... One FBI agent calls the photographer and says, 'Spread these calipers...spread her out to .375, get us a picture, and we'll bring it back and we'll give it to Dr. Aiken. And that...was the proof of a baton strike to the head...

"This is not evidence...of an intentional baton strike. Every doctor has told you that. You know that from your common sense. You know if you were struck...with that baton, what it would do... So, I go back to you and I say, 'Where is the evidence of willfulness?' ...They say you can convict him on the basis of head strikes. You heard the evidence. There's not one shred of evidence that this officer intentionally struck Otto Zehm in the head. The medical evidence...proves to you that that didn't occur... We can quibble about whether things are vertical or diagonal, how he holds his baton, that he didn't hold it right. We're going to come in here and convict him of a crime because he didn't hold his baton right? The only thing Karl Thompson did was what he was trained to do. He used his police tools... Counsel said to you, 'What could Otto Zehm do? After all, Karl Thompson had his arm.' Well, what could he do? How about just stop fighting. How about what Steve Braun told him? 'Stop, quit fighting.' When Karl Thompson told him, 'Drop the bottle,' how about just doing that?

"Karl Thompson said, 'If he didn't have the bottle, I wouldn't have used the baton.' You know that. You saw what police presence is. You saw the expected response when Karl Thompson came in the door and there was a fellow in the gray shirt who just raised his hands up. That's what Karl was looking for.

"I want to talk to you about this lunge statement. The government...wants to say, 'Well, this guy created a web of lies." ...Look the testimony over and over and over. Mr. Moses, first time before the Grand Jury, no conversations...taken into the room, wire-brushed by the government, shown the video, "Oh, yeah, this is you doing this.' Shown an animation, some re-creation by the government, 'We know that you did this.' Then the same thing with Sandra McIntyre, a woman who you heard not one time, two times, but three times threatened. 'We're going to investigate you. You're either going to say it the way we want it or you're going to get charged.' And then a target letter threatening her with prosecution because they wanted it the way that they wanted it, scaring the lights out of her. And then getting her into a Grand Jury room where there's no one else, it's into the court of law, there's no judge, there's no defense lawyer, and getting them to agree with what they say. And then getting them to say, 'Well, gee...how were you treated?' What do you expect that witness to say if they were intimidated... Do you really think that someone that's afraid is going to get by themself in a Grand Jury room with the very people that are working on them and say, 'You scared the daylights out of me.'? The answer is predictable.

"Karl Thompson got up there and told you exactly what happened that night. He told you what his conversation was with the officers at the scene, explained to you, 'This is what I said.' He didn't tell anybody there was a lunge. He explained, as best that he could quickly, what he had interpreted, and then it got mis-relayed and the police chief made a comment. And what did Karl Thompson do? ...When the interview was getting set up, he told...Miss Ferguson, 'Tell the chief to correct that. There's no lunge...'

"You've got to make the determination, ladies and gentleman, as to whether or not this is a man who is going to create or who needs to create a web of lies. He looked at you on the witness stand, answered every question that any lawyer put to him as best that he could, to the best of his recollection... This is a man who voluntarily gave a statement...who did not want to be influenced by a video. He wanted to say things as he remembered them... So, he got some things wrong. You know that memory is fragmented, fractured, temporally out of sequence. That's what Dr. Lewinski told you. You've got to make a determination whether this man...was in there telling them as best that he could, and...he had just learned about Otto Zehm's death right before that. He said to you it had an emotional effect on him. He said it was a profound tragedy...for the Zehm family, for him, for the community. We know under those

224

circumstances that we don't get things right... You don't need an expert to tell you that. You've got a whole life experience to tell you that...

"There are all kinds of reasons for doubt... It's a man that didn't act with a bad purpose, a man who acted with a legitimate purpose, a man who was in there doing the best that he could. A man that stands for something...so much that his co-employees wanted him to be police chief... So if Karl Thompson is in the interview on March 18th, 2006, and makes a mistake, he doesn't commit a crime in making a false statement. He does what many of us do, he made a mistake. You have to decide that. You have to decide...whether this man has worked all of his life...to make life better, saves lives, gets an award for saving lives, negotiates with...hostage takers... Is he the liar the government wants him to be?

"You know that he's not, and you know that he went in there to do his job. And so I would ask you, ladies and gentlemen, after five and a half years of this, to acquit this defendant. We cannot second-guess this type of decision-making. This is an innocent man doing his best who should not be here in a criminal court of law. Thank you."

Allowed 10 minutes to respond to Oreskovich's closing argument, Boutros began, "I was struck by how little the defendant said about what happened on March 18th, 2006. That's what this case is about. We try acts, not people. This is not about what the defendant did in the 60s, 70s, or 80s. It's about what happened on March 18th, 2006.

"The defendant talked about reasonable doubt. It's not 'any reason to doubt.' It's 'reasonable' doubt. It's not based purely on speculation. Look at the instruction.

"The bad purpose that's being talked about here is just this: that he's acting willfully if he acts in open defiance or objective disregard of a known and definite constitutional right, the right to be free from objectively unreasonable force... The question is, did he intend to use unreasonable force? And willfulness is different from motive. Motive is not an element that we're required to prove. We may never know. Otto Zehm never knew why the defendant hit him. You may never know that either, but you don't have to know why. This case is not about why he did what he did. It's about what he did... And the relevant intent...can be formed in an instant. He didn't have to have that intent when he was in the car. He didn't have to have it when he walked through the door of the Zip Trip. Any time he used a strike knowing that it was unreasonable force and did it willfully, that's a conviction for Count I.

"He says, 'Well, what if it was a mistake or carelessness or accident?' You decide. Was it a mistake? Was the first strike a mistake? How about the second? How about the third or the fourth or fifth or sixth or thirteenth? Or the Taser? He wasn't acting carelessly or mistakenly. He was acting intentionally and willfully.

"He says, 'Well, he was just there as a police officer.' ...That doesn't mean he didn't act willfully. Willfully is completely separate from that. So don't mistake that...as meaning that a police officer can never act willfully to deprive someone of their...right against unreasonable force.

"He says, 'Well, you know the defendant had to make a split-second decision.' ...Sometimes officers do have to make split-second decisions, but sometimes they don't, just like doctors... Not every stomach ache requires you to cut into the stomach and pull out the appendix. Sometimes it's just a stomach ache, and sometimes a suspicious circumstances call is just a suspicious circumstances call. How do we know that there was no need to make a split-decision in this case? Because of Officer Braun. He had exactly the same information as the defendant. Did he run in...with his baton drawn? No, he applied his training...took his time...evaluated the situation...looked carefully. He thought about which door to go in. He didn't pull his baton until it became necessary. That is how you know this was not a split-second decision.

"And recall the testimony of Mr. Bragg. You can't create your own exigency. The defendant knew that. You can't run out in front of a car and then begin shooting because you're in jeopardy of deadly force. You can't create your own emergency and then cite the resistance that you caused as a justification for your additional force. The defendant knew that. That was part of his training. The defendant talked about his use of force experts, Mr. Preuninger and Bowman. Notice that...every police officer that you saw the defendant put up is SPD, Spokane Police Department. You're permitted...to take that into account when you evaluate their creditability.

"He says, 'Well, he's just doing his job.' ...His job was to uphold the Constitution of the United States, to protect citizens like Mr. Zehm from the use of unreasonable force.

His job was not to go in and beat an unarmed man who posed no threat.

"He says, 'The eyewitnesses are all over the place.' Not on the important details. The eyewitnesses speak with one voice with the exception of Mr. Colvin, who came to the scene at the very end. The witnesses tell you no punches, no kicks, no aggression with the pop bottle, no boxing, no verbal responses by Mr. Zehm. They're remarkably consistent, even five years after the fact...

"He says, 'Oh, well, Dr. Aiken and Dr. Smith don't agree.' Don't be misled by that... What Dr. Aiken said is this is blunt force trauma. All these injuries are blunt force trauma, and they're consistent with a baton... And she says the one on the brow ridge, because it's a pattern injury which is really rare...more likely than not that's a baton. She says these are consistent with a baton, but they're not pattern injuries, so we can't just look at the injury itself and know the instrument that caused it. But in the clinical context and with the variety of witness statements you have, you know that it was caused by a baton. Nobody, no police officer, no civilian witness, not even the defendant said that Mr. Zehm hit his head on shelving. Nobody said floors. They created these hypothetical possibilities of alternative causes of injury, but nobody has corroborated them. The only thing that everybody says is he was hit with a baton.

"He says, 'Well, what the defendant wanted is...what Mr. LeBlanc did, put up his hands...' Go back and look at the video. Mr. LeBlanc saw the defendant running towards him for eight seconds. How much time did the defendant give Mr. Zehm to respond? Less than two-and-a-half seconds.

"He says, 'Well, Dr. Lewinski talked about fractured memory.' You know what, Dr. Lewinski talked about a lot of different experiments and he told you, 'I'm not saying a thing about the defendant. I have no opinion on how any of this applies to the defendant.' More importantly, most of his research was about stuff cops don't remember. He says they get in stressful situations and they forget all kinds of important things. But look at the defendant's 35-page transcript. He wasn't forgetting things. He was adding things. He wasn't getting things out of order and mixed up. He was making them up out of whole cloth...

"And the other thing you have to remember is that this is an incident that involved a pop bottle and no injury to the defendant. The defendant says he's been in all sorts of more dangerous situations with serious weapons, deadly weapons, where people have been injured. Are you to believe that in all those circumstances his statements were as erroneous as this one was? Are people going to jail because his statements are as erroneous as this one is? If this one had this many errors, how many errors would you expect in a case that's far more serious with a real deadly weapon, with real injuries at stake?

"Lastly, the defendant talked about himself being the victim. The five-and-a-half years, and the defendant is the victim. Don't forget what happened to Mr. Zehm. Don't let the defendant distract you away from the terror and the panic that Mr. Zehm suffered as he was beaten over and over and over without any recourse, no way to stop the acts from continuing. To his dying words, he never understood why the defendant had beat him. 'All I wanted was a Snickers.'"

*

After deliberating for three days, in the presence of the Zehm family the jury returned a verdict of guilty on both counts-24 votes for guilt, none for innocence. As federal marshals led Karl Thompson away, "Present Arms!" resounded in the courtroom and 50 officers of the Spokane Police Department stood and saluted Thompson. Then they turned their backs to the Court!

Shortly after the verdict was delivered, Prosecutor Timothy Durkin commented to the press, "It's not something we take any joy in. But it's a very important case, and we still have a lot of work to do."

Spokane Police Officer Kevin King promptly posted on the We Support Karl Thompson Facebook page, "Karl is a better man than me. If this can happen to him, then it can happen to me. I've always felt supported by our community. I no longer feel that... I'll be at work tonight with my brothers and sisters. We will support each other while we are threatened, spit upon, assaulted, and put our lives on the line-for you. My heart is with you, Karl."

CHAPTER TWENTY ONE

Within hours of the Spokane police officers' "above the law" courtroom display, Mayor Verner and Chief Kirkpatrick offered written apologies to the Zehm family. Incredulously, Kirkpatrick said to the press, "They were showing their honor and support of Karl. The disconnect is that the community is thinking that this officer has been convicted by his peers. Why aren't (Thompson's fellow officers) accepting it? I do think that this community needs a reset button here... We as a Police Department need to be unified and show that we share the values of this community, and the community needs to believe the Police Department is reflecting their values."

Meanwhile, Jeffry Finer commented on behalf of the Zehm family. "They didn't salute Otto. They didn't grieve Otto... As before, his voice and options have not been taken into account by a significant portion of our law enforcement. Healing starts with recognition."

Breean Beggs repeated his suggestion for reconciliation. "We continue to call to the city and the department to repudiate any type of policy that would result in this type of death, and when they do so, the community can heal."

U.S. Attorney Mike Ormsby cautioned, "Many may be tempted to read messages into this verdict that I would not suggest be done. This case was about a single police officer and what he did on one evening in one situation and the steps that he later took to impede and impact the investigation. This is not an indictment of our entire police department, and it should not be an excuse for any of us to ignore the good work that our police officers do every day and every night in our community to protect us."

Soon after the trial concluded, Carl Oreskovich indicated he would appeal the verdict based on the observations of a paralegal assistant, Jodi Dineen, who claimed she'd seen "at least two jurors exposed to a ticker on Northwest Cable News TV that mentioned the 'beating death of a mentally ill janitor' on November 1 and November 2 during breakfast at the hotel in Yakima." In the appeal, Oreskovich asked to question the jurors about influences on their verdict.

Judge Van Sickle deferred ruling on the appeal. But, citing Thompson's lifelong service in law enforcement, his exemplary military service in the Vietnam War, and complying with all conditions of his release prior to his four-week trial in Yakima, he allowed the defendant to be released from prison pending sentencing.

The jury had decided not to comment to the press about its deliberations, but the defense's allegation of outside influence elicited a response from the forewoman, Diane Riley. In an e-mail to the Spokesman-Review she stated, "I do not believe for a moment the jury was influenced by anything outside the courtroom; the conclusions and ultimately the verdict were based fairly and honestly on what was seen and heard in the courtroom."

After convicting Thompson of using excessive force and obstruction of justice, Riley said she couldn't sleep "the whole night. We convicted this police officer of something that will be forever with him. You still walk away and say, 'These are the facts. This is what he failed to do in the scope of his job.' Yet, he's still a human being and you don't want to make a mistake. There is always that little spark of doubt about whether we did the right thing." She indicated that on the morning after the trial concluded she went to her computer and read the news coverage of the Zehm encounter. "First, I learned about his mental condition, and two, he didn't have any drugs in his system. I was like, wow, we did make the right decision. I slept like a baby the next night."

According to Ms. Riley, "We were all on the fence until Tim Moses took the stand. That man gave everything away. You could tell by his attitude and how he presented himself. You don't get that way unless you are guilty of something or hiding something. It was just a gut instinct that this man was covering something up... And when McIntyre took the stand and followed suit, I remember somebody saying that the feds really must have done a number on her to make her cry like that. I said, 'That's a possibility...but if I'm in trouble, I cry.'"

She indicated she waited until the case was completed before she made up her mind, "Just like the judge asked. I have three daughters and 13 grandkids. I learned that you have to hear all sides of the story to be fair." She related,

"There were about four jurors who felt (Thompson) was the fall guy for the department. Everybody felt 100 percent there was a cover-up. But the four felt that Thompson was the victim of the department cover-up. That's why they couldn't say at first that he intentionally, willfully obstructed justice.' When the jury listened to Thompson's March 22, 2006, interview, the four jurors "couldn't get past the department cover-up. I said, 'Let's pretend there was no department cover-up. Let's just look at the statement.' Regardless of whether the word was 'lunged'...or whether Zehm 'came at' Thompson, it doesn't matter the word. Did Otto Zchm do something that could be construed as aggressive? It was a resounding, 'No.'"

Ms. Riley added, "Most of us had never heard of this case. We didn't know the particulars. But one of the jurors had an acquaintance who lived in Spokane... She said politics in Spokane are corrupt and dirty. That was the only person that had a sense of what was going on."

The Thompson defense team used Riley's comments to press their request to interview the jurors. According to the Spokesman-Review, "Karl Thompson's lawyers say jury forewoman Diane Riley's statements to media...are further evidence of the need to examine whether outside information was considered in deliberations. Riley told the Spokesman-Review no jurors considered information not presented at trial...but she also said a juror knew someone who lived in Spokane and that politics here are corrupt and dirty. The fact that the alleged corrupt or dirty politics of Spokane was discussed...is particularly alarming given the fact that the jury made its determination regarding Defendant Thompson's guilt based on its belief that 'everybody felt 100 percent that this was a police cover-up,' attorney Courtney Garcea wrote... 'Whether there was or was not a police cover-up was not an issue to ever be considered by the jury.'

"Garcea points to Riley's comment that, 'Most of us had never heard of this case,' as acknowledging that outside information such as Zehm's mental illness or his purported innocence could have been considered. She also points to statements Riley made to KREM 2 News that jurors suspected Otto Zehm may have been disabled by looking at photos of him as a sign that jurors improperly considered that information when reaching the verdict."

When Ms. Riley learned that her comments were being used by the defense team to bolster its appeal, she sent a lengthy letter to Judge Van Sickle explaining her remorse at having communicated with the media about the jury's deliberations. Referring to the allegation that jurors were influenced by news reports while staying at the hotel in Yakima, she stated, "There was NO indication-subtle or direct-that could lead to the conclusion that any of the jurors in the room had learned from news reports, or any source, that Mr. Zehm had a mental condition. It is true that in answering questions about Mr. Zehm's unusual behavior in the Zip Trip that the jury discussed hypothetically the possibility of a cognitive disability... We agreed unanimously that we COULD NOT use Mr. Zehm's mental condition as a factor to find Mr. Thompson guilty or not. We asked the question of ourselves: Did Mr. Thompson use premeditative excessive force when he entered the Zip Trip to apprehend a suspect--regardless of who the suspect was or what the victim's mental state was? The answer was: Yes... The facts are the facts, and the facts say that Mr. Thompson knowingly and willfully applied excessive force on an unsuspecting suspect. That was the basis we used to reach the verdict."

When Judge Van Sickle ruled on the ticker issue, he said that had he been alerted him to the exposure at the time, he "could have made inquiries and taken appropriate corrective action... As it was, the Court repeatedly admonished jurors to ignore media reports concerning the trial in the event they encountered them... The presumption is that jurors followed those instructions." However, he granted Oreskovich's request to interview the jurors. During that hearing the alternate juror who had indicated in prior correspondence to Oreskovich that he disagreed with the verdict reiterated his view. The inquiry found no evidence of juror misconduct.

Originally scheduled for January 24, 2012, the sentencing hearing was postponed after Judge Van Sickle received a letter from Grant Fredericks, a forensic videographer who had been listed by both sides as an expert witness but was not called to testify. Court records indicated that in 2006 Rocco Treppiedi hired Fredericks, formerly a police officer in Vancouver, B.C., to analyze the Zip Trip video and that before Fredericks completed the work, he told Detective Ferguson his report would include "no liability to the city."

Later in 2006, federal authorities hired Fredericks to do the same video analysis after challenging several of his assertions, including that the video did not show any baton strikes for one minute and 13 seconds. During the initial meetings, Fredericks told federal investigators that he first became involved at the request of Jack Driscoll, the chief deputy Spokane County Prosecutor. But the investigators learned that Fredericks actively encouraged the city to hire him by promising favorable conclusions. Federal prosecutors called Spokane Police Department Officer John McGregor, who had prior professional dealings with Fredericks, to appear before the grand jury that eventually indicted Officer Thompson. He testified, "It was actually Fredericks who initiated contact with the SPD and made an unsolicited offer to 'help' the SPD after viewing media portions of the Zip Trip video. McGregor also told the grand jury that Fredericks said it was his belief...that the video depicted the 'two-liter bottle being used as a weapon.' It was this observation that...'triggered (Fredericks) to want to get involved in helping the police.'"

In July, 2012, the Justice Department submitted its objection to the lengthy delay of sentencing. On August 31, 2012, the hearing to address Fredericks' claims was reported by the Spokesman-Review. "When arguing for a new trial, Oreskovich said that a report on a meeting between FBI Special Agent Lisa Jaangard and Fredericks was inaccurate and mischaracterized Fredericks' opinions, which would have proven favorable to Thompson's defense.

"In his first report, Fredericks said the video did not show any baton strikes for the first minute and 13 seconds of the confrontation. He was later questioned and hired by the FBI to do the same analysis. Fredericks then wrote a second report, and later testified under oath to a grand jury, that the video actually showed baton motions that were consistent with baton strikes within seconds of Thompson confronting Zehm.

"In his ruling, Van Sickle agreed that favorable evidence was withheld from the defense but said, 'The possibility of a different outcome is not great enough to undermine confidence in the verdicts the jury entered.'"

The sentencing hearing was scheduled for November 15, 2012. Prior to the hearing each side made recommendations concerning Thompson's sentence. The prosecution argued for a sentence of eight to ten years while the defense sought no prison time. An independent probation officer reviewed the case and recommended a sentence of 27 to 33 months.

According to the Spokesman-Review, "Durkin said in court records that the probation officer who completed the presentence report only talked to witnesses provided by the defense, 'all of whom provided information favorable to Thompson... 'It does not appear that the Probation Officer interviewed (former) Assistant Chief Jim Nicks or the Kootenai County Undersheriff who critically evaluated Defendant's work and performance. Nor did Probation interview others having similar knowledge and favorable information about the victim, Mr. Zehm.'"

Durkin felt that Thompson should be sentenced under the recommended guidelines for aggravated assault, which did not include the option of a probation-only sentence. Meanwhile, Oreskovich argued that Thompson should have that option available because the crime did not meet the criteria for aggravated assault as Thompson did not intend to or succeed in causing Zehm bodily harm. According to Oreskovich, "There is no evidence supporting the government's contention that Mr. Zehm suffered a serious bodily injury as a result of Defendant Thompson's conduct. Injuries attributed to Defendant Thompson's actions were limited to muscle bruising (contusions), a small laceration from Taser probes, and hematomas (excluding subgaleal hematoma which could not be medically linked to Defendant Thompson's baton by a preponderance of the evidence). As pointed out by the government, serious bodily [injury] 'should be something more than ordinary scratches, scrapes and bruises.'

"It is also significant to point out that the injuries ultimately sustained by Mr. Zehm were not foreseeable. Defendant Thompson's conduct did not set in motion the chain of events which ultimately led to Mr. Zehm's death. Any chain of causation argument asserted by the government is flawed because it fails to take into account Mr. Zehm's own behavior in continuously resisting arrest."

CHAPTER TWENTY TWO

Prior to leaving office at the end of 2011, Mayor Verner created the Use of Force Commission to review the city's handling of the police confrontation that resulted in the death of Otto Zehm. She selected Gonzaga University executive vice president and former Law School Dean Earl "Marty" Martin to lead the commission. Bill Hyslop, U.S. Attorney for Eastern Washington from 1991 to 1993, was chosen to be vice chairman.

In January, 2012, the remaining three members and an expanded role for the commission were announced. Recently retired Washington State Supreme Court Chief Justice Gerry Alexander agreed to serve, joining Ivan Bush, the Spokane Public School's equal opportunity officer, and Susan Hammond, director of outpatient and psychology services for Spokane Mental Health. Chairman Martin indicated the commission would not focus solely on how the city handled the Zehm confrontation and the legal issues that resulted but would also review police procedures and training and civilian police oversight. "The issue is bigger than one individual case."

Having stated when hired in 2006 that she planned to stay "for about five years," in March, 2011, Chief of Police Kirkpatrick signaled her intent to leave the job. She said she would remain in the position through the first few months of 2012 while the city searched for a new chief. However, in early November, 2011, a verdict awarding damages of $722,000 from the city was reached. The award resulted from the manner in which the Police Department disciplined Detective Jay Mehring, who had been acquitted in October, 2008, of the charge that he threatened to kill his wife during their divorce. The award included $250,000 in punitive damages for Kirkpatrick's actions in the matter.

Subsequently, in a November 6, 2011, letter to Mayor Verner, Chief Kirkpatrick stated her departure date would be January 2, 2012, citing a desire to retire to spend more time with her family and stating, "I'm at a great age for new things." She denied that turmoil in the department over Thompson's conviction and the Mehring verdict affected her decision to leave earlier than planned. When asked if the Police Department is making changes after trainers testified they supported the use of force by Officer Thompson that jurors subsequently found to be criminal, she stated, "Some things are being addressed. I'm not ready to comment on what those are right now... I inherited Otto Zehm. I said I would carry it, and I did carry it. I said I would stay to see that come to closure. I'm just doing what I said I would do."

Assistant Chief Nicks had stated that he planned to retire when Chief Kirkpatrick left and, at the time of the announcement of her departure date, was on medical leave from the department. Spokane Police Major Scott Stephens was appointed Acting Assistant Chief in October, 2011 and in late December, 2011, became the Interim Chief of Police.

Mayor-elect Donald Condon urged that the selection of a new police chief be delayed until he took office. "I believe a national search conducted at this time won't yield highly qualified candidates. Qualified candidates will want to know that they have the support of the new mayor. I want all options on the table as we work not only to find a new chief but reform the department as a whole."

Condon assumed the duties of Mayor on January 4, 2012, intending to assess and perhaps change the management of some of the city departments after several months on the job. Events forced him to act sooner.

Police Sergeant Brad Thoma had been fired from the Police Department in 2009 following an off-duty drunk driving hit-and-run incident. Thoma protested his termination, arguing that the city was discriminating against him for being an alcoholic. Former city prosecutor Howard Delaney, hired as City Attorney by Mayor Verner in 2008, led the negotiations resulting in an agreement to rehire Thoma and give him $275,000 in back pay. Mayor Condon reportedly found the agreement distasteful but signed it nevertheless. However, in February, 2012, an angry City Council unanimously rejected it. Just prior to the vote Councilman Mike Allen asked, "Is our system...or our process so broke that the staff and legal council for the City think this is a justified outcome for our citizens?"

On March 1, 2012, Mayor Condon fired Howard Delaney and named Nancy Isserlis to the position. City spokesperson Marlene Feist said the change was not about any "single issue... The mayor was looking for new leadership in the City Attorney's Office. Nancy Isserlis is the fit he's looking for." On April 2, 2012, the fifty-seven year old attorney left the Spokane firm of Winston and Cashatt and a successful career in bankruptcy law to manage the City Attorney's Office with its staff of 35 and annual budget of $4.6 million.

Ms. Isserlis was well known in the community as the chairperson of the Health Sciences and Services Authority and previous chair of the Ethics Commission. When she had worked with Mayor Condon on the board of Spokane Neighborhood Action Partners, they had found common ground despite different political philosophies, and she had assisted his transition team. After indicating a strong desire to "restore trust and move forward," she stated, "I'm a firm believer that opportunities come your way for a reason and at a time when you can embrace them."

In early April, 2012, Spokane Chief Financial Officer Gavin Cole informed Pam Schroeder of her dismissal. She had been hired by Mayor Hession as the city's Risk Manager in 2006 when Rocco Treppiedi's dual role of Assistant City Attorney and Risk Manager was split. Cole stated, "This is part of a broader review of city risk management."

Cole and Isserlis had been studying the city's risk management strategy in part because of allegations that the firm that had the contract to handle portions of the city's risk management responsibilities pressured police and a city employee to hide potentially incriminating details about a collision involving a city vehicle that had paralyzed a pedestrian.

Soon after taking office, Mayor Condon stripped Rocco Treppiedi of his role as the Police Department's legal adviser. The change of leadership would not have an immediate impact on Treppiedi's future, however. While the mayor had reiterated during the campaign that he wanted Treppiedi out of the City Attorney's Office, the City Charter gave the power to fire assistant attorneys to the City Attorney. The mayor expressed his concerns about Treppiedi to Isserlis but said he had not and would not direct her to dismiss him. "She is doing a full review of all our processes... She has reviewed all the files on all employees who are under her direction."

Two weeks after taking charge of the City Attorney's Office, Nancy Isserlis fired Rocco Treppiedi.

*

Immediately following the 2011 release of the summary of Assistant Chief Nicks' anticipated testimony at the criminal trial, specifically that Thompson's use of force violated departmental policy and detectives had improperly investigated the Zehm encounter, Mayor Verner stated that she intended to pursue "all courses of action" to settle the civil suit. Prior to that de facto acknowledgment of culpability, the city's position had been that its 2009 legal reply to the civil suit, which blamed Otto Zehm for his death, was valid. But progress toward resolution of the civil claim was not apparent to the public during the remainder of her term.

The city's liability insurance policy with American International Group required it to pay the first one million dollars of a liability claim, AIG the next ten million, and the city, any additional amount. The "first one million" included legal expenses paid by the city in defense of a claim, which in this case included the money the city had paid Carl Oreskovich for Thompson's defense. In assessing its risk, an insurer has its lawyers review the evidence, including evidence the judge has not permitted in the related criminal case. Spokane attorney Bob Dunn, who had successfully sued the city in liability claims previously, commented to the Spokesman-Review, "If the case goes to trial, the city runs the risk of allowing a jury to decide both actual and punitive damages, which are unlimited... It depends on how incensed a jury would be after viewing the videotape, and a lot of things not allowed in the criminal case would be allowed in the civil case. The fact that (Zehm) hadn't committed a crime may make him much more sympathetic to a jury."

*

In 2011 two attempts at enhanced police oversight failed. The Spokane City Council was forced to remove from the police ombudsman's powers the right to investigate police misconduct independently from the Police Department after

238

a successful legal challenge by the Police Guild. The use of body cameras on police officers to record their interactions with the public had been proposed. While body cameras can protect citizens treated improperly by officers and prevent frivolous lawsuits against the police, the program was felt to be prohibitively expensive by Mayor Verner and, being a work condition that had not been bargained in the current contract, was blocked by the Guild. That contract expired at the end of 2011, and both matters soon resurfaced in the deliberations of the City Council.

In February 2012, Spokane City Council President Ben Stuckart proposed a resolution intended to institute a body camera program as existed in several nearby communities. Spokane Police Ombudsman Tim Burns had recommended the body camera program in his annual report to the Council in 2011, and Spokane County Sheriff Ozzie Knezovich previously had asked the county commissioners to fund a camera program for his force. Mayor Condon endorsed the proposal. "We will be investigating their use and what's the best equipment and policies and procedures about how to use them." Officials now were ready to spend $600,000 for a camera program for the Police Department and County Sheriff's Office.

After the resolution passed, Spokane's Interim Chief of Police Scott Stephens was asked how the police force felt about wearing body cameras. He explained, "(They) are very welcoming of them but also want to know how will you precisely implement this program. They just want to make sure that however we choose to implement is fair and balanced toward them."

The resolution restored the police ombudsman's power to investigate police misconduct separately from the Police Department's internal investigation. Stephens commented, "I believe the officers actually developed kind of a favorable opinion of the stronger police ombudsman (ordinance). We don't have objections to that in principle... They felt like things were being done to them without their input, and that's why they threw the roadblock up there."

The resolution also provided for the use of the ombudsman's rulings in police disciplinary determinations. Stephens stated, "The chief needs to be the one that has the final discipline authority, but I have no objection to looking at whatever information the ombudsman would provide and considering that in the overall picture of the discipline."

Commenting on Mayor Verner's 2011 request that the Department of Justice review Spokane Police Department practices, Stephens said, "It might provide some comfort for the citizens of this city to have this department's practices and patterns viewed by an outside body who can put perspective in it to say, based on what we see nationwide and looking at current trends in policing, either we're doing everything the way we're supposed to be doing or we need to change a couple of things."

*

In February, 2012, city officials and attorneys representing Ann Zehm and the estate of Otto Zehm announced that they would enter mediation to settle the civil suit. In office just more than one month, Mayor Condon stated in a news release, "It's time to move this long-standing case toward resolution... Resolving the Zehm suit is a high priority for me and our community."

Representing Zehm's mother and estate, Breean Beggs said in the release, "The Zehm family believes that mediation is the most constructive way to move forward towards resolving this dispute." Beggs also explained the agreement to keep those negotiations secret. "We thought the mediation would be more productive if the specific proposals were kept confidential until it was clear that there is an agreement."

In April, Interim Chief Stephens publicly acknowledged that mistakes were made during the investigation of the Zehm incident. While he was in charge of the detectives assigned to the investigation, Stephens said that Assistant City Attorney Rocco Treppiedi had had greater access to the investigation than he did and that Mayor Condon had put an end to the city attorneys' unfettered access to criminal investigations. "I think we have to own the mistakes we've made, acknowledge that and take measures that they don't repeat. My desire is that we restore the public trust and confidence in their department."

Upon hearing Stephens' statement, Otto's relative Sandy Zehm said, "This is what we've waited to hear all these years, and they've refused to say it for whatever reason. We don't want any other family to have to go through the same incident that caused Otto's death."

In the same month, in the course of the extended legal battle by Thompson's attorneys to obtain a new trial, U.S. Attorney Aine Ahmed filed grand jury transcripts showing that Officer Jason Uberuaga and three other officers were allowed three days before they were asked to write incident reports about their role in the confrontation. Uberuaga had told the grand jury that neither he nor the other officers involved, including Officer Erin Raleigh, wanted to give an oral statement on the night of the incident because they felt the detective was treating them like suspects. They asked to have guild attorney Hilary McClure present when they wrote their reports, and Uberuaga said he was allowed to consult with McClure, who read his report before it was submitted. Uberuaga also testified that the interval of three days was provided by a department protocol that allowed officers a couple of sleep cycles to improve memory.

Breean Beggs and Jeffry Finer immediately called for police officials to say who authorized the officers to write their reports as a group with the help of an attorney. Interim Chief Stephens responded several days later that the detectives in the case, Mark Burbridge and Terry Ferguson, arranged to have Uberuaga, Raleigh, and the two other officers gather to write their reports on March 21, 2006. Sergeant Joe Peterson had handled the day-to-day supervision of the detectives and told Stephens he was aware that Uberuaga and the other officers wanted to provide a written statement. "And the guild wanted an attorney to be there," Stephens said. "The earliest they could make those pieces fit was" three days after the confrontation. Stephens explained that in 2006 it was an accepted practice to have a guild attorney consult with officers as they wrote incident reports, "But it's not accepted today." He explained further that while officers are allowed to have an attorney present during questioning following a critical incident, the same right afforded to citizens, present policy prohibits more than one officer in the room during the interview.

*

In 2007 U.S. District Judge Michael Hogan of Oregon assisted in the mediation of the $104 million agreement to settle the claims of sexual abuse by priests in the Archdiocese of Portland. In 2012 he was mediating a similar claim against the Catholic Diocese of Spokane. When the parties to the civil suit agreed to have Judge Hogan oversee the mediation, Judge Suko ordered the attorneys for the Zehm family and estate, Spokane City Attorney Nancy Isserlis, and the attorneys for the city's liability insurance carrier, AIG, to meet on May 14 and 15, 2012. Sandpoint, Idaho attorney Ford Elsaesser was asked to assist Judge Hogan in the two-day mediation session.

Heading into the mediation, the plaintiff's original demand of $2.9 million had risen to $14.5 million based on additional information about the Zehm encounter and the subsequent police investigation, which Assistant U.S. Attorney General Thomas Perez labeled "an extensive cover-up."

Mayor Condon attended both days of mediation, and at the end of the second day, a settlement of the suit was announced. The City of Spokane pledged to pay the Zehm family $1.67 million, to spend $350,000 to certify all Spokane police officers more than one year from retirement in Crisis Intervention Training, and to commit $50,000 to pay a consultant to assist the Spokane Police Department in the transition to a new use of force policy. The City agreed to apologize officially to the family and establish a memorial to Otto in one of its parks. The city was required to pay $720,000 of the monetary settlement, having spent $280,000 on private attorneys.

Jeffry Finer later described some of the challenges during the mediation. AIG, the insurance carrier, had been told by the city's former counsel that there was no liability and, as Zehm had no dependents, no damages. Furthermore, after Officer Thompson's conviction on federal criminal charges, AIG had a strong defense against liability. Judge Hogan convinced AIG's attorneys to re-evaluate the company's exposure in light of the city's support of the suffocating hog-tie and prone positioning by the back-up officers while informing the plaintiff's attorneys that the damages were limited by the small size of Zehm's estate.

Nancy Isserlis stated that the city settled the case "because it's the right thing to do." The City Council quickly ratified the agreement. At the press conference announcing resolution of the suit, Mayor Condon was joined by the members of the City Council, leaders of the Police Department, and employees of the City Attorney's Office. Condon said, "Today we not only have finality for our citizens but also for Mrs. Zehm. Truly we cannot change the past, but we can acknowledge our mistakes and move toward a better future for our community." He apologized to Ann Zehm for the encounter and the way the city handled the dispute, announced comprehensive police training based on the Memphis Crisis Intervention Training Model, and promised that the city would pay for an independent use of force consultant.

Judge Hogan responded to the question posed to the mayor as to why the city had blamed Zehm for his death. "We have some new people here now, and these people have been completely open about the facts of the situation with me from the first day I began to work on this. With regard to explaining the response of others at another time, that's for other people, frankly. I can say for client's lawyers, for the mayor and the City Attorney, they have been completely open, transparent, forthcoming..." He indicated he would ensure the agreement is implemented as specific terms are worked out and added, "I'm hopeful we will see a new day...for the relationship between law enforcement and the public of Spokane. What was remarkable was the openness for constructive suggestions to resolve the matter and put it in the city's rear view mirror... There will be an apology for any allegations that Otto Zehm had committed a criminal violation and for the manner the confrontation was handled and its tragic result."

Dale Zehm, Otto's cousin, said, "I know he would have been happy. We don't want this to happen to anybody else ever again." He had been in the courtroom when Spokane police officers saluted Thompson as he was taken into custody and added, "That was not enjoyable. Hopefully, we can get over that with what's happened in the last two days. We are looking forward to the change and some closure."

Councilwoman Nancy McLaughlin, the only city leader remaining in office from the time of the Zehm encounter, said, "My heart goes out to Mrs. Zehm." She indicated she was grateful for the settlement. "The very first time I saw the video, red flags were going off... City legal staff stressed...the tapes didn't have audio...and that there was other evidence that needed to be considered. It made me wonder if (Treppiedi) just didn't see it because of his aggressive nature and the way he defended cases for the city."

Breean Beggs commented, "There were political reasons and legal strategies and collective bargaining. All those factors were in play, and I think bad decision-making in the past, and that can't be undone."

In early June Mayor Condon personally delivered the city's official apology to Ann Zehm after the family's attorneys approved the language. Nancy Isserlis suggested the mayor present her a version written by hand, and he gave her the letter during a meeting in the conference room of her apartment building.

Dear Mrs. Zehm,

I very much regret, and I sincerely apologize for, the death of your son, Otto. I understand that Otto was a loving and supportive son who enjoyed his work and enjoyed spending time with you, other family members, and friends. His death is a loss not only for you, but for our entire community.

You, and our community, waited too long for resolution in this matter. For me, blame was clearly misplaced in this case, and I fear that compounded the pain for you and many others.

I cannot change the past, but I can ensure a better future. Since Otto's death, the City has committed to instituting procedures to protect citizens like Otto.

In addition, to honor Otto's memory, I will recommend to the Park Board that it name a pavilion for Otto and place a plaque stating that the pavilion is offered: "In Memory of Otto Zehm."

Again, please accept our profound apologies for the loss of your son.

Very truly yours,

David Condon

After telling him about Otto and how she missed him, Mrs. Zehm accepted his apology. Nancy Isserlis commented, "I've never really witnessed something so genuine and moving as watching Mrs. Zehm talk to the mayor. Sometimes in the practice of law, you don't get to bring closure to stuff like this."

In August, 2012, the Park Board accepted the mayor's recommendation to honor Otto in Mission Park where his mother indicated he had spent his most enjoyable time. On what would have been his 43rd birthday, the memorial plaque on the stone support of a picnic pavilion in Mission Park was unveiled in a ceremony attended by Mayor Condon, the Chief of Police, and members of Otto's family. Otto's cousin, Johanna Gallegos, placed a 2-liter Pepsi bottle and a bouquet of chrysanthemums beneath the plaque, which appeared in the photograph of Ann Zehm touching the plaque from her wheelchair that was published in the Spokesman-Review to commemorate the occasion.

CHAPTER TWENTY THREE

During the campaign Mayor Condon said his top priority would be to restore citizen's trust in the Police Department. By the end of May, 2012, federal officials still had not responded to his predecessor's request for a pattern and practice review, and a new Chief of Police had not been selected. Spokane County Sheriff Ozzie Knezovich advocated for a single force for the city and county, and the mayor indicated he'd consider the suggestion in matters such as property crime.

The mayor re-launched the search for a new police chief on June 1, established a deadline of June 30, and stated that applications from within the department would not be accepted. Interim Chief Stephens was no longer under consideration. Mayor Condon explained, "I want somebody who has a full understanding of a metro-policing model. When I look at the type of police chief and the major initiatives we want to implement, I owe it to the citizens to find that person."

The Use of Force Commission was fully engaged by June, 2012, when multiple community forums were held. The topics discussed included dealing with special populations and people with mental illness, citizen oversight and independent review of police actions, and how the City Attorney's Office handles claims of excessive force. Chairman Martin indicated the Commission would investigate the policies in place in the City Attorney's Office to prevent the conflict of interest that occurred in its handling of the Zehm matter. At the end of June, Spokane Police Advisor Mary Muramutsu told the Commission that Nancy Isserlis had changed procedures in the City Attorney's Office to prevent conflicts of interest when representing city employees and to ensure that the city attorneys stay out of criminal investigations of the city's employees. "We're looking at...a new way of thinking."

After the Use of Force Commission completed its schedule of community forums, Chairman Martin announced that there would be members-only conferences and study of the reports of two consultants when available before a list of recommendations for the Police Department, City Council, and Mayor was drafted. He also stated that the Commission would hold a public hearing after the draft was presented prior to finalizing the recommendations.

Mike Painter, director of the Washington Association of Sheriffs and Police Chiefs, said that 56 agencies in the state, including the Spokane County Sheriff's Office, are accredited by his organization and 10, including the Washington State Patrol, by the Commission on Accreditation for Law Enforcement Agencies. Both organizations have established extensive standards that must be met to achieve and maintain accreditation. Painter added that many police unions are uncomfortable with accreditation, but Mary Muramutsu indicated that city leaders have a strong interest in the process. "Accreditation is crucial. It's key."

*

Only 13 applications for the position of Chief of Police were received, and some city leaders were unenthusiastic about the two finalists, Donald Mahoney and Frank Straub. Mahoney was the commander of the Ingleside Police Station in the San Francisco Police Department, and Straub had just resigned in anticipation of a vote of no confidence by city leaders in Indianapolis after a two-year stint in management of its Police and Fire Departments. A panel of law enforcement professionals that included Sheriff Knezovich advised the mayor to reopen the search. However, after reviewing the Indianapolis metro policing model as a potential plan for Spokane and having asked Straub earlier in the year to apply, Mayor Condon selected him for the position.

Frank Straub was highly educated, holding a bachelor's degree in psychology, a master's degree in forensic psychology, and a Ph.D. in criminal justice. He had worked in security for the Diplomatic Service, as a special agent for the U.S. Department of Justice, as assistant director for counterterrorism for the New York Police Department, and as commissioner of police and fire services in White Plains, New York, prior to moving to Indianapolis.

Reportedly, Straub had a strained relationship with the Indianapolis police union. But Indianapolis Councilman Duke Oliver said, "It's a credit to him because we needed some reform. The reform he wanted to institute met with some resistance." Concerning the potential vote of no confidence, Oliver stated, "That was more about politics than Straub... If you put him in charge, he's going to lead."

After his selection was announced, Straub pledged to institute a community policing model in Spokane and discussed change in policing. "If you really want to be innovative...and you really want to get things done in policing, you can get much more done in a department this size than you do in an Indianapolis-size department or in Chicago or New York. You have the opportunity to be very creative...to really be in that intimate connection with the community."

Interim Police Chief Scott Stephens, a 27-year veteran of the Spokane Police Department, indicated he would remain as assistant chief and said, "(Straub) is going to need that institutional knowledge and our support. We are going...to make sure he has everything he needs to be a great chief."

Sheriff Knezovich conceded, "The mayor has made his decision, and we are willing to work with Mr. Straub to make sure he is successful in Spokane."

Police Ombudsman Tim Burns added, "There are some opportunities for the community and the Police Department to benefit from his past experience."

Breean Beggs, attorney for the Zehm family, said he hoped the new chief could "steer the department and entire city through substantial change in culture and strategy. The fact that (Straub) met resistance in his previous job shows that he knows what it takes to move Spokane forward. It's going to take the entire city government and community to create a new vision of community policing and move forward, even if there is resistance inside or outside the department."

Soon after Straub assumed the role of Director of Law Enforcement, it came to light that Internal Affairs investigators for the Spokane Police Department found no problem in all 492 uses of force in the previous five years, 60 of which generated a complaint of excessive force. Chief

Straub indicated he had spent 12 years of his career investigating alleged misconduct by federal and state officers and explained, "My first priority is not to go back and do retroactive investigations. But what I can tell you is that when those cases come to my desk, they will get a very thorough investigation."

CHAPTER TWENTY
FOUR

The probation officer who reviewed the case against Karl Thompson recommended a sentencing range of 27 to 33 months based on guidelines for simple assault. Prosecutor Boutros began his presentation at the sentencing hearing on November 15, 2012, with an explanation of the difference between simple and aggravated assault. "You pull a gun on someone, you don't actually hit them with it, you don't shoot them with it, but you scare them with it... That's a frightened category of assault. And then you can actually physically assault them and cause bodily injury, however severe, however minor, you can cause bodily injury. So it's a distinction between the frighten kind of assault, which falls in the minor assault category, and the bodily injury kind of assault, which falls in the aggravated assault category... Or, whether you have a dangerous weapon or not, if serious bodily injury results, that's another way to get to aggravated assault."

Having made his argument for the proper starting point for the sentencing calculation, he explained the sentence the prosecution thought appropriate. "The government has taken the crimes of former Officer Thompson seriously, and in the interests of justice and the safety and integrity of the community and its police officers, today requests a sentence of 108 to 135 months as provided by the Federal Sentencing Guidelines... As a trial attorney for the Civil Rights Division of the Department of Justice, I travel all over the country investigating many criminal violations of civil rights, including 242 (assault by a police officer), and this is a particularly egregious 242 violation. Often in 242 cases you have an unsympathetic victim with a lengthy criminal history who is accused of a very serious crime on very solid and consistent information, who may have dangerous weapons (and) a history of violence, who may be high on drugs, who may actively and undisputedly provoke the officer, who may be larger and physically more imposing than the officer... Here, by contrast, we have Otto Zehm... There's been enormous emphasis during the trial, for legal evidentiary reasons, to focus on Mr. Thompson's point of view. But to really understand the nature of the circumstances of this case, we must also understand something about Otto."

Boutros described Otto as "squeaky clean and very vulnerable" and stated, "I think it's fair to say that in the absence of the rush to strike first and ask questions later, Otto Zehm is here. He's known as a very gentle person as we, as the defendant knew from his training with those who shared the same disability as Otto Zehm, they're far more likely to be gentle than violent. As those who knew Zehm best testified or told us, that was exactly true of him. And that emphasizes the significance of this sort of crime. The risk of officers who choose to willfully use excessive force, as the defendant did in this case, is that innocent citizens like Otto Zehm are not safe and that, in the worse cases as this one, innocent men lose their lives.

"In the course of the trial there was a strong emphasis on trying to put yourself in the defendant's shoes. What has been, I think, particularly distressing is understanding the circumstances from Otto Zehm's shoes... 'When is it going to stop? When will it ever stop?' These are the questions that must have been going through Otto Zehm's mind. And foremost, first and foremost, 'Why? Why is this happening to me?' And with his simple mind, he never understood. And it just got worse... As he was thinking about it, 'What was I doing when this thing all started?' he says, 'All I wanted was a Snickers.' He's thinking back, 'I was turning toward the candy aisle when I first got struck.' That is a horrible, horrible last day for Otto Zehm. It's horrific. I wouldn't wish it on anyone. And that is the cost of police officers, in whom we place this great trust, abusing their authority, abusing their power...

"And while this story didn't get to the jury, it is important for the Judge, for you, Your Honor, to consider as you weigh the circumstances of this case."

The Court listened to a number of victim impact statements. Dale Zehm was the first family member to speak:

"Saturday, March 18th, 2006, changed my life. Otto was my cousin. After attending the trial of Karl Thompson, I continue to struggle each day with the realization of what Otto went through the last hour of his life. I cannot imagine what it would have been like if that had happened to me.

"Now, at sentencing, it should be known that Otto was innocent. He did nothing wrong... Karl Thompson's excessive force and escalation of actions resulted in Otto's brutal, senseless, and unnecessary death. Karl Thompson took his actions against Otto without any explanation to Otto.

"It is very troubling to listen to testimony by the police, Spokane police officers, during the trial that was in contradiction to the actions I saw on the video. As bad as it was to know that Karl Thompson had no reason to beat Otto, it was just as bad to see his efforts to cover up his wrongdoing, blaming Otto for the attack, blaming him for the way he was treated, blaming him for everything. I never heard one time where Karl Thompson said anything but that Otto deserved what happened. Even when he testified that Otto's death was tragic, it seemed he meant his being put on trial for it was the tragedy.

"I was disgusted with the behavior of the many police officers after Karl Thompson's custody hearing on November 4th, 2011. These officers, upon command, stood in front of our family and saluted Karl Thompson as he was led out of a federal courtroom. He nodded back to them as he was led away. The officers showed no respect for our family or for the legal system that they are sworn to uphold.

"I know I have never seen Karl Thompson show remorse for what he did or try to explain to others why it was wrong. All we see is his defiance.

"Otto lived a good, happy life. I was glad for the short time we had together but sad that that I've lost my cousin forever. I want Karl Thompson to be held accountable for his actions. I never want this to happen to anyone else ever again.

"It's been over six years, and we need to let our healing begin. I wonder how Mr. Thompson would have felt as a parent if this would have happened to his child."

Sandy Zehm echoed her husband's sentiments. After describing her resentment of the Spokane police officers' courtroom behavior, she added, "The same lack of consideration and respect was reflected in pages and pages of Facebook postings by fellow officers supporting Karl Thompson's actions. These actions, along with the photographs taken by investigators of officers smiling after the confrontation, were very offensive to our family."

Jeffry Finer addressed the Court, "On behalf of this family and the others who knew and loved Otto very much... There's a part that is hard for them to discuss, and they have asked me to bring this out. I want you to know because I think it's indicative of the issue. The lasting impact is not just the horror and grief of losing Otto but, also, a fear and a loss of security.

"This family has a child who is disabled. He's 40; he's doing well. But when this happened to their cousin, their nightmare as a parent with a child who has a stigmatizing disorder, who has mental issues, was compounded, not only just that they would have to face that someone would take advantage of them or that some opportunistic person would harm them, but their whole faith and belief that the child would have the protection of the law was destroyed. And it's affected them every day-they have been fearful for their child. Mrs. Zehm has been fearful. Anyone with a child like this, adult or young, would be fearful...

"And I think, as I talked to them, the worst has been the fear of a lack of respect for law. I was with them in the courtroom when the salute was given... We were there when the statements were given by the Chief of Police blaming Otto Zehm. We were there when the civil filings came in blaming Otto Zehm and...for the interview statements as they were read into court blaming Otto Zehm. And we were there at trial where much of the defense was an effort to blame Otto Zehm. And in view of the respect this family has for law, I will say, they are deeply troubled, and on the obstruction, they are dumbfounded."

Then Breean Beggs read a letter from Ann Zehm:

Dear Judge Van Sickle,

Thank you for letting me write the Court this letter about sentencing Karl Thompson. I'm afraid to appear in court after seeing the news about what has been done before, so I'm hoping that you will let my attorney read this letter in open court.

Otto Zehm was my only son. I gave birth to him and raised him to be a good man.

At the time of his death, he had a good job, lived in his own apartment, and was a talented musician. He could do almost anything with his guitar.

From a young age, Otto showed that he was a gentle person. He was always concerned with the welfare of animals, people, and even insects that he found in the house.

He followed current events and was interested in the world.

He was a smart kid and I always enjoyed talking with him.

He graduated from North Central High School and paid me rent until he moved out on his own.

Every night after dinner Otto called me on the phone to talk and to tell me he loved me.

He would take me out for dinner and buy me things that he thought I would like.

I think about Otto every day. I often cry for him. It took over six years for the City of Spokane to apologize to me for its officers attacking and killing my son.

I'm still waiting for an apology from Karl Thompson.

I forgive Karl Thompson. I want Karl Thompson to spend time in prison so that he knows that he did wrong. I hope that you send him there on the day he is sentenced.

He will someday be released to his family. Otto is never coming back to me.

Every night I will still miss his phone call and hearing him say, 'I love you.'

Sincerely,

Ann Zehm

Leona Eubank gave a statement. "I work with Skils'kin. I'm the project manager at Fairchild (Air Force Base), and I was Otto's supervisor for about six years while he worked with us

254

when he was a janitor. I would like to thank the Court for allowing me the opportunity to speak about Otto and his co-workers and the impact his death had on his co-workers.

"Skils'kin's mission is to provide support and services to adults with disabilities to expand their living opportunities. For Otto and many other area adults with significant disabilities, we accomplish our mission via the Ability One Program, which is a federal program that creates jobs and training opportunities for people with significant disabilities, empowering them to lead more productive and independent lives.

"Otto was a great example of that success. Not only did Otto enjoy the independence and freedom that comes with earning your own paycheck, he also enjoyed the friendship of his co-workers. Otto was soft-spoken, kind, never aggressive, and often assisted many of our other 70 disabled employees by mentoring them on life skills or technique. Very rarely did you ever see Otto without a smile on his face, a pep in his step, and a song on his mind. Otto came to work early every day so he could say 'Hi!' to everybody, and on his way out the door, he said goodbye to everybody, making sure that everybody had a good day.

"Otto was well-liked by his peers and by me and is dearly missed. The circumstances of Otto's death caused a great deal of anxiety and fear amongst his co-workers. A goal Skils'kin hopes for our employees is to live an integrated, ordinary life in their neighborhoods and communities of choice. Otto was living an integrated life when some very unfortunate events occurred, resulting in his death. Otto's co-workers couldn't help but wonder, 'If that could happen to Otto, it could happen to me, too.' After all, Otto was just visiting a convenience store to buy soda and a candy bar."

Then it was Carl Oreskovich's turn to speak. "We come here, and I come here on behalf of Karl Thompson, to ask you to sentence the man...fairly, and sentence him on the basis of what he did, what his actions were, in the context in which he engaged in those actions...in which he had the information to act...in which he exercised his judgment. I heard Mr. Boutros...saying to you today, 'Impose a sentence because an innocent man is dead.' I argue to you, Judge, that is improper reason in terms of considering what type of sentence that you should impose...because you as the independent fact-finder have the ability not to be moved by emotion, or be persuaded by our emotion, not to do that which is politically correct.

"When one of the lawyers asks you to heal the community, Judge, he's asking you to impose a sentence that would be politically acceptable. But you know and I know that's not what we're here for. We are here to look at what Karl Thompson did, to determine whether or not his judgment, his actions, his frailties in judgment, how that should be held accountable in this particular courtroom...

"This has been such a tragedy. It has been a tragedy to every single person that's been involved in this case. It has been a tragedy for the Zehm family daily. They have told you that... It has been a tragedy, Judge, for Karl Thompson and his family. This man that's before you is not a villain. This is a man that...has lived a life that has been exemplary, absolutely exemplary, until... March 18th, 2006. We know that, although we don't think it's the right verdict. And I tell you sincerely, we accept the verdict..."

Oreskovich argued that sentencing should be calculated by the guidelines for simple assault because Thompson had been trying to control rather than harm Zehm. 'There was not one witness who said...that Officer Thompson said things in any way, used...a swear word or any word that was in any way disrespectful of Otto Zehm. What they said is that there were commands given...about dropping the pop...about, 'Stop fighting or I'll Taser you.' ...My point is that is someone who obviously has no intent to injure...and both bodily injury and serious bodily injury require the specific intent to injure, none of which is present in this particular case... When there (were) enough officers to control Mr. Zehm, Officer Thompson withdrew.

"Officer Thompson didn't engage in gratuitous violence. He didn't engage in the type of violence where there were racial epithets, there were kicks, there were gratuitous acts of violence, there were instructions to fracture him-to break his bones. That's not the case that we have here.

"This is an officer who was trying to do his job, and albeit the jury concluded not the right way, but an officer who was trying to do his job, and when there were enough people to control, removed himself from the scene. That is not the mindset, Your Honor, of someone who has a specific intent to injure anyone."

Oreskovich attacked the evidence supporting head strikes and reviewed several witness statements intending to demonstrate that those witnesses didn't think Zehm was in that much pain. Then he argued for a reduced sentence based on Thompson's acceptance of responsibility for his actions. "The Sentencing Guidelines themselves and the case law clearly establish that a defendant who accepts responsibility for his actions, regardless of whether he does it pretrial or not, still can qualify for the two-point reduction for acceptance of responsibility... Officer Thompson said...he disagrees with the jury verdict. Officer Thompson tried, in his mind, to act appropriately that night... And although he disagreed with the outcome, he accepted that as being their outcome, and he accepted the responsibility for his acts... I think one thing that comes clear to this Court...is that this is a man that has always taken responsibility..."

Concerning how the obstruction charge affects Thompson's acceptance of responsibility, Oreskovich stated, "If you think about, for instance, some of the witnesses testified...well, the commands were given prior to the baton strikes. And then witnesses were shown the video and changed their testimony. I think the record itself shows just how susceptible someone can be to having their own memory being different than perhaps that with which it is recorded. That's what he did. Now, he did that in a circumstance that perhaps wasn't a good judgment. He forms a memory under a confusing, tense, threatening time-in the middle of a struggle...that wears him out in 30 seconds-and he comes forward and gives statements that ultimately lead to his conviction. But he has never said, Judge, that 'I didn't give those statements.' He has said, 'This is what I decided to do. I thought I was doing it right. This is what my memory was. I wanted to live by what my memory was. I'll accept the consequences if I'm wrong.' That's acceptance of responsibility, Your Honor... So I know that it's got to be bothersome to have the obstruction charge. It makes it a harder argument, frankly, to make. But it doesn't deprive someone of the right to (the reduction)."

Then Oreskovich asked for a variance, a sentencing reduction at the judge's discretion, based on Thompson's personal history and circumstance. "Judge, you're going to sentence a man that's 65 years old, who has lived with this case for six and a half years now...lived with an indictment for approximately three and a half years... This man's life is not reflected by the fact that he has no criminal history... I'm asking you to vary saying to you, this is a man who has lead an absolutely exemplary life, one that has been devoted to public service, one that has been marked by honors and respect, both in terms of people respecting him and his respect for others.

"I know the Zehm family is hurting, and I hear what they say about having children who suffer a mental illness and being worried about whether they will be protected by the police because of this event. And the great irony and what no one knows, Judge, is that this man is the man that goes out and trains and teaches. And this man knows hurt more than anyone because he has mental illness in his own family with one of his children.

"This circumstance couldn't hurt any more than it does, Judge... The tragedy couldn't be any more significant than what he faces here today. And it just, it tears at you when you look at how fragile life can be and how it can twist, how you can live a way to be a certain person and how it can flip and then become the villain, when really all he was really trying to do was to do his job.

"Look at the Sentencing Guideline and the statutory scheme that you know so much better than I and recognize that a fair sentence, a reasonable sentence for this defendant is not to put him in prison for the entire term or perhaps at all... It seems to me that a fair sentence and a reasonable sentence would recognize who he is and recognize the very unique circumstance of what happened here, both in terms of the offense and the person that acted."

Then Karl Thompson took the stand and read from a prepared statement. "Especially to Mrs. Zehm, also to the family, I'm deeply sorry for the loss of Mr. Zehm. I'm also a parent. I know nothing equals the love of our children.

"I have dedicated my life to the protection of the public. I've always tried to live a life of integrity, respect, and compassion for others. I did not intend to harm Mr. Zehm that night, nor did I act with any malice. His death was the opposite of everything I have dedicated my life to.

"Mr. Zehm will always be a part of me. I've lived with the events of that night continuously. I am and have always been responsible for my actions. That includes my errors in judgment. I accept responsibility for my actions.

"Again, I am deeply sorry for this tragic loss."

Prosecutor Boutros responded to the arguments made by defense counsel and to Thompson's statement. He repeated his previous assertion that sentencing should be for aggravated assault and stated, "The last piece of the guidelines calculation is the acceptance of responsibility. And, honestly, much of what the defendant said during his oration was a restatement of their position at trial. It was not an admission of the offense. It was, 'I maybe made a bad judgment, I made a mistake, I got-I misremembered some things.' That's not a crime...not what he was convicted of. He was convicted of willfully using excessive force. He was convicted of knowingly giving false statements. And the obstruction part of the story was largely ignored...and really undermines the acceptance of responsibility."

Then Judge Van Sickle addressed the courtroom. "The jury having found you, Mr. Thompson, guilty of Count I, Deprivation of Rights Under Color of Law, and Count II, Falsification of Records in a Federal Investigation, the Court determines that you are guilty of those crimes as charged based upon the verdict of the jury as to each of those counts.

"The next part of the sentencing process entails making a determination of the Sentencing Guidelines. I have reviewed the Presentence Investigative Report. I find it to be a well done report. I think most of the objections are addressed correctly, but I...determine that report to be accurate except as I otherwise indicate.

"It seems to me the serious bodily injury certainly does apply. I'm inclined to believe that... this circumstance involved a serious bodily injury involving, I think, extreme physical pain when you combine the use of the baton, the strikes that involved strikes to the head in particular, but also head and neck, and then the use of a Taser...

"And the evidence reflected in the testimony of the medical witnesses, particularly the Medical Examiner, Dr. Aiken, shows that there were strikes to the head and the neck. This is different than the Presentence Investigative report, and so the extent that I am making these statements that differ from it, it would be changed and the objections so responded to accordingly...

"Now, the issue is whether or not there should be acceptance of responsibility. That guideline has a note that says, 'Conduct resulting in an enhancement under the provision involving obstructing or impeding the administrative justice ordinarily indicates the defendant has not accepted responsibility for his criminal conduct. There may, however, be extraordinary cases in which adjustments under both of these sections should apply.'

"I'm not persuaded that this is a circumstance here, that this is such an extraordinary case. I am mindful that Mr. Thompson chose to exercise his constitutional rights and dispute the facts that were presented to a jury. And, while he acknowledges responsibility for what conduct he did, he does not acknowledge any violation of law or culpable conduct under the criminal law. I think that, combined with this obstruction of justice provision, results in the determination that there is no reduction for acceptance of responsibility...

"I've learned that whatever determination I make will be viewed by some as not severe enough and by others as too severe... In looking at this circumstance involving the guideline range that's been indicated of 108 to 135 months, (I have) determined that a variance is appropriate... I do think that this unusual conduct on the part of Mr. Thompson (is) clearly out of character. The service in Vietnam...was laudatory... He did receive awards and medals for his conduct...and that was reflecting on the fact that he did things that were above and beyond, seeking to protect and save fellow soldiers. The same kind of conduct keeps continuing as you go through his law enforcement career and is exemplary in all other respects. This isn't a person who's on the edge, who has a lot of disciplinary actions in a file someplace, and that he was a questionable officer... There's no showing of that.

"Having taken all those things into consideration, it is the determination and judgment of this Court that you, Mr. Thompson, be committed to the custody of the United States Bureau of Prisons for a period of imprisonment of 51 months concurrent as to each count, I and II... Given the circumstance and reviewing the financial circumstance, I'm not persuaded you have the ability to pay a fine. A fine is waived."

After Carl Oreskovich asked that Thompson be released pending appeal in light of his good behavior during the post-trial legal proceedings, Assistant United States Attorney Mike Ormsby, director of the Attorney General's Office for the Eastern District of Washington, took the stand. Sputtering with indignation, he stated that none of the exceptions to the immediate incarceration of a sentenced defendant established by case law and court opinion exist in this case. Then he added, "There's another very important consideration here, too, Your Honor, and that is what this says to the community. And I think the Court rightly talked about that as a factor in sentencing. I also think that's a factor in when this defendant should be required to...begin his incarceration. If anyone else in this community were found guilty of something that equaled an assault and they were also found guilty of obstruction of justice, there would be no question that that person would report immediately for incarceration. When you talk about the rift that has developed in this community between law enforcement officers and those they are sworn to protect, that rift is only going to get worse if people in the community believe there are two sets of rules-one set of rules that applies to men and women who happen to wear uniforms and have badges and another set of rules that applies to all the rest of us. That just is not going to underscore the importance of the rule of law."

Ormsby concluded, "So we would respectfully urge the Court to stick with its ruling and that Mr. Thompson be ordered to report to the Marshals today to begin his term of detention."

Escorted by federal marshals, Karl Thompson left the courtroom headed immediately for prison.

*

One month after the sentencing hearing, Timothy Durkin filed documents asking Judge Van Sickle to force Karl Thompson to pay Otto Zehm's medical bills from Deaconess Medical Center, the wages he would have earned had he worked to age 65, and the legal fees paid to the attorneys who had represented the Zehm family and estate. The amount requested, $824,163, would be split between Ann Zehm and the City of Spokane, which had incurred considerable costs in settling the civil suit. Durkin wrote, "The millions of dollars of local community resources that were expended to defend Defendant's criminal, obstructive conduct in the civil suit do not appear, unfortunately, to be recoverable in a restitution judgment." By that time Van Sickle had approved payments of $564,188 to Oreskovich's firm to cover the costs of defending Thompson and $30,294 for transcripts of the trial and sentencing hearing.

Oreskovich's response, delivered in January, 2013, argued that most if not all of the expenses Durkin specified had been resolved as part of the $1.67 million judgment that settled the civil suit. He claimed that the estate "has fully

261

recovered Mr. Zehm's medical expenses." If additional restitution were due, he wrote, "Some of the injuries sustained by Mr. Zehm were not a result of Defendant Thompson's...conduct that formed the basis of his conviction." Oreskovich noted that Thompson only had contact with Zehm for about 90 seconds, but the confrontation lasted another 15 minutes as other officers struggled to subdue him. "The injuries sustained by Mr. Zehm were complex and cannot be attributed to Thompson in their entirety."

Pertaining to the amount of lost wages, Oreskovich argued that Zehm's employers had noticed "unusually erratic and disturbing behavior" from Zehm. "As a result of this dramatic change in behavior, Mr. Zehm was no longer capable of working until he received a psychological evaluation. Whether or not Mr. Zehm would return to work and when is unknown; therefore, the calculations are based on speculation."

Oreskovich concluded his response by pointing out that Thompson will be nearly 70 years old when he is released. "Finding employment after incarceration will be difficult. Any future ability to pay restitution is nominal."

Judge Van Sickle rejected Durkin's request that Thompson make restitution. He ruled that the City of Spokane had accepted responsibility for its failure to adequately train and supervise the police force and paid Zehm's family $1.67 million to settle a civil lawsuit. He stated that Ann Zehm is not entitled "to recover twice for the same losses." He also rejected the request to require Thompson to reimburse the city as Zehm's injuries were not solely his fault, explaining, "It is likely though by no means certain" that Zehm's death resulted from the way he was restrained by other officers on the scene and not by Thompson's actions. However, he did note that Thompson "provoked Zehm's resistance" and, for a time, directed other officers on the scene. "The City bears at least partial responsibility."

Breean Beggs pointed out that Thompson's attorney fees were paid by the government after a judge found that he was indigent. "It's...another situation where the taxpayers are paying for Thompson's actions."

CHAPTER TWENTY FIVE

In December, 2012, the Use of Force Commission released its draft of 26 recommendations for the City of Spokane and the Police Department. After acknowledging the skill, courage, and dedication of the city's police officers, Chairman Martin said, "Any great organization must be clear about what it stands for. This department needs to be clear about its values in all that it does." Specific recommendations included:

- Conduct a culture audit of the department.

- Bring greater transparency to the city's negotiations with the Police Guild and other unions.

- Revise the Police Department's mission statement.

Chief Straub and other command staff should maintain an open dialogue with the community.

- Affirm the de-escalation of potentially violent encounters as a primary goal of the department.

- Improve the use-of-force reporting system.

- Improve the investigative practices in use-of-force incidents.

- Equip officers with body cameras.

- Create a Citizen Advisory Board for the Office of the Police Ombudsman.

- Give the Police Ombudsman the authority to open and conduct independent investigations into operations, actions or omissions by the Police Department.

- Change the role of the City Attorney's Office in defending, advising, and providing legal assistance in reviewing police department policies and procedures.

The Commission indicated that two public hearings concerning these recommendations would be held in January, 2013, prior to the delivery of its final recommendations to the mayor.

The next day Chief Straub announced that the Police Department would be undergoing a major reorganization with the goals of making more efficient use of resources and reducing crime. The department's new strategic plan called for adding a sergeant in the Internal Affairs unit, revamping training processes, and equipping officers with body cameras. He indicated that many of the changes he wants to bring to the department will require the city to hire more officers and purchase an upgraded computer-aided dispatch, criminal analysis computers, and software to operate the body cameras. He stated that several departmental functions would be streamlined to allow officers to react more quickly to information from the street and that civilians would take over the budgeting, accounting, and human resources work.

Straub emphasized that the strategic plan can incorporate the recommendations of the Use of Force Commission and, being flexible by design, can change as challenges with smaller budgets and new crime trends appear. "In the past, the...Department has relied on a traditional, vertical organizational structure, with separate bureaus designed around specific functions. In reality, most police work takes place laterally, moving across different units... By reorganizing into a flatter, more horizontal and connected organization, we can match units to their functions."

Mayor Condon immediately announced his intention to implement as many of the recommendations of the Use of Force Commission as possible and that he would seek a tax increase the following August to help pay for the changes outlined in the Police Department's new strategic plan. "We as a community have to decide what we can afford... It's the administration's job to come up with the financial plan."

*

The Spokane City Council created the Police Ombudsman's position in 2008 after receiving the approval of the Police Guild. The Ombudsman's power was amended to include the independent investigation of alleged police misconduct in 2010. That change was challenged by the Police Guild, however, and the council withdrew the independent investigative power provision after an arbitrated settlement of the dispute.

Subsequently Councilmen Mike Allen and Steve Salvatori proposed putting to a vote an addition to the City Charter empowering the Police Ombudsman to independently investigate alleged police misconduct with a five-person oversight commission. The proposition had the unanimous support of the City Council and the support of Mayor Condon.

Rick Eichstaedt, the current executive director of the Center for Justice, said the proposition "would really hard-wire independent (police) oversight into our system of government."

The proposition was approved in February, 2013, by 70% of those who voted. However, certain language in the proposition, that the ombudsman will have independent authority within the limits of state labor law, would require a change of state law for full implementation. Nevertheless, Councilman Allen explained, "Placing the ombudsman's office within the City Charter depoliticizes police oversight... The ombudsman needs stability and steady, strong rules."

Police procedure expert Michael Gennaco, a consultant to the Use of Force Commission, found that Spokane Police officials sometimes did a great job documenting the use of force by its officers. He also found cases in which investigators failed to ask officers key questions, asked leading questions, did not obtain officers' statements in a timely manner, or failed to interview all potential key witnesses. Use of Force Commission Chairman Martin concluded, "We want competent and thorough use-of-force investigations. You are only going to get that outcome if you have good processes. That includes interviewing all witnesses...and not using leading questions or getting answers by email or phone messages. These investigations are one of the visible ways that the public decides to find trust."

The Use of Force Commission submitted its final report to Mayor Condon in February, 2013, the month officials of the U.S. Department of Justice informed the mayor that they would arrive soon to review police shootings and the use of batons and other physical but nonfatal methods employed by Spokane police officers to subdue suspects. The federal process would be a Technical Assistance Project instead of a full "pattern and practice" review of the department's policies and procedures. The program was only the second of its kind conducted by the Justice Department's Community Oriented Policing Services and would pay for consultants to work with police officials to identify practices needing modification.

U.S. Attorney Mike Ormsby applauded Mayor Condon and Chief Straub for their willingness to work with the federal officials and added, "Because it's a collaborative process, meaning all the parties working together, I have no reason to believe that the city is not going to be committed to implementing the recommendations."

Under the Technical Assistance Program, if the Police Department does not accept the recommendations of the Department of Justice, a consent decree can be entered in which a federal judge forces it to make the changes advised. Chief Straub commented about the program, "It's the carrot, not the stick, but the stick is right there."

*

On April 24, 2013, the Spokesman-Review reported that County Prosecutor Steve Tucker had confirmed that Officer Timothy Moses would resign from the police force and plead guilty in Municipal Court to a misdemeanor charge of making a false statement to a public servant. While under oath in 2009, Moses had told investigators that immediately after the encounter Thompson told him Zehm had lunged at him and that he had struck Zehm in the head, neck, and upper torso with his baton. He had relayed the sites of the baton strikes to AMR personnel at the scene. However, soon after being contacted by Thompson's defense team ten months later, he told investigators he did not remember Thompson using the word, 'lunge,' and had not told AMR personnel of baton strikes to those areas of Zehm's body.

The plea bargain allowed Moses to avoid a felony charge and concluded the investigation of his alleged lying to FBI agents and federal prosecutors. The misdemeanor charge had a maximum penalty of one year in jail and a $5,000 fine.

When Officer Moses resigned from the Spokane Police Department and pleaded guilty to Judge Mary Logan on May 7, 2013, he was sentenced to 12 months of probation and fined $2,500. She told him, "I agree this has taken a long time...with much loss on everyone's behalf. You are precluded from doing that which you are most trained to do ...by your own hand."

Others saw the matter in a different light. His brother, FBI agent Keith Moses, blamed media coverage for his brother's situation. Chris Bugbee, his attorney, said afterward that his client hadn't lied but had "caved in" to the pressure of saying things he actually didn't remember. "This is a good man who was an outstanding police officer... He has support in law enforcement despite what happened."

Timothy Moses stated, "I believe I have served this community well. My integrity has never been negotiable." He stated that he had pled guilty "to allow this unfortunate incident in 2006 to finally be put to rest. I hope this brings some closure to the Zehm family."

Jeffry Finer, the attorney who represented the Zehm family in the civil suit against the City of Spokane, explained that the impact of a misdemeanor conviction on a police officer is significant because it will "terminate his usefulness as a law enforcement officer. It will follow him, and it will eliminate his ability to take the stand because he can be impeached for having a conviction involving dishonesty."

According to the Spokesman-Review, "Finer said he understands why federal prosecutors would agree to move the case to Municipal Court, but he called the development 'bittersweet. This may be a good decision from the standpoint of resources, but I would expect this will disappoint a lot of people.'

"U.S. Attorney Mike Ormsby declined to comment on the case... (and) on the status of the investigation relating to Officer Sandra McIntyre. Her attorney, Rob Cossey, confirmed last year that he also had entered discussions with prosecutors about potential charges relating to her testimony during the federal investigation into Thompson... McIntyre testified three times before the Grand Jury in 2009. She admitted during her testimony at Thompson's 2011 trial that she met with an assistant city attorney who suggested that she answer, 'I don't recall,' to questions about the incident when, in fact, she did remember some portions of the event."

*

During 2013 the City of Spokane committed $1.1 million of its reserve capital to implement the recommendations of the Use of Force Commission. In August, 2013, Chief Straub reported to members of the Use of Force Commission, Mayor Condon, the City Council, the city department heads, a group of Police Department employees, and a number of community leaders that significant progress had been made on all 26 recommendations. After describing the recommendations as focusing on the Police Department's culture, policies and practices, citizen oversight, and the city's administrative role, he suggested three courses of action: training, transparency, and standardization.

Straub informed the group that, to date, one-third of all patrol staff had received crisis intervention training pertaining to dealing with individuals with mental health issues. He announced the anticipated purchase of body cameras that would be worn by officers at all times. He had a police officer demonstrate the use of a body camera and present the specific Taser and collapsible baton to be used by every officer in the future. Then he claimed that a drop in the city's crime rate and improved morale among its officers is clear evidence of the benefits of the new strategic plan.

Use of Force Commission Chairman Martin questioned why transparency had not been apparent in the negotiations between the police union and the city. Nancy Isserlis explained that the current negotiations were governed by an old agreement that allowed only a mediator to comment to the public about them. When questioned by Commissioner Bush, formerly the equal opportunity officer for Spokane Public Schools, Chief Straub said the department is "particularly attentive" to seeking diversity when hiring new officers. Commissioner Hammond, formerly the director of outpatient and psychology services for Spokane Mental Health, said she was glad to see that officers are being trained in how to deal with individuals with mental health issues and reminded those present that the confrontation with Otto Zehm and its handling by the Police Department had been the reasons for the formation of the Commission.

On September 23, 2013, the Spokane City Council authorized the purchase of 220 body cameras and upgraded Tasers.

*

Released in late 2013, Mayor Condon's budget for 2014 provided for hiring 25 additional police officers as promised. However, the employment contract to which he and the Spokane Police Guild agreed did not include independent investigative power for the Office of the Police Ombudsman because state labor laws require such power to be bargained with the union. As the City Charter was amended by popular vote in February, 2013, to invest that office with independent investigative power, the City Council could not ratify the contract. Council President Ben Stuckart subsequently wrote to the mayor asking him to reopen negotiations with the Guild to address investigative powers for the ombudsman's office.

Early in 2014 Mayor Condon and Chief Straub proposed that the ombudsman participate in all Police Department internal investigations and be empowered to contract with an independent agent to continue investigating any case the Ombudsman's Commission felt had not been thoroughly investigated. The contract ultimately negotiated included those concessions and also gave the ombudsman the right to conduct an investigation when the Police Department declined to open one and to obtain interviews pertaining to complaints filed with the ombudsman's office before the department has started an investigation.

In a celebratory press release the mayor said the new five year contract "includes the elements requested by the City Council and the public and delivers to the community unprecedented independent oversight of its police department."

Councilman Stuckart commented to the Spokesman-Review, "This comes pretty darn close to the intent of my letter, as close as you're going to get in a negotiation. The council spoke, the mayor listened, and we have a good path forward."

However, police reform advocates pointed out that the contract limits the ombudsman's right to investigate alleged misconduct independently from the Police Department. Breean Beggs said, "Under the Charter, you can't limit (the ombudsman's) independent investigative power."

The new labor contract, which provided for an annual 2% pay increase for police officers from 2012 through 2015 and raised the pension contribution in 2016, was ratified by the City Council in February, 2014. Just one of the seven councilpersons opposed the contract, arguing only that it was too lucrative for the Police Guild.

The Guild approved the contract by a vote of 201-14. Soon afterward the Spokesman-Review reported, "(Council President) Stuckart said he doesn't think there is a way to make everyone happy, and the new contract contains more independent oversight than any police department he's familiar with in the northwest. 'I think it meets the intent of the charter. This is a huge win for the citizens.'"

In *Brady v. Maryland* the United States Supreme Court ruled that prosecutors must provide defense attorneys with any evidence that could clear the defendant of guilt. In a motion to the trial court after the verdicts in *U.S.A. v. Thompson*, Carl Oreskovich had claimed that statements made by forensics expert Grant Fredericks were withheld from the defense and that opinions Fredericks expressed in a meeting with Special Agent Lisa Jaangard had been mischaracterized and would have proven favorable to the defense.

In response, Judge Van Sickle stated that favorable evidence was withheld from the defense but ruled, "The possibility of a different outcome is not great enough to undermine confidence in the verdicts the jury entered." Oreskovich then appealed to the 9th Circuit Court of Appeals, arguing that by withholding some of Frederick's statements and misrepresenting others in materials provided before the trial, the government had violated Thompson's constitutional rights. He argued further that testimony about Zehm not fleeing from police undermined Thompson's claim that Zehm could have used the soda bottle as a weapon, that the jury instructions were flawed, and that juror misconduct had occurred. He asked the appellate court to set aside the verdicts and order a new trial.

Oral arguments pertaining to the defense's appeal were presented to a panel of three judges of the 9th Circuit Court on June 2, 2014. Oreskovich indicated the defense did not receive Fredericks' grand jury testimony that what he saw in the video footage was consistent with baton strikes but could have been other actions. He claimed that had the defense attorneys been aware of that statement prior to trial, they could have questioned the conclusions of all of the witnesses who testified about Thompson's excessive use of force. Accordingly, "He (Fredericks) would have changed the trial strategy."

Judge Paul Watford asked Oreskovich whether he was interpreting Fredericks' statement with more certainty than was intended. "It's not as though he says, 'Absolutely not, there's no way that video evidence can be seen as consistent with a strike.'"

Responding for the prosecution, Department of Justice attorney Jennifer Eichhorn pointed out that the video of the encounter made up only a portion of the evidence presented.

She argued that as all the other evidence presented at trial rebutted Thompson's version of events, any prejudice the jury may have experienced from not hearing all of Fredericks' thoughts about the video was negated. "None of the eyewitnesses corroborated Thompson's version of what Mr. Zehm's actions were."

However, Judge Margaret McKeown said that turning over all of Fredericks' statements about the case would have affected the trial strategy of Thompson's defense. "It's hard to see how that wouldn't have impacted how they constructed their case."

Nevertheless, on June 17, 2014, the panel of 9th Circuit Court judges upheld the verdicts of the criminal trial. "The government's pretrial disclosures put Thompson on notice of potentially favorable opinions in Fredericks' reports; Thompson was thus not deprived of the opportunity to develop a defense strategy that utilized those opinions. Finally, the nondisclosure did not impede Thompson's ability to cross-examine the government's witnesses."

The next day the Spokesman-Review reported Oreskovich saying that he will consider seeking a full review of the decision of the three judge panel by the 9th Circuit Court.

*

In May, 2014, the Spokane Police Department received accreditation by the State of Washington, which must be renewed every four years. Major Crimes Detective Terry Ferguson retired from the force shortly before the Thompson case came to trial. Sandra McIntyre continues to work as a Spokane police officer.

Epilogue

The arc of the moral universe is long, but it bends towards justice. Dr. Martin Luther King, Jr., paraphrasing abolitionist Theodore Parker

How often the investigation of a tragedy uncovers converging blunders, none sufficient by itself to produce the outcome. Otto's death resulted from such a perfect storm.

The schizophrenia-spectrum diseases are complex neuropsychiatric disorders that usually appear in adolescence or early adulthood and require lifelong treatment by specialized providers. Otto's behavior was regulated by olanzapine. However, noncompliance due to side effects is frequent with this and related medications, and Otto stopped taking it when drowsiness and weight gain became intolerable. His ability to function at work deteriorated, so his supervisors at Skils'kin insisted that he meet with his healthcare provider for re-assessment of his condition. What were his options?

Along with hundreds of others with mental illness, Otto's access to psychiatric expertise through the community mental health organization, Spokane Mental Health, was terminated in 2003. The treatment of most of them was transferred to the Community Health Association of Spokane, a group of state-funded clinics with insufficient staffing and expertise to manage a large number of psychiatric patients.

Otto's February, 2006, appointment there was with a nurse practitioner whose response to his complaint of unacceptable side effects from his medication was to have him sign a statement that he would continue to take it. Perhaps that was what she was supposed to do, and it may have been the only thing she knew to do. But what he needed was re-evaluation of his condition and adjustment of medication to minimize the adverse effects he was experiencing while managing his symptoms.

His behavior unregulated, on March 18, 2006, Otto arrived too late to deposit his paycheck in the north central branch of Washington Trust Bank. The young women using the ATM were frightened when he approached on foot, got close to them, and acted oddly, so they drove away and called 911. Although he ran when he noticed the women following him in their car, he was calm after entering the convenience store and went about his usual routine until interrupted by a policeman bearing down on him with a baton in strike position.

While he was driving to the Zip Trip, Officer Braun asked the dispatcher to verify that the suspect had taken the complainant's money and was told that the caller was not sure. That response came precisely when Karl Thompson was exiting his patrol car and rushing into the store. Uncertain that a crime had been committed, Braun approached circumspectly. Did Thompson hear that dispatch?

Dressed like his heavy metal heroes in a leather jacket, jeans, and boots, with long hair and a stocky build perhaps Otto did look menacing. But why did Thompson abandon the prudent caution of a veteran police officer and hurl himself into a physical encounter with so little at stake? Was his ambition to be Chief of Police so intense that he interposed himself in this call and didn't wait for back-up? How fearful was he of failing to get the top job again?

Did the back-up officers punish Otto for resisting Thompson's force? Personal ambition aside, Karl Thompson belonged to a police force that had become exceedingly militaristic. His brutality to a retreating man captured by the often rebroadcast video of the encounter and the analysis of the misguided internal investigation brought that culture into focus. That perception was reinforced by the trial testimony of two firearms trainers for the Spokane Police Department, Detective Bowman and Officer Preuninger, concerning Thompson's use of force during the encounter.

There is no legitimate argument that the City of Spokane tried to make Karl Thompson the scapegoat for its culpability in Otto's death. Thompson was provided with competent private legal counsel after his indictment and had the support of the Police Department and City management long after it was palatable to the public, a quintessential example of the difference in resources available to those accused of police brutality compared to its victims.

However, had the Zehm family's claim been settled soon after the release of the video showing none of the aggressive behavior cited to justify Thompson's force, would the federal investigation and the changes in the leadership and policies of the Police Department and the City have occurred? As had happened in previous cases of injury from arguably excessive force by Spokane police officers, the Zehm ripple in the status quo likely would have died out, leaving its causes unaddressed. But the City's intransigence in face of the video of Thompson's unprovoked assault unleashed forces that turned the ripple into a tidal wave.

Did Thompson's defense succeed? He did not enter prison until six and a half years after the crime and a full year after his conviction in federal court. The sentence he is serving is half the full sentence allowable for his crime, which the prosecution had sought. Faced at the outset with the video evidence of the encounter and the Department of Justice as its opponent, isn't it likely that the realistic goals of the defense were to keep Thompson out of prison for as long as possible and to convince the judge to grant a variance in sentencing?

The Zehm story had legs. Without a doubt, Otto's character was pivotal in keeping the story alive, and many individuals contributed. Popular Spokesman-Review columnist Doug Clark, who started the OTTO button campaign, was an early and persistent critic of the Police Department's investigation and the failure of the City and County Prosecutor to address the matter openly and objectively. The editorial staff of the Spokesman-Review maintained the newspaper's commitment to cover the story to its conclusion, and reporters Thomas Clouse, Jonathan Brunt, and Shawn Vestal did a superb job. Center for Justice attorneys Breean Beggs and Jeffry Finer managed the complaint and civil suit with poise, avoiding mudslinging that would have distracted the public from its concerns about the quality, integrity, and transparency of the police force and the City Attorney's Office. Through vindicating Otto, the Department of Justice demonstrated that its mission and resources extend to a region as remote and sparsely populated as eastern Washington.

*

In their wisdom Ann Zehm and the attorneys of the Center for Justice sought from the outset to use Otto's death as a focal point for change in community policing, hoping to prevent similar assaults and needless injuries in the future. They didn't get everything they wanted, didn't achieve everything they set out to do. But they sure came close!

In the years following Otto's death, the media and prominent members of the community held the city's feet to the fire, and new leaders eventually redirected the policing philosophy. But cultural change within a large police department can only evolve slowly. Integrity in internal police department investigations and training in the use of force require the public's continual attention. Secured by those who stood up on his behalf, Otto's enduring legacy is the impetus to maintain that attention.

About the Author

Andrew Gabriel Britt is a 2012 honor graduate of Eastern Washington University where he majored in sociology. He is an avid reader and gardener. *Frenzy and Cover Up* is his first literary work.

Andrew will begin training for a career in the law in the fall of 2015.